THE CRISIS OF SOUTH AFRICAN FOREIGN POLICY

Diplomacy, Leadership and the Role of the African National Congress

MATTHEW GRAHAM

I.B. TAURIS

LONDON · NEW YORK

Published in 2015 by
I.B.Tauris & Co. Ltd
London • New York
www.ibtauris.com

International Library of Africa Studies 42

ISBN: 978 1 78076 635 5
eISBN: 978 0 85773 948 3

A full CIP record for this book is available from the British Library
A full CIP record is available from the Library of Congress

Library of Congress Catalog Card Number: available

Typeset in Garamond Three by OKS Prepress Services, Chennai, India
Printed and bound by CPI Group (UK) Ltd, Croydon, CR0 4YY

Matthew Graham is Lecturer in South African History at the University of Dundee. He is also Research Associate at the Centre for African Studies, University of the Free State. He specializes in the history of the African National Congress (ANC), post-colonial nationalism, and South African foreign policy.

To Bill, Lorraine, Rachael and Iris

CONTENTS

ACRONYMS

AAM	Anti-Apartheid Movement
AAPSO	Afro-Asian Peoples' Solidarity Organization
ANC	African National Congress
APRM	African Peer Review Mechanism
ARMSCOR	Armaments Corporation of South Africa
AU	African Union
BCM	Black Consciousness Movement
BNP	Basotho National Party
BRICS	Brazil-Russia-India-China-South Africa Partnership
CODESA	Convention for a Democratic South Africa
COSATU	Congress of South African Trade Unions
DA	Democratic Alliance
DFA	Department of Foreign Affairs (South Africa)
DP	Democratic Party
DRC	Democratic Republic of Congo
EC	European Community
EFTA	European Free Trade Area
FLS	Frontline States
FRELIMO	Liberation Front of Mozambique
GEAR	Growth, Employment and Redistribution Strategy
GNU	Government of National Unity
IBSA	India-Brazil-South Africa Partnership
IDASA	Institute for a Democratic Alternative for South Africa
IDC	Industrial Development Corporation
IFP	Inkatha Freedom Party

IMF	International Monetary Fund
MAP	Millennium Partnership for the African Recovery Programme
MDC	Movement for Democratic Change
MK	Umkhonto we Sizwe (Spear of the Nation)
MMD	Movement for Multiparty Democracy
MPLA	People's Movement for the Liberation of Angola
MPNP	Multi Party Negotiating Process
NAM	Non-Aligned Movement
NCACC	South African National Conventional Arms Control Committee
NCC	National Consultative Conference
NEC	National Executive Committee
NEPAD	New Partnership for Africa's Development
NGOs	Non-governmental organizations
NP	National Party
NPT	Non-Proliferation Treaty
OAU	Organisation of African Unity
PAC	Pan-Africanist Congress
PAFMECA	Pan-African Freedom Movement of East and Central Africa
PAIGC	African Party for the Independence of Guinea and Cape Verde
PAP	Pan-African Parliament
PASOK	Panhellenic Socialist Movement
PCAS	Policy Co-ordination and Advisory Service
PCFA	Portfolio Committee on Foreign Affairs
PFP	Progressive Federal Party
POLISARIO	Popular Front for the Liberation of Saguia el-Hamra and Rio de Oro
PRC	People's Republic of China
RCD	Congolese Rally for Democracy
RDP	Reconstruction and Development Programme
RENAMO	Mozambican National Resistance Movement
ROC	Republic of China (Taiwan)
SAAF	South African Air Force
SACP	South African Communist Party
SADC	Southern African Development Community

SADCC	Southern African Development Co-ordination Conference
SADF	South African Defence Force
SAIIA	South African Institute of International Affairs
SAIC	South African Indian Congress
SANDF	South African National Defence Force
SAOM	South African Observer Missions (Zimbabwe)
SASOL	South African Coal and Oil Ltd
SAUF	South Africa United Front
SCFA	Sub Council on Foreign Affairs
SCOPA	Standing Committee on Public Accounts
SWANU	South West African National Union
SWAPO	South West Africa People's Organisation
TANU	Tanganyika African National Union
TEC	Transitional Executive Council
UDF	United Democratic Front
UN	United Nations
UNIP	United National Independence Party
UNITA	National Union for the Total Independence of Angola
ZANU PF	Zimbabwe African National Union Patriotic Front
ZAPU	Zimbabwe African People's Union

ACKNOWLEDGEMENTS

The research and writing of this book has been aided immeasurably by the support and assistance of a large number of people and organizations, to whom I owe a great deal.

My wholehearted thanks and gratitude go to Ian Phimister, who has inspired, encouraged and challenged me from the moment I began my academic interest in southern African history. His guidance and support has been invaluable to the process. Numerous people across the United Kingdom and South Africa have been of enormous help in my research journey through the sharing of ideas, reading and editing my draft work, and aiding me on my travels. Special mentions go to: Peter Vale, Arrigo Pallotti, Miles Larmer, Abdul Bemath, for indexing the book, Kate Law, Matt Carnell, Daniel Spence, Shani D'Cruze, Lyndsay and Peter Walker, Ian and Olive, Joanna Tyler, Cathy and William, Alice and Pat Ashwell, Ivy Kinnear, Lize Kriel, Neil Morris, Andy Cohen, Marijke Vermaak, and Shonagh and Graham Lowe. I wish to express my sincerest thanks to all the people who kindly agreed to an interview, taking the time to answer my seemingly endless questions. They have added a deeper understanding to the rich tapestry of this topic. Furthermore, I would also like to thank all my friends and colleagues, too many to mention individually, but nevertheless incredibly important. I am also grateful to the School of Humanities at the University of Dundee, which has provided plenty of support during the final stages of writing this book, as well as the Centre for African Studies, at the University of the Free State where I am currently a Research Associate.

I have been helped enormously by a number of organizations whose generosity made this book a reality. Thanks go out to the Royal

Edinburgh Society, the Middlemore Educational Foundation, the William Piddock Foundation, the Sir Richard Stapley Trust, the Petrie Watson Exhibition, the Royal Historical Society, the Gilchrist Educational Trust, the University of Sheffield History Department Research Travel Award and the University of Sheffield Learned Society Fund. To all of these contributors I am extremely grateful.

For assistance in finding documents and material for the research, I would like to thank the extremely helpful staff at: the ANC Liberation Archive (University of Fort Hare); Historical Papers and the South African History Archive (University of Witwatersrand); the Mayibuye Archive (University of the Western Cape); the Foreign Affairs Archive (Pretoria); the Institute of Commonwealth Studies (London); and the Bodleian Library (University of Oxford).

I must give a special mention to Clive and Mary Harber, because without whom my whole fascination with Africa may never have happened. As a child, their stories of travelling around Africa captivated me, and when they moved to South Africa in the mid-1990s I was fortunate enough to experience the continent for the first time. I have not looked back.

Finally, I am deeply indebted to Bill, Lorraine, Rachael, and Iris. They have unflinchingly supported my academic endeavours, providing me with all the support I could ever have needed during this process.

CHAPTER 1

INTRODUCTION

Since 1994, the policies of the democratic government of South Africa, led by the African National Congress (ANC) have been under intense scrutiny. After decades of racial domination by a white minority, the emergence of Africa's newest democracy was regarded as a high-water mark for international ideals of human rights and democratic governance. Equipped with a visionary, human rights inspired foreign policy, the 'new' South Africa was cast by domestic and international observers alike as a rising force for global change. There was a widespread belief, if not expectation, that the newly elected ANC-led government would be able to translate these new-found ideals into an effective and meaningful foreign policy for South Africa. Yet, by the time Thabo Mbeki, South Africa's president from 1999 to 2008, stepped aside, both the country's and the ANC's international reputations had been severely damaged. President Nelson Mandela's assertion in 1993, that human rights 'will be the light that guides our foreign affairs' appeared to have been long forgotten.[1] Commentators from either side of the political spectrum had lined up to bemoan the failures and inconsistencies of the ANC government's international record. While there have been numerous high-profile successes for the fledgling democracy's foreign policy, these are often obscured by an underlying sentiment of missed opportunity and damaging contradictions. For many critics, the question is 'how and why did it go wrong' for South Africa?

A mistaken assumption is that the 'new' South Africa began with a clean slate in 1994, and the problems of ANC foreign policy emanate solely from this period. This is incorrect for many reasons, particularly because such an approach expressly excludes what preceded it. The historical legacies of apartheid South Africa and the ANC as a national liberation movement have continued to cast a shadow over the modern political arena. Undoubtedly, the ANC's own policy choices and decisions have significantly contributed to the perception of failure, but little or no consideration is given to how the past has shaped the present. Such an occurrence is perhaps understandable, because the 1994 elections marked an era of hope, optimism and, above all else, a focus on South Africa's post-apartheid future. However, this tendency has obscured the fact that the ANC is indelibly shaped by the experiences of its past. The history of the ANC has largely been separated into three distinct periods; the ANC in exile (1960–90), South Africa's transition from apartheid to democracy (1990–4) and the ANC in government (1994–the present), which has created artificial divisions in the movement's trajectory. The result is that important continuities and discontinuities within the ANC as a political movement and in its foreign policy perspectives and activities are frequently overlooked. Rather than focusing narrowly on the democratic era, this book takes a 'long view' and expands the analysis and assessment of the ANC out into South Africa's transition period, and the key events and experiences in the movement's exiled liberation struggle. Therefore this work of history evaluates the so-called 'crises' in post-apartheid South Africa's foreign policy against the context of the past, up until Thabo Mbeki resigned from the presidency in 2008; it will not focus on the presidencies of either Kgalema Motlanthe or Jacob Zuma.

From its inception in 1912, the ANC has had an international dimension to its activities in its struggle against formal segregation in South Africa. Fully aware that the intransigent white minority were unlikely to change, the ANC – in what was a farsighted approach for the time – quickly appreciated the importance of international opinion and pressure in assisting their cause. Although the ANC's early attempts at petitioning the British government were unsuccessful, these initial international activities began a long and important series of interactions with external actors. The movement's focus on the international community as an agent of change became more urgent after 1948 when the new National Party (NP) government set about extending and furthering institutionalized racial segregation through the system of apartheid. In April 1960, following the protest and subsequent massacre at Sharpeville, the ANC, alongside all other African opposition groups, were banned by the NP government. The inability of the ANC to operate legally in South Africa forced the movement into indefinite exile, scattering it across the world. The ANC was forced to turn to the international community for help, and its links with the Soviet Union and the newly independent governments of Southern Africa became crucial after 1960. Indeed, without such support the ANC's very survival would have been in doubt. External assistance sustained and shaped the movement throughout its 30-year exile, and significantly influenced its perceptions of the world.

The decision by South African President, F. W. de Klerk to unban the ANC in February 1990, was to set in motion South Africa's transition from apartheid to democracy. Over this four-year period, the negotiation process saw many important decisions made that would transform the country and pave the way for democratic rule. However, in terms of assessing post-apartheid South Africa's foreign policy, the transition period has been widely neglected. This was a pivotal moment in South African history, with a number of converging interests and pressures influencing and impacting the democratic government's initial room for manoeuvre. The demise of global communism, the role of the Western-dominated international community, the efforts by the apartheid-era civil service to direct the negotiation process and the emerging splits within the ANC, would all be crucial. Moreover, it is important to stress that the unbanning of the ANC did not mark a sudden sea change in its ideological perspectives; important continuities in its global outlook remained, particularly amongst the grassroots supporters. By examining the events and decisions of the transition, this book provides a clearer interpretation and new explanations of some of the ANC's policies in government from 1994, until the end of Mbeki's presidency in 2008.

Furthermore, in order to fully understand the evolution in the ANC's foreign policy, it is impossible to separate it from the nature, ideology and structure of the movement as a whole. Indeed, the character of the ANC, both as an exiled movement and a governing political party, has had a significant effect on the shape and direction of its foreign policy. During its exile, the ANC leadership repeatedly demanded that the movement maintain a monolithic unity in order to survive in its fight against the apartheid state, a practice that has since continued until the present.[2] However, the attempts to display an external unity of purpose and direction have begun to crumble, revealing the conflicted internal nature of the ANC. In reality, the ANC is a mass nationalist movement, one that harbours a range of ideological doctrines, encompassing anything from socialism to neo-liberalism, and everything in between. Yet the ANC is also an elite-dominated organization, with decision-making confined to a relatively small number of people, an enduring legacy from its exile struggle. This centralization of power, which continued through the transition and has become increasingly apparent in government too, means that decisions go largely uncontested, with little opportunity for internal debate or dissent within the ANC.

However, precisely because the nature of the movement and what it actually represents is not entirely clear given the divergence of opinions within its ranks, it is very difficult for the leaders to speak for 'the' ANC. The consequence is that behind the ANC's façade of unity there are underlying tensions not only amongst the movement's supporters but also its leadership. Many of these tensions have found expression in the ANC's foreign policy between 1960 and the present. Consequently, this book will address the ideological incoherence and structural composition of the movement, and analyse how this has shaped the direction and implementation of a democratic South Africa's oscillating foreign policy under ANC stewardship, through until the end of Mbeki's administration. The book allows for these tensions and contradictions to be explored in greater depth, illustrating how the conflicted and contradictory nature of the ANC has had an important bearing on the evolution and implementation of its foreign policy, particularly in government. It is therefore impossible to separate the historic activities of the ANC as an exiled liberation movement, from the ANC as the ruling political party of South Africa. Indeed, the important hold that the past has upon the ANC, particularly after 1994, is a theme that will be emphasized throughout the book.

In order to establish the continuities and discontinuities in the foreign policy of the ANC, and the impact that this had upon the democratic South Africa, the book is split into three main sections. The first section assesses the ANC's exile, 1960–90, examining some of the key events and decisions and the ways in which the movement formulated and implemented its nascent foreign policy against the context of a challenging international environment, and highlighting the important role of external actors throughout the period. The second investigates South Africa's transition to democracy, 1990–4, uncovering the myriad of twists and turns during the process, demonstrating the historic continuities within the ANC, and pointing towards the influences of various groups on the final outcomes that shaped the democratic government. By building upon the platform of the ANC's exile experiences, and the widely overlooked pressures and influences during the pivotal period of negotiations during the transition, the final section focuses on post-apartheid South Africa under the leadership of Presidents Nelson Mandela and Thabo Mbeki. It examines the constraints of the past on the democratic South Africa and the efforts by the ANC government to implement its foreign policy ideals, and investigates the accusations of incoherencies and contradictions. By establishing historic continuities, emphasizing the pivotal moment of the transition and disaggregating 'the' ANC, the book offers new ways of interpreting the 'crises' in post-apartheid South African foreign policy.

CHAPTER 2

THE ANC IN EXILE, 1960-76

Following three decades of exile from South Africa, the African National Congress (ANC) had become one of the world's most significant and respected national liberation movements. By 1990, the ANC had successfully mobilized global support and achieved international legitimacy in its bid to isolate the South African regime. Yet, the fact that it took the movement 30 years to force the apartheid government to the negotiating table, illustrates the immense difficulties it faced in exile. One observer analysing the ANC's record in exile in 1985, claimed perhaps cruelly, that it was 'the world's least effective liberation movement'.[1] The fortunes of the ANC certainly fluctuated, from being effectively moribund in the 1960s, to a widely fêted international movement by the end of the 1980s. Such a dramatic transformation was in no way inevitable, and was achieved in part by the tireless efforts of the ANC's leaders to engage and garner support from a wide spectrum of international actors, and the generosity that was reciprocated to them in return, most notably by the Soviet Bloc, Western-based campaigning organizations and independent African states. Without sustained support, for example, in areas such as military training, education, financial donations and the provision of refuge, the ANC would not have been able to survive in exile, let alone wage such a comprehensive international campaign against apartheid. The importance of external support to the ANC was emphasized by the South African Communist Party (SACP) leader Joe Slovo, who claimed in 1986 that 'in this day and age there is no struggle which can be separated from the international context, but in the case of South Africa the international factor plays a unique role; because the evil of apartheid, like no other issue, cuts across the world ideological divide'.[2] Although internal opposition definitely played its part in bringing about the end of apartheid, a significant factor in its demise was the concerted efforts of the ANC (plus the activities of internal organizations such as the United Democratic Front (UDF), and the global Anti-Apartheid Movement) to internationalize the South African struggle from 1960.[3]

The ANC's 30 years of exile began in March 1960, after a protest organized by the rival Pan-Africanist Congress (PAC) culminated in the Sharpeville massacre, which left 69 people dead. The incident sparked a week of demonstrations and protests across South Africa, after which the National Party (NP) government declared a state of emergency, banning the ANC and the PAC.[4] Plans to form an external section of the ANC had been discussed in December 1959, 'to carry abroad the message of its vision and solicit support for the movement', but in the aftermath of Sharpeville this had to be accelerated.[5] In the course of these early discussions the ANC leadership had nominated its Deputy President Oliver Tambo to leave South Africa and head an External Mission to co-ordinate the ANC's international efforts. Tambo secretly left the country in April 1960, first making his way to the British Protectorate of Bechuanaland (now Botswana), and then on to Tanganyika (now Tanzania).[6] He quickly set about the task of raising awareness and gaining support for the ANC by touring friendly states and creating links with international backers that enabled Tambo 'to establish ANC missions in Egypt, Ghana, Morocco and in London'.[7] However, despite the South African government's banning of the ANC, there was no immediate exodus of its members; many remained in South Africa to carry out clandestine activities. Only after the arrest of the ANC's leaders at Rivonia in July 1963, and their subsequent imprisonment, did the organization finally abandon its formal structures within South Africa.[8] Until 1963, the ANC had managed to maintain an illegal presence in the country, albeit one that was severely limited by sustained repression and harassment by the state. Although the bulk of the leadership had remained, its ability to direct the struggle effectively was greatly diminished. The internal military and political structures of the ANC were thoroughly destroyed after the Rivonia Trial, and with its leaders in prison or in exile, control of the organization shifted to the External Mission.[9]

This and the following chapter will examine the ANC's foreign policy in practice, but as will be illustrated, it was by no means consistent nor coherent. The very nature of being an exiled political movement meant that for practical purposes the ANC had to be relatively flexible in its approach to external actors, as world events unfolded over which it had little or no influence. Although the ANC espoused socialist ideals throughout its exile (that in turn were not always consistently expressed), the movement appealed to both Western and communist nations for help; quite clearly a different message was required for these very different audiences. For the purposes of political expediency, a fluid approach to foreign policy was thus required. Additionally, as will be seen here and in Chapter Three, the ANC did not produce many clear statements of what its foreign policy actually was. The two clearest examples were the Freedom Charter, written in 1955, before its exile, and the Report of the Commission on Foreign Policy tabled at the 1985 Kabwe Conference.[10] While these two documents provide some insight into the ANC's priorities, they are rather limited in scope, with a lack of information about its foreign policy ideals. It is therefore important to take into account the many limitations the ANC faced in developing an explicit and consistent foreign policy in exile.

The burgeoning literature concerning the ANC's exile experiences is vast, spanning a diverse range of themes and approaches.[11] This study focuses on the most important events in the chronological evolution of the ANC's foreign relations in exile, concentrating primarily on southern Africa. These include: the impact of the 1969 Lusaka Manifesto; the formation of alliances with like-minded Soviet-sponsored liberation movements; the decolonization of Portuguese Africa and the 1985 Kabwe Conference.

The 1960s

The first decade of exile was a traumatic and turbulent experience for the ANC. The movement found itself ill-prepared for its banning and subsequent life in exile.[12] Major problems challenged the very existence of the ANC during the 1960s. Primarily, the ANC was left entirely dependent on the goodwill and benevolence of newly independent states such as Tanzania and Zambia for refuge, as well as the Soviet Union and the Eastern Bloc for financial and military support. It must be noted that without the largesse of the Communist Bloc throughout the entirety of the exile period, the ANC would have faced enormous difficulties in waging its struggle against the apartheid state. Moreover, a growing concern for the movement was the co-ordination of its international efforts, as the ANC leadership was dispersed across Africa and Europe, almost completely cut off from its domestic support base.[13] Additional crises faced the ANC including: unanticipated competition for African support and patronage from its rival movement the PAC;[14] a mutiny amongst members of its armed wing Umkhonto we Sizwe (known as MK)[15] after the defeat of its guerrilla fighters during the Wankie and Sipolilo campaigns of 1967–8[16] and expulsion from Tanzania in 1969 by the president, Julius Nyerere.[17] Despite these substantial difficulties, the 1960s was not as bleak for the ANC as it may first appear. The achievement of simply surviving as a (largely) unified movement in the first decade of exile was in itself a major accomplishment. Furthermore, although the ANC became dependent on external aid, it was relatively successful in attracting international support for its cause; it began the process of forging alliances with Southern African liberation movements such as the Zimbabwe African People's Union (ZAPU) and it was involved in the process leading to South Africa leaving the Commonwealth in 1961.

The ANC had envisaged that its exile from South Africa would be only temporary, but the leadership had realized the pressing importance of attracting external support. In 1960, the primary foreign policy goals of the External Mission were to isolate South Africa internationally and secure material and moral support for the cause. Initial efforts to win external backing and to isolate the apartheid regime were predominantly focused on Britain, as the former colonial power, and international organizations such as the UN that were thought capable of exercising influence over South Africa.[18] However, the failure of Western states (excluding Scandinavia) to back the ANC or take effective action against apartheid, forced the movement to look towards communist states as an alternative base of support. The Eastern Bloc, led by the Soviet Union but with important contributions from states such as Cuba and the German Democratic Republic (GDR), became a vital and consistent ally of the ANC throughout its exile. These nations provided financial backing, military hardware and instruction, education, visas for travel and even temporary refuge.[19] However, this turn to the East further reinforced the West's negative perceptions of the ANC as a Soviet-backed terrorist group. In the context of the Cold War, the white minority governments of Southern Africa were perceived by the West to be bulwarks against the spread of communism in Africa, and were thus supported economically and politically, at the expense of national liberation movements.

A major practical problem that dogged the ANC, particularly during the first few years of exile, was the geopolitical climate of southern Africa, as South Africa was buttressed by a series of white minority regimes.[20] Moreover, the composition of Southern Africa was not simply located within a framework of race, but also within a common political and, more crucially, economic interdependency. As a direct legacy of British colonial rule, the various region states (especially the smaller territories such as Swaziland) were characterized by a considerable degree of interconnectivity, chiefly with South Africa as a hub. Therefore, no matter what regional governments' opinions of apartheid were, their independence was severely curtailed. In 1960, the British Protectorates of Bechuanaland (Botswana) and Northern Rhodesia (Zambia) were the primary destinations for South Africans fleeing the country, but the apartheid state was able to exercize its economic and political leverage throughout Southern Africa to prevent the ANC from settling in these countries. The extent of regional interdependency meant that it was extremely challenging for the ANC to negotiate an international position for itself in Southern Africa due to the reach and dominance of the apartheid state. It was an issue that persisted throughout the ANC's exile. Even after a wave of decolonization and independence had swept the region by the mid-1960s, South Africa's dominance over its neighbours ensured that the ANC was still kept a considerable distance from its borders.[21] Dr Hilgard Muller told the South African parliament in June 1965 of the extensive 'administrative links, the interwoven economy of the region and the existing technological co-operation' particularly with Basutoland, Bechuanaland and Swaziland.[22] There is considerable evidence of British colonial authorities in Northern Rhodesia arresting and deporting ANC members back to South Africa for imprisonment.[23] Therefore, in 1960, the nearest safe haven for the ANC was Dar es Salaam in Tanzania, leaving the movement over 1,500 miles away from the borders of South Africa.[24] It was only as states with a greater degree of independence from South Africa became independent, such as Zambia in 1964, that the ANC could begin to establish more permanent bases from which to wage its struggle. Although states such as Tanzania generously sustained the ANC in the 1960s, the movement often had strained relationships with host governments, naturally finding itself beholden to their decisions and interests.

The South Africa United Front and the Commonwealth, 1960–62

An early and significant achievement in the struggle against apartheid was the mobilization of international opinion against South Africa's continued membership of the Commonwealth. This resulted in part from the activities of the short-lived South African United Front (SAUF), which was officially launched in September 1961 by the exiled representatives of the ANC, the PAC, the South African Indian Congress (SAIC), and the South West African National Union (SWANU).[25] In a bid to isolate South Africa internationally, these organizations temporarily put aside their differences, allowing them to raise funds jointly and speak with one voice. Apparently formed as a result of pressure by African states such as Ghana, the SAUF established offices in London, New York, Accra and Cairo.[26] During its 18-month existence the SAUF published information about apartheid to mobilize opinion and lobbied international organizations such as the UN to apply sanctions.[27] According to Yusuf Dadoo, the SAIC representative to the SAUF, 'much was achieved in the early stage of the United Front's existence ... We succeeded in winning wide international support for our cause.'[28]

The SAUF was fortunate that the South African government provided it with new grievances against which to campaign. In October 1960, at the request of President Hendrik Verwoerd, a whites-only referendum was held to decide whether South Africa should become a republic. By a narrow margin of 52.14 per cent to 47.42 per cent, the majority voted in favour and it was announced that South Africa would become a republic in May 1961.[29] The international consequence of the referendum was that it required South Africa to re-apply for its Commonwealth membership.[30] British Prime Minister Harold Macmillan had been keen for South Africa to remain a member of the organization, but a groundswell of opposition from the British public and recently independent Afro-Asian nations mounted against Pretoria's re-application. In the run-up to the

Commonwealth meeting in London, representatives of the SAUF visited or wrote to member nations, to argue the case for South Africa's expulsion.[31] At the London Conference of Commonwealth Prime Ministers in March 1961, pressure was put on Verwoerd to alter South Africa's racial policies, particularly by Canada and the Afro-Asian block, but he proved immovable on the issue.[32] After protracted discussions broke down, an official communiqué announced 'that in the light of the views expressed on behalf of other member Governments, and the indications of their future intentions regarding the racial policy of the Union Government, he [Verwoerd] had decided to withdraw his application for South Africa's continuing membership of the Commonwealth'.[33] The SAUF heralded it as 'a significant victory for all opponents of Dr Verwoerd's racial policies. It marks the point beyond which the world will not sit idly looking on while South Africa continues practising inhuman policies ... this heralds the beginning of a rapid world movement towards the complete isolation of South Africa.'[34]

However, the success of the SAUF was fleeting and South Africa's 'departure from the Commonwealth ... did not have the damaging consequences' that had been predicted, with the links between South Africa and Britain remaining strong.[35] Moreover, the unity between South African movements proved only temporary, and the incompatibility and mutual hostility of the ANC and PAC leaderships quickly came to the fore. A number of factors contributed to the collapse of the SAUF. These included regular attacks by the PAC, via the shared Voice of Africa radio station, including criticisms of the ANC's links to communism. A complete breakdown in working relations occurred during the Pietermaritzburg All-in Conference, in March 1961.[36] The result was that on 15 March 1962 the SAUF was formally disbanded.[37] The collapse of the SAUF had damaging consequences for the ANC's foreign policy in Africa that will be explored further in this chapter. A contributing factor to the ANC's declining international fortunes was that PAC propaganda led many African leaders to believe the ANC was overwhelmingly communist and controlled by whites. Prominent ANC member Ben Turok later observed that 'the PAC had persuaded Africa's leaders that the ANC's multiracialism was a mechanism for domination by white communists'.[38] According to Slovo, during the early 1960s the PAC successfully cultivated a 'myth' that it was a 'more militant and more revolutionary movement' than the ANC.[39] The result was deepening suspicions from pan-Africanist nations such as Ghana. Although the PAC had considerable weaknesses, the assertion that there was a strong communist streak running through the ANC was well placed. The links to the Soviet Union began to pose a dilemma for the ANC, caught between the need for practical assistance, but mounting African suspicions.

Mandela's 1962 Tour of Africa

In January 1962, Nelson Mandela secretly left South Africa to attend the Conference of the Pan-African Freedom Movement of East and Central Africa (PAFMECA) in Addis Ababa, after which he embarked on a tour of independent African states.[40] Mandela's tour helped fulfil some of the ANC's foreign policy objectives, namely: the isolation of South Africa; gaining international support for the movement and, more importantly, securing funds and training for its guerrilla fighters. This latter point was the primary purpose of his trip.

The ANC's decision to wage an armed struggle was perhaps the most significant event of the 1960s, and one that shaped the course of the entire exile period. The turn to violence was made by the remnants of the internal leadership in June 1961, and strongly advocated by Mandela. Although the decision to adopt violent methods was officially announced in December 1961, the first group of cadres had already been sent to China for military training in early 1960, far in advance of MK's launch.[41] However, it was not a unanimous decision, especially because of the ANC's long-stated commitment to non-violence.[42] Mandela revealed that debates about the use of violence had been ongoing since 1960 but, sensitive to internal opposition, the new armed wing was kept separate from the political wing. It was only during the Lobatse Conference in 1962 that the ANC officially confirmed its ties to MK and the armed struggle.[43] The official announcement in December 1961 was marked by a series of attacks against government installations throughout South Africa. However, the timing proved embarrassing for the ANC, as its President Chief Albert Luthuli received the Nobel Peace Prize the same month (although it had been awarded in 1960). The award angered the NP government, which was forced to allow Luthuli to leave the country to accept it, wary of the negative international publicity if it refused.[44] The award of the Nobel Peace Prize was highly symbolic and a propaganda coup for the ANC in the West, though

Mandela later acknowledged that it made launching the armed struggle somewhat awkward.[45] The consequence of this turn to violence was that from this moment on, the primary (but originally unintended) priority of the External Mission was to seek support for MK operations. The focus on military aims would come to dominate the ANC's international efforts.

At the PAFMECA conference, Mandela addressed the collected heads of state about the situation in South Africa and stressed the vital importance of African assistance to the ANC.[46] Mandela saw the conference as an 'opportunity to furnish important connections for the ANC ... and [the] best chance for us to enlist support, money, and training for MK'.[47] Many of the conference delegates were united against apartheid, prompting a number of countries such as Algeria, Ethiopia, Morocco and Nigeria to pledge finances and military training to the ANC.[48] Initial signs were that African states would unite behind the ANC's struggle. One tangible outcome was that a number of MK cadres were sent for military training in the aforementioned nations over the following few years. After the conference in Ethiopia, Mandela embarked on an extensive tour of the continent (along with a brief stop in London) to meet leaders, ascertain their commitment to the ANC and to secure training for MK.[49] During his visits to Morocco and Ethiopia, Mandela met with several other African liberation movements, including Algerian freedom fighters, who discussed tactics with him and provided a course of basic military instruction.[50] Turok argued that Mandela was 'highly successful at winning important commitments from many heads of state who received him as an equal'.[51] Yet, further escalation of the armed struggle was stalled soon after Mandela's return to South Africa in August; the NP government arrested its most wanted fugitive.

However, problems soon emerged. A key issue was the activities of the PAC during and after the PAFMECA conference, which had a considerable effect on the ANC's relations with African states and movements. The ANC found that its multi-racial character and close links with the SACP compromised its nationalist credentials.[52] Many delegates, particularly from counties such as Ghana with strong pan-Africanist ideals, were hostile to the involvement of whites in the ANC. For example, during Mandela's stop in Ghana, the president, Kwame Nkrumah, declined to meet him, and he also endured hostility from some government officials who were ideologically closer to the PAC.[53]

Kenneth Kaunda, the leader of the United National Independence Party (UNIP) and future president of Zambia, similarly expressed his apprehension about the ANC's links to communism.[54] In his autobiography Mandela articulates his growing concern as 'one African leader after another had questioned our relations with white and Indian communists, sometimes suggesting that they controlled the ANC ... In the rest of Africa, most African leaders could understand the views of the PAC better.'[55] It was an early indication of the ANC's fractious and insecure relations with the rest of Africa.

In May 1963, at the Conference of Independent African States in Addis Ababa, the Organization of African Unity (OAU) was established, providing enormous symbolic assistance to Africa's remaining liberation movements.[56] In order to accelerate the decolonization process, distribute funds and co-ordinate the activities of liberation movements, the OAU created the Liberation Committee. The OAU stood as a beacon against white minority rule until the 1990s, although the removal of apartheid did not become its priority until the 1980s. The explanation for this stance was encapsulated by the notion, often known as the 'Domino Theory'; all efforts at overthrowing colonialism should be targeted at the weakest white/colonial regimes. Once one regime had succumbed to majority rule, it would hopefully spark off a chain reaction and others would fall in quick succession. This policy advocated by the OAU meant that in Southern Africa, the Liberation Committee's priority was the Portuguese colonies of Angola and Mozambique, followed by Rhodesia (Zimbabwe), Namibia and finally South Africa, with the level of support provided to each liberation movement corresponding to its position in this chain. Therefore, the ANC (and PAC) were last in the queue, and consequently received relatively little assistance from the OAU. Understandably the ANC was less than impressed. However, the movement had quickly realized that financial problems in the OAU drastically curtailed the meaningful implementation of its rhetoric. The consequence was that the ANC was forced to seek alternative forms of assistance to ensure its capacity to wage its guerrilla conflict. Ultimately, the inability to provide sufficient funds diminished the OAU's influence over the strategies of the ANC's struggle.

Despite continental concerns about the ANC's close links with the Soviet Union, it was an alliance that proved extremely beneficial. The ANC, through members of the SACP, had established close working

contacts with the Soviet Union and the Eastern Bloc.[57] Following
Sharpeville there was an upsurge in assistance from the Soviet Union,
which began to provide financial aid from 1963 onwards.[58] The benefit
of communist assistance to the struggle in the early 1960s (and the
ANC's gratitude for it) is reinforced by high-profile cadres such as Mac
Maharaj who was posted to the GDR, and by Ronnie Kasrils who was
sent for military training in the Soviet Union.[59] Without this help the
ANC's struggle would certainly have been forestalled. Yet, despite a
large number of communists within the ANC leadership and a close
ideological affiliation to the Soviet Bloc and its geopolitical goals, the
decision to court communist assistance was also practical. The lack of
meaningful Western and African support ensured that the only logical
ally was the Soviet Bloc. In discussions concerning whether to seek
Soviet support, one ANC leader, Joe Matthews, later recalled that 'it's
not a question of ideology, it's a question of practicality ... We knew
that the African states, generally speaking, were too weak.'[60] The
alliance certainly manifested itself in a practical sense, enabling the ANC
to sustain itself, train its fighters and (in the long run) forge closer links
with other Soviet-sponsored liberation movements such as the
Mozambique Liberation Front (FRELIMO). Callinicos observes 'that
the steady widening of the composition of the movement, bringing with
it a spread of ideological tendencies ... [was to be] the turning point for
the ANC [and] was to have profound repercussions in the movement's
international ... relations for decades to come'.[61] Indeed, this is
something that is still evident today. Therefore the ties with the Soviet
Union must not simply be viewed through the prism of ideology. The
disillusionment within the ANC regarding the failures of the wider
international community, encompassing the West, the UN and the
OAU in supporting its aims, provides an important framework for
understanding the turn to the Soviet Union. It would prove to be an
extremely profitable association for the ANC and consequently meant
that the support of others diminished in importance.

Despite the negative perceptions concerning the ANC's ties to the
Soviets, the movement had, by 1962, successfully established offices in
Algiers, Rabat, Cairo, Dar es Salaam, Lusaka and London, with all its
African offices geared to supporting MK activities.[62] After the Rivonia
raids in 1963 had dismantled the internal structures of the ANC,
complete control of the struggle passed to the External Mission.[63]

Once the baton had been passed to the External Mission, the ANC located its provisional headquarters in Tanzania, the closest available point to South Africa. The establishment of its headquarters in Dar es Salaam was actively encouraged by President Julius Nyerere, who provided facilities for and support to the movement.[64] Despite Tanzanian largesse, relations were not always good. For example, in 1964, only a year after settling in Dar es Salaam, the ANC was forced to relocate to the provincial town of Morogoro, because Nyerere decreed that only four representatives from each liberation movement could reside in the capital.[65] The decision was far from ideal for the ANC, removing it far from the international milieu. Yet, this was the price the ANC was repeatedly forced to pay for being sheltered by independent African governments. The movement, not entirely unreasonably, was beholden to their hosts' decisions without chance of recourse. However, Nyerere and his government's position towards the ANC was far from certain. Rhetorically they were firmly behind the struggle, but would then regularly and openly criticize the ANC. Much of the criticism stemmed from the Tanzanian government's closer identification with the ideals and outlook of the PAC, rather than the ANC.[66] It left the leadership uncertain of the movement's position in the country.

Following Zambian independence in 1964, President Kenneth Kaunda similarly opted to permit the ANC to settle in Lusaka. The ANC immediately established a presence in the country, slowly building up its infrastructure, until in 1967 it located the military headquarters and its president's office in Lusaka.[67] Although Kaunda was a firm supporter of the ANC's struggle, he walked a delicate tightrope. The support was tacit, but Kaunda could not be too vocal nor outspoken because Zambia was directly exposed to potential South African, Rhodesian and Portuguese military actions. The ANC had wanted to locate itself in Zambia because it was closer to South Africa, but the very nature of hosting the movement meant that Zambia was susceptible to potential reprisals. Regardless of the fact that the ANC were clearly present in Zambia, UNIP's official policy was that guerrilla fighters were not allowed to operate from the country. In a bid to maintain this mirage, any fighters entering the country were forced to surrender their weapons, allowing the state to exert some control over the ANC.[68] Conversely this arrangement ensured that the ANC leadership could enlist Zambian assistance in maintaining discipline over its cadres.

Despite these official restrictions on military activity in Zambia, the country provided the platform for the first significant military engagements by the movement: the joint ANC-ZAPU incursions into Rhodesia.

The ZAPU Alliance and the Wankie Campaign

By the mid-1960s, demoralization had set in amongst the ANC's cadres. The movement was scattered across Africa, South Africa remained largely unaffected by its posturing, and MK fighters were left frustrated and unused in their camps, with little prospect of engaging the enemy. Frustrations about a lack of combat activity became a recurring problem throughout the ANC's exile. By 1966, the ANC had organized training for MK cadres in China, Ethiopia and the USSR, but these fighters remained redundant, thousands of miles from South Africa. These exiles had joined MK in order to fight the apartheid state, yet several years later they languished in bases, having achieved nothing. A key obstacle to their return was the lack of underground structures in South Africa and the inaccessibility of the border from their current locations, a problem that the ANC repeatedly failed to overcome.[69]

In 1966, MK cadres in Tanzania increasingly frustrated by the lack of action and the poor conditions in the camps commandeered a truck in an attempt to express their grievances to the ANC leadership. The group never reached Morogoro, because the Tanzanian army intercepted and arrested them when they were accused of being deserters by the ANC.[70] The interception of the group by the Tanzanian army was a significant incident, of a type repeated throughout the ANC's exile, in which the leadership willingly utilized the military of allied governments to suppress internal dissent. What these incidents demonstrate is that the ANC leadership had sufficiently close relationships with many of its hosts to persuade them to assist in this manner.[71] Although no disciplinary action was taken, it prompted the leadership to explore seriously the possibilities of accelerating the infiltration of MK fighters into South Africa. It was not just the ANC's cadres that were getting impatient. Many of the movement's African allies were frustrated by the lack of any demonstrable progress; the armed struggle had not even started. Embarrassingly, the ANC in exile had failed to infiltrate a single guerrilla fighter back into South Africa. This failure was made more acute by the guerrilla activities of FRELIMO in Mozambique.[72]

With internal and external pressures on the ANC mounting, the leadership sought to act on its rhetorical claims of engaging militarily with South Africa. One solution was to announce, in October 1967, a military alliance between the ANC and ZAPU.[73] The communiqué marked an important stage in the ANC's foreign policy, in that it started the process of establishing alliances with like-minded liberation movements in Southern Africa. Tambo described at the time how the alliance with ZAPU developed:

> We have had close political relations with ZAPU and these developed into relations at the military level until we were in a position to fight together. We are facing a common enemy, fighting for a common purpose, hence a combined force for a common onslaught against the enemy at every point of our encounter as we march down for the liberation of our respective countries.[74]

The ANC and ZAPU planned to infiltrate their forces into Rhodesia to create 'liberated zones', from which MK aimed to establish a 'Ho Chi Minh trail' to the South African border.[75] In August 1967, the first unit, known as the Luthuli Detachment, crossed into Rhodesia, starting the Wankie Campaign.[76] Although Rhodesian security forces quickly spotted the guerrilla incursion they were, according to ANC sources, initially shocked by the ferocity of the MK offensive.[77] This prompted *Sechaba* to claim somewhat dramatically that 'the enemy has suffered untold casualties'.[78] The 'success' was somewhat short-lived as the better armed Rhodesians, aided by South African reinforcements, regrouped; the counter-offensive saw most guerrillas captured or killed, while a few managed to escape into Botswana.[79] Those who retreated to Botswana, including the detachment's political commissar and future MK Commander Chris Hani, were arrested, given prison sentences, and subsequently deported to Zambia in 1968.[80] In late 1967 and early 1968 further incursions (the 'Sipolilo Campaign') commenced, with similar results. The ANC claimed victory, but it was obvious that its forces had been defeated.[81] The defeats of 1967–8 starkly exposed the limitations of the ANC's military strategy; its forces had not even come close to South Africa's borders.

These military failures in Rhodesia were nevertheless an important turning point for the ANC and marked the true beginnings of the armed struggle. The Rhodesian offensive demonstrated the ANC's willingness to engage South Africa militarily (albeit not where it had hoped to) while proving to its detractors a determination to take action. The military activities also helped to quell discontent within the movement, and re-establish its credentials in the eyes of its international supporters as a truly revolutionary movement. Furthermore, the campaign created the ANC's first martyrs for the armed struggle and provided symbolic evidence of resistance to apartheid. Although unsuccessful, the Wankie Campaign furnished the ANC with vital propaganda opportunities, because 'the movement was largely in the doldrums, it had to be presented as being engaged in armed struggle in the same way as FRELIMO [Liberation Front of Mozambique], MPLA [People's Movement for the Liberation of Angola] and PAIGC [African Party for the Independence of Guinea and Cape Verde]'.[82] Yet the manner of the defeats prompted a bout of soul searching within the ANC. The desired boost to cadre morale did not materialize effectively and dissatisfaction remained widespread. Eventually, in April 1969, in a bid to stem mounting criticism from the rank and file, the ANC leadership convened the Morogoro Conference so that grievances could be aired and tactics formulated for the next stage of the struggle.

1969: A Year of Upheaval

For the ANC, 1969 was a year of upheaval, but also one that opened up several opportunities to advance the liberation struggle. During 1969, the ANC enhanced and cemented alliances with Soviet-sponsored Southern African liberation movements at the Khartoum Conference and held its own consultative conference at Morogoro. However, in the course of the year the ANC was expelled from Tanzania and, worryingly, witnessed the rise of greater African co-operation with the apartheid state, epitomized by the adoption of the Lusaka Manifesto

The Khartoum Conference

In January 1969, the first International Conference of Solidarity with the Peoples of Southern Africa and the Portuguese Colonies was held in the Sudanese capital, Khartoum. It was attended by six Marxist inspired liberation movements, namely the PAIGC (Guinea and Cape Verde), MPLA (Angola), FRELIMO (Mozambique), ZAPU (Zimbabwe), the South West Africa People's Organization (SWAPO) (Namibia) and the ANC (South Africa).[83] The Khartoum Conference was sponsored by the Soviet Union, organized jointly by the Afro-Asian Peoples' Solidarity Organization (AAPSO) and the World Council for Peace, and was attended by delegates from across the world.[84] Given the mounting problems for the ANC, the invitation to the conference came at a crucial moment, and was treated with the utmost importance by the leadership. The importance attached to the conference was demonstrated by the ANC's delegation to Sudan; of the 64 countries and 13 international organizations present, the ANC had the fourth largest party.[85] The size of the delegation offers a clear indication that the leadership viewed the conference as a unique opportunity to move the struggle forward. The conference proceedings called upon all democratic and progressive governments and organizations to offer greater moral and material support for the six liberation movements. However, it was the decision to extend exclusive recognition to the invited liberation movements that was to have the most significant impact on the ANC's foreign policy and one that still has repercussions today in Southern Africa. This was a significant moment, as the notion of authenticity and legitimacy still remains an important and binding concept for the governing parties across the region. The result was the formation of the Khartoum Alliance, a bloc of 'legitimate' or 'authentic' liberation movements, all backed by the Soviet Union and united by a common political and ideological association.[86] Thus, the conference had defined the ANC's 'natural allies' in the region, providing a degree of international legitimacy to its struggle. Additionally, the alliance established a network of solidarity and co-operation in the region, endorsing the ANC's foreign policy; the six movements subsequently combined to lobby as a bloc at international organizations such as the UN and OAU.[87] However, the full impact of the Khartoum Alliance was not felt until after 1975, following the Portuguese withdrawal from Angola and Mozambique. Once in power, both the MPLA and FRELIMO governments immediately opened up their territories for the ANC to establish diplomatic and military bases closer to South Africa. The alliance also created splits in the regional struggles by explicitly challenging the authority of the OAU and creating an unofficial group of 'non-authentic' movements sponsored by China including the Zimbabwe African National Union (ZANU), the National Union for the Total Independence of Angola (UNITA) and the PAC.[88] In the case of Zimbabwe, following its independence in 1980, relations between President Robert Mugabe and the ANC were extremely frosty, reflecting the dynamics of this regional split.

The Morogoro Conference

While the Khartoum Conference was in session, Chris Hani was being deported from Botswana to Zambia. On his return from prison, Hani was shocked to discover the poor organizational state of the ANC in Zambia and identified the movement's failure to learn the lessons of the disastrous Wankie Campaign as a major cause for concern.[89] Accusations were made that Wankie was poorly planned and (more worryingly) that it had been a way of eliminating dissenting elements. In early 1969, Hani and six others voiced their dissatisfaction and grievances to the leadership by penning the critical 'Hani Memorandum'.[90] Given the Stalinist nature of the ANC's exile structures, the Memorandum disturbed a leadership unused to being criticized. The document aired grievances about some key ANC individuals (particularly MK Commander-in-Chief Joe Modise) and expressed the growing malaise within the movement. The 'Hani Memorandum' laid bare criticisms including: the absence of a debriefing after the Wankie Campaign; accusations that the ANC leadership in exile was 'careerist' and 'divorced from the situation in South Africa'; that MK and the ANC were run separately from each other with no co-ordinated strategy; and that the Security Department of the ANC was internally focused, handing out brutal punishments to cadres in the camps without fair trials.[91] For having the temerity to criticize the leadership, Hani and the other signatories were immediately expelled from the movement by a tribunal (they were later reinstated) and sentenced to death, saved only by the vigorous appeals of Mzwai Piliso.[92] The Memorandum was a reflection of the immense dissatisfaction amongst the ANC's rank and file about the state of the movement and the underwhelming progress. There was also a realization that the struggle had largely failed. According to the ANC journal *Mayibuye*, it had become 'clear that the External Mission as then constituted was not organizationally geared to undertake the urgent task of undertaking this role'.[93]

Now acutely aware of the growing discontent within the movement, the leadership acted swiftly and decisively to resolve the situation;

in April 1969 it announced that a National Consultative Conference would be held at Morogoro. The conference provided an opportunity for all ANC cadres to participate, if not in person, then through written submissions. The conference was presented with 53 documents, 19 of which originated from various units of the ANC, and 34 of which were individual contributions, covering a wide range of subjects, criticisms and opinions.[94] An example submission was Turok's scathing memorandum entitled 'What is Wrong?', which was a highly critical assessment of the struggle.[95] Over 70 delegates attended the conference, which initiated, in the words of the ANC, a rare process of self-reflection 'in an atmosphere of complete frankness'.[96]

One of the most important documents tabled at the conference, written largely by Joe Slovo, was 'Strategy and Tactics', which described the current situation and outlined a future direction for the struggle.[97] Slovo had keenly advocated that the ANC should explicitly commit itself to the revolutionary strategy of a peoples' war – an approach that was enthusiastically embraced by the delegates. 'Strategy and Tactics' argued that the revolutionary struggle was 'the only method left open' to achieve freedom in South Africa; to accomplish this vision, the armed wing had to take centre stage.[98] However, the document struck a note of caution, urging the ANC to 'reject all manifestations of militarism that separate armed people's struggle from its political context'.[99] The document recognized that without the politicization and active participation of the masses, the armed struggle could not possibly succeed. Yet, this warning was never heeded, and the ANC consistently failed to prioritize the political struggle. Throughout its exile, the ANC was unable to establish 'liberated areas' or create sufficient cells within South Africa with the capability to shelter or supply an infiltrating guerrilla army. The not too surprising result was that most fighters that did successfully enter South Africa were largely on their own, leaving them more vulnerable to detection by the apartheid security forces.

One significant outcome of the conference was the decision to officially allow non-Africans to join the ANC; this had not hitherto been permitted, despite the non-racial approach adopted in the Freedom Charter. Paradoxically, several leading members of the SACP and MK, such as Dadoo, Slovo and Kasrils were non-African and, despite living in exile and sharing the principles and goals of the ANC, had been prevented from becoming members.[100] 'Strategy and Tactics' declared that 'those belonging to the other oppressed groups and those few White revolutionaries who show themselves ready to make common cause with our aspirations, must be fully integrated on the basis of individual equality'.[101] The decision allowed the ANC to fulfil its pledge of a non-racial struggle that had originally been envisaged in the Freedom Charter. Although non-Africans were admitted for the first time, they were still prevented from joining the highest structure of the movement, the National Executive Committee (NEC), due to lingering suspicions amongst 'Africanists'.

Following considerable criticism of the leadership in the build-up to Morogoro, the conference also proved an ideal opportunity for the ANC to restructure and streamline the External Mission; a task that had not been addressed since its creation. The aim was to create a more dynamic movement and to align the military and political wings under an umbrella structure. A Presidential Council and a (multi-racial) Revolutionary Council were established 'to improve efficiency and decision-making'.[102] The creation of the Revolutionary Council was 'an expression of the hope that greater effectiveness could be achieved if the direction and oversight of the armed struggle were made the responsibility of a specialized body free from other tasks'.[103] Additionally, the NEC, which had been regarded as unwieldy due to the number of representatives, was reduced in size, with the aforementioned structures made accountable to this body.[104] Moreover, in a bid to appease complaints about the unaccountability of the leadership, new officials were elected; Oliver Tambo stepped down as acting president general at the start of the conference, only to be unanimously reinstated.[105]

Understandably, the primary focus of the Morogoro Conference was on internal restructuring and planning strategies for the future. These overriding priorities meant that other important dimensions of the struggle, such as the role of external support, were not explicitly discussed. Clearly, the decision to escalate the armed struggle had an important impact on the ANC's foreign policy. Indeed, the conference reiterated that the task of the External Mission was to ensure the success of the armed struggle and to promote internal mass activism. However, these two separate yet intertwined aspects of foreign policy were never effectively linked by the movement. The ANC continued to insist that armed insurgency would be the primary politicizing tool, a strategy that was repeatedly prioritized over efforts at creating internal political structures.

The failure to address the issue adequately would overshadow the rest of the exile struggle. The only discussions at the conference about the international situation were set out in the NEC's 'Political Report', which discussed ongoing Southern African issues. The international plans were reported in *Sechaba*, which focused on the recent Khartoum Conference and the subsequent alliance.[106] The discussions at Morogoro were a tentative step forward in the ANC's foreign policy, something that had never been addressed before. However, it proved somewhat of a missed opportunity for the movement as the outcomes were far from sufficient, resulting in the predominance of military concerns.

The Lusaka Manifesto

In early April 1969, immediately before the Morogoro conference, the Fifth Conference of East and Central African Heads of State convened in Lusaka to discuss the situation in southern Africa. At the summit, delegates from 14 states agreed upon a landmark document known as the Lusaka Manifesto.[107] The Lusaka Manifesto is, in general, perceived as a significant step forward in African, and more specifically southern African states' support for the liberation struggles of the region. The Manifesto publicly committed independent southern Africa to opposing the racist regimes in the region. On the face of it, the Manifesto offered greater opportunities to the liberation movements. However, the Manifesto expressed two important ideas: firstly, an affirmation that the region's struggles had to be dealt with one by one, in accordance with OAU thinking; secondly, it explicitly distinguished the illegal regimes of Rhodesia and Portuguese colonialism from what it classed as the 'legitimate' state of South Africa. The ANC was far from pleased by the official announcement.

The Lusaka Manifesto began by condemning racial subjugation in southern Africa, criticizing apartheid and demanding self-determination for the people.[108] However, the change was that the document adopted a conciliatory tone and appeared to reject armed struggles in favour of peaceful change. The stance seemed out of kilter with unfolding events, since Tanzania and Zambia had exerted pressure on the ANC to engage in military activities. This air of conciliation was a serious problem, because only weeks later at Morogoro, the ANC advocated the intensification of its armed struggle. Furthermore, some of the signatories of the Manifesto who hosted the ANC had knowingly allowed the movement to use its territory for military bases. This apparent volte-face by Southern African governments did not correlate with the ANC's own perspectives on the struggle. There was little the movement could do and the Manifesto was subsequently endorsed by the OAU and the UN as the preferred course of action for regional decolonization.

The second pertinent issue for the ANC was that it had always maintained that the South African regime was illegal according to international law. However, the Manifesto challenged this assumption by arguing that 'South Africa is itself an independent sovereign State and a Member of the United Nations ... On every legal basis its internal affairs are a matter exclusively for the people of South Africa.'[109] Effectively, the region claimed it could not interfere with, nor alter, the policies of the apartheid government. The heads of state not only recognized South Africa's legitimacy, they openly declared a policy of non-interference in what they hoped would be a peaceful transition. In many ways this was a simple acknowledgement of the realities of Southern African geopolitics, as there was not really anything these states could do to effect change. It just had not previously been expressed this way. Thus, any political or social changes would have to be the prerogative of the South African government. Given the continued power of the NP government, such an outcome was highly unlikely. This tactical retreat by Southern African governments was far from positive for the ANC's struggle.

To exacerbate matters, none of the Southern African liberation movements had been invited to the conference, nor been consulted on a declaration which was to have drastic repercussions for them. The Lusaka Conference thus stood in stark contrast to the earlier Khartoum Conference in which the six Marxist-inspired Southern African movements had actively participated. The SACP's *African Communist* wryly observed that in contrast to Khartoum 'unfortunately and conspicuously ... none from the fourteen states ... were represented at Lusaka'.[110] The journal scathingly condemned the heads of state for 'their failure to speak out unequivocally [which] can only arouse lively apprehensions of a real, and not merely a verbal sell-out'.[111] Its most damning observation was that the independent African states that endorsed the Manifesto had gained their independence relatively easily, and the Lusaka Manifesto was thus 'insufferably patronising and even arrogant'.[112]

The outcome of these developments was that the ANC increasingly found itself unsure of its standing in the region. Thomas Karis and Gail Gerhart argued that the Manifesto meant that 'now even the continued support by Tanzania and Zambia and, in general, the solidarity of African states with the liberation struggle appeared shaky'.[113] The movement relied on the benevolence of these nations, so could not afford to be overly critical, yet privately it was furious at what it interpreted as a betrayal. The Lusaka Manifesto was a stark warning about the ANC's tenuous position in the region. By the end of the decade the ANC's struggle was faltering in almost every way and importantly, it could no longer rely on the unwavering support of independent African governments. Moreover, the ANC's troubles, highlighted by the Lusaka Manifesto, were deepened further by the concurrent efforts of a number of African governments to pursue a policy of 'Dialogue' with the apartheid regime.[114] The Dialogue Process, championed by the Ivorian president, Houphouet-Boigny, sought to establish closer links with South Africa, as a way of encouraging change. This process posed a serious threat to the ANC's struggle, and will be examined later in further detail.

The ANC's Expulsion from Tanzania

If the Lusaka Manifesto was an impediment to the ANC's struggle, its expulsion from Tanzania was a catastrophe. By the end of the 1960s Tanzania and Zambia were under increasing pressure from neighbouring white minority ruled states. Although they were never targeted to the extent of other Southern African states, Rhodesia and South Africa had repeatedly threatened them with military action.[115] For example, Vorster had threatened in 1967 to 'hit Zambia so hard that she would never forget it'.[116] The Tanzanian and Zambian governments were ever more vigilant about potential threats in the wake of sabotage attempts against key infrastructure including the oil pipeline between the two countries.[117] They could not compete militarily with the white regimes, and 'many (including Zambia) for solely economic reasons needed or wanted to trade' with South Africa.[118] The only reason behind this threat to their sovereignty was their protection of the ANC. The consequence was that as the military and economic threats escalated, official attitudes towards the ANC hardened. The Zambians made the first move when Kaunda ordered the complete withdrawal of all MK fighters from the country. Although the threat was never fully implemented, the announcement was an apt demonstration of the ANC's increasingly uncertain position.[119] Instead of expelling the movement, in September 1969 Kaunda ordered the ANC to provide lists of all members in Zambia, insisting that no military personnel could reside in the country. The ANC's freedom in Zambia was drastically curtailed.

Rather than threatening the ANC, President Nyerere took decisive action by expelling the movement from Tanzania. The decision was not simply due to the mounting external threat, but also the ANC's political actions in the country. Oliver Tambo had become embroiled in the treason trial of former Tanzanian Foreign Minister Oscar Kambona, against whom he refused to testify. Tambo insisted that as guests, the ANC should remain neutral in the affairs of other countries, to which Nyerere and the Tanzanian government took exception.[120] The consequence was that in, July 1969, the ANC was ordered to vacate the military camp at Kongwa within 14 days; the official reasoning was because MK posed a security risk.[121] Nyerere's decision sparked panic amongst the ANC leadership, as there was no possibility that MK could infiltrate its fighters into South Africa in such a short period of time. Furthermore, following the Lusaka Manifesto, no other African state was willing to act as host for so many fighters. The ANC was in serious trouble, saved only by its close alliance with the Soviet Union, who came to the rescue. An airlift of all ANC cadres from Tanzania to the Soviet Union was organized, resulting in the ANC's ally sustaining the movement's entire fighting force for nearly three years.[122] The ANC's expulsion from Tanzania marked an inglorious finale to the decade. The ANC was left increasingly short of allies, particularly in Africa, and by 1970 was now located further from South Africa than ever before.

The Early 1970s

After a decade in exile, the ANC's standing in Africa was weaker than it had been in 1960. The armed struggle had not progressed in the manner expected, discontent was rife within the movement, and its expulsion from Tanzania and subsequent relocation to the Soviet Union was a serious setback. Additionally, the Lusaka Manifesto hinted at the increasing willingness of African governments to treat South Africa as a legitimate state, which undermined a key tenet of ANC foreign policy –

the international isolation of the apartheid regime. The ANC's malaise continued through until the mid-1970s, exacerbated by the growing links between independent Africa and the apartheid regime. The initiative known as the Dialogue Process witnessed concerted efforts by South Africa to break its international isolation through formal political and economic relations with amenable African states.[123] Naturally the Dialogue Process infuriated the ANC, but with little influence over the governments involved, the movement was left merely watching on and shouting from the sidelines.[124] According to ANC activist Jack Simons, the movement 'was stagnant in the frontline areas, had undergone a loss of purpose, made little contact with people in South Africa, and was suffering from arrested development'.[125] It was only in 1975 that the ANC's fortunes began to change. Decolonization in Angola and Mozambique proved the catalyst for African liberation in southern Africa. Two 'authentic' movements of the Khartoum Alliance took power, which opened up new opportunities for military bases and the infiltration of guerrillas into Rhodesia and South Africa. After Portugal's retreat from Africa, the ANC's vibrancy and viability was further boosted by the Soweto Uprising in 1976, which resulted in a new wave of young, militant South Africans fleeing the country and joining the ANC. This section will examine how these events affected the ANC's foreign policy during this stage of the struggle.

The Dialogue Process

The emergent Dialogue Process proved a serious threat to the ANC's relations with a number of African governments. Talk of openly establishing links with the apartheid regime was a taboo for many African governments. However, in private, matters were entirely different, as there had been a growing trend of developing secret relations with South Africa. Before Dialogue began in earnest, Malawi's President Hastings Banda was a rare example of an African leader publicly establishing official economic and political relations with South Africa in 1967.[126] Banda's decision incurred the wrath of the ANC, whose mouthpiece *Sechaba* repeatedly condemned the activities of Malawi, labelling the president as an 'African Judas' committing acts of 'brazen treachery'.[127] Yet Banda defended his policy claiming that African states that criticized him were hypocrites: 'while they are criticizing me for trading with South Africa openly, they themselves are trading with

South Africa secretly'.[128] Banda's outspoken statements were an indication of the double standards of some African governments and their increasingly close ties to South Africa. Following the Lusaka Manifesto's conciliatory tone and aided by his success at winning over Malawi, President Vorster accelerated the process of pragmatically reaching out to receptive African states.[129] As a consequence, a number of African leaders grudgingly accepted the apartheid regime and expressed privately the desire to forge closer ties.[130] If the Lusaka Manifesto was a setback to the ANC's foreign policy, the Dialogue Process posed an even graver threat. Its hard work of establishing diplomatic and military links with independent Africa was rapidly being eroded by the overtures of South Africa. In spite of revolutionary rhetoric and claims of overt support for the struggle, African states had been increasingly seduced by the economic advantages of relations with Pretoria. The irony is that a similar approach would later be replicated by the ANC in government, when it established ties with nations on the edge of the global mainstream in return for economic benefits. The standard-bearers of the Dialogue Process were Presidents Houphouet-Boigny of the Ivory Coast and Banda, who were also joined by leaders from Ghana, Gabon, and Madagascar.[131] They justified Dialogue through a desire for peaceful coexistence in Africa and, perhaps more importantly, economic factors. The prime minister of Ghana criticized the ANC's armed struggle as 'sending a few people to slaughter', and Houphouet-Boigny argued that, instead of violence, diplomats should invade South Africa peacefully.[132] Although only a minority of African leaders made public statements about rapprochement with Pretoria, by mid-1971 it looked increasingly likely that South Africa's efforts at wooing African support would be successful.

The ANC was alarmed and incensed by this dramatic shift in African attitudes. Yet the reality was that there was very little it could do to alter continental opinions. The movement denounced all African states that embraced Dialogue, accusing them of damaging African unity, betraying the struggle for liberation, and succumbing to the forces of racism and fascism. *Sechaba* asserted that Dialogue was 'a slap in the face ... for those men of vision who held such high hopes in the sixties ... what a retreat from the ideal of African freedom ... as espoused by the founders of the institutions of African Unity'.[133] The ANC even questioned whether the pro-Dialogue governments had been 'captured' by Western governments and made to reappraise their stance towards apartheid.[134] The Dialogue controversy was not properly considered by African leaders until the 17th Session of the Council of Ministers of the OAU, in June 1971. Despite the inroads made by Vorster and backed by the vocal bloc of pro-Dialogue nations in the OAU, the majority of the Council rejected the idea, and 'emphatically declar[ed] that there exists no basis for a meaningful dialogue' with South Africa.[135] Moreover, an important outcome of the meeting was that the OAU announced it would from then on consult with the liberation movements. After the divisiveness of the Dialogue debate, the OAU chose to reaffirm its unconditional commitment to the ANC's struggle.[136] The defeat of the Dialogue Process came as a relief to the ANC leadership, safe in the knowledge that the majority of the OAU backed its struggle, while offering a modicum of security that had been previously lacking.

The rejection of Dialogue certainly blunted South African attempts at breaking its isolation, but it did not stop links between Pretoria and some southern African states from continuing, albeit covertly. Following the failure of the Dialogue Process, South Africa's outward looking policy was not deterred. In 1974, a new period known as détente soon began, after Vorster offered Africa 'the way of peace'.[137] It was a message well received by African leaders such as Kaunda, who described it as 'the voice of reason'. However, détente's constructive diplomatic potential was severely undermined by South Africa's invasion of Angola in 1975–6, bringing to an end Vorster's hopes of breaking the country's isolation. For the ANC, the developments drew a line under what had been an immensely troubling period in its diplomatic history. More importantly, key allies such as Zambia had continued to offer support and shelter.

The Internal and External Situation of the ANC in the Early 1970s

By the early 1970s the ANC had started to diversify its international sources of financial and material aid. The Soviet Union still remained its most important ally in terms of financial and diplomatic assistance, but the ANC had successfully reached out to Scandinavian countries. For example, in 1973, it received its first direct aid from Sweden, earmarked for non-violent activities such as administration, education and living expenses.[138] This signalled the beginning of a long and close relationship between the ANC and Scandinavian governments, while also establishing an important diplomatic foothold in the West. Perhaps more importantly for the international projection of the ANC and its ideals, it was granted observer status at the UN General Assembly and its Special Committee against Apartheid in 1974. Not only did the ANC now have access to sources of funding, the invitation provided a platform from which it could visibly make its case against apartheid.[139] This was a considerable success for the ANC and it effectively utilized the position throughout the rest of its exile to publicize the struggle and the movement.

Although the ANC was left largely isolated from the internal political undercurrents in South Africa, there was limited evidence of continued activity by the movement. Various tactics were used by the ANC to keep it in the public consciousness, including smuggling in and distributing pamphlets and journals and, from the late 1960s, regular broadcasts from Zambia (it later also transmitted from Angola, Ethiopia, Madagascar and Tanzania), via Radio Freedom.[140] There were also a number of high-profile trials of several ANC activists, including Winnie Mandela, demonstrating that there was still some internal political dissent against apartheid.[141] However, such activities were conducted haphazardly and, with few security precautions in place by the ANC, often led to the swift arrest and detention of activists. It would be incorrect to extrapolate from these isolated events that the ANC was particularly active inside South Africa in this period. Put simply, the underground structures had not recovered after being dismantled in the mid-1960s, and the South African security forces continued to successfully subdue dissent.

The ANC was eager to resolve the problem of establishing underground structures, and it actively sought to boost its presence within South Africa. The plan was to achieve this through focusing upon military objectives. Having failed to infiltrate guerrillas by land, a new plan was developed in 1971 to land an invading force by sea. Based on the experience of the Cuban revolution, the plan, known as 'Operation J', was to sail from Somalia and land approximately 45 cadres on the South African coast.[142] According to Joe Matthews, the ANC had discussed these plans with Soviet military officials for some time. Interestingly, during a visit to Moscow in 1970, they were warned of being too hasty, because 'without a proper and secure machinery which could receive and sustain guerrillas at home, any plan was doomed to failure'.[143] The ANC remained confident of its plans because of Castro's successful revolution, but the Soviets 'considered the success of the Cuban revolution as a fluke ... and should not be repeated'.[144] Despite the lack of internal structures and Soviet misgivings, the ANC pressed ahead. The ANC procured a ship in the Mediterranean and put a guerrilla unit through intensive training, including in the Soviet Union.[145] The plan was however scuppered, not by South African interception, but the failure of equipment on two separate occasions, prompting Slovo to consider whether saboteurs were to blame.[146] Not to be defeated in its efforts to escalate internal activity, the guerrillas were flown to Botswana and Swaziland and infiltrated into South Africa; they were swiftly intercepted by South African security forces and put on trial.[147] The failures yet again underlined the lack of viable underground structures to receive and support armed units in South Africa. Slovo later admitted that from 1971 to 1976, the ANC repeatedly and unsuccessfully attempted to infiltrate guerrillas. However, he argued that these failures had raised public awareness, as 'here was a committed and dedicated group which was just going to continue knocking their heads against this wall until somehow there was a crack in it. I think this was a very important side-product of the efforts.'[148]

The ANC was further weakened in this period by a split within its leadership. After years of simmering discontent, eight members led by Tennyson Makiwane accused the movement of having been hijacked by communists.[149] The so-called 'Gang of Eight' were branded by the leadership as dissidents, intent on destabilizing the movement, and were promptly expelled in 1975.[150] Even for the most optimistic supporters of the ANC the situation looked bleak. There was little hope of an imminent return home; the leadership appeared to be on the verge of fragmenting and the support from its African allies was far from guaranteed. Karis and Gerhart argue that 'despite minor advances, the liberation struggle seemed stagnant and on the defensive'.[151]

The Decolonization of Angola and Mozambique, 1974–6

While this book is not concerned with the fine detail of Portuguese decolonization in Southern Africa, it was nevertheless the most significant event to befall the region during the exile period of the ANC. In Portugal, a coup in 1974 by dissatisfied military officers overthrew the fascist rule of Marcelo Caetano, and, on taking power, pledged an immediate withdrawal from Portugal's African colonies.[152] The coup shaped the subsequent course of history in southern Africa, and of even more significance brought the Cold War directly to the region. The Portuguese withdrawal from Angola and Mozambique in 1975 resulted in two Marxist governments taking power, both of which directly supported African liberation. In Angola, decolonization was far from simple, as a bitter civil war erupted between ideologically competing parties, and also drew South Africa into the fray. South African military involvement set a dangerous precedent, as from 1975 onwards the apartheid regime adopted a more assertive, militaristic stance in the region, including the later destabilization of neighbouring states and repeated invasions of Angola.[153] Without events in Portugal, there is little doubt that the advancement of black emancipation from white minority rule would have been further delayed across Southern Africa. Portuguese decolonization came as a major surprise, with neither the regional liberation movements nor the white minority regimes anticipating the suddenness of the withdrawal. The importance for the ANC of these developments in Angola and Mozambique was twofold. For the first time, the protective shield of white-controlled states had crumbled, affording the movement greater opportunities to infiltrate into South Africa. The struggle could now be brought directly to the apartheid regime. This was enhanced by the staunch support from two of the ANC's closest allies, the MPLA and FRELIMO, who once in power willingly and generously provided facilities and support to the movement. Not only could the ANC now move its operations closer to South Africa's borders, it could also escalate its liberation struggle, to a previously impossible level.

The Soweto Uprising, 1976

Despite the welcome international developments, the ANC remained largely isolated from the masses in South Africa, and was thus out of touch with the undercurrents of a new political awakening in the country. Although the ANC claimed to speak for the masses, it was in reality a small, centralized, exile movement, disconnected from the people it was supposed to represent; in 1971–2 the ANC had only roughly 100 members living in exile in Lusaka.[154] In the absence of an overt internal presence, leadership of the struggle against apartheid had passed to the

Black Consciousness Movement (BCM), led by Steve Biko and supported by militant, disaffected youth.[155] On 16 June 1976, an estimated 14,000 school students gathered to protest in Soweto about the introduction of Afrikaans as the medium of education.[156] The police fired upon the protestors, killing 23 people and sparking unprecedented nationwide unrest. Soweto became a national and international symbol of apartheid repression, and provided a powerful propaganda tool for the ANC. Although the ANC benefited from the uprising in a number of ways, it had no direct role in it, despite subsequent claims by some activists.[157] Many of the protesting students had little or no knowledge of the ANC or the PAC, and certainly had no association with the established liberation movements.[158] Yet, in the aftermath of the uprising, many youths fled the repression in South Africa, and ended up enlisting with the ANC in exile. Ronnie Kasrils expressed his shock about these new exiles, who were 'in a sense, blank about the history of the struggle, the role of the ANC, of MK in the earlier period ... what struck me was the extent to which that generation had really grown up with the absence of that kind of political culture'.[159] It was a damning indictment of the ANC's failure to politicize the South African masses. Before Soweto the movement had been in serious danger of becoming an irrelevance, as a new era of activism took hold amongst the young. This dislocation from events meant that the ANC was left unprepared for such eventualities and was unable to offer effective guidance or leadership to the protesters. Future UDF leader Murphy Morobe highlighted the ANC's isolation from the South African milieu, recalling: 'we thought we were the first people to fight the government. We did not know about the Defiance Campaign and the school boycotts in the 1950s.'[160] Looking back at the Soweto Uprising, Tambo candidly admitted:

> it was however true that in 1976–77 we had not recovered sufficiently to take full advantage of the situation that crystallised from the first events of June 16, 1976. Organisationally, in political and military terms, we were too weak to take advantage of the situation created by the uprising. We had very few active ANC units inside the country. We had no military presence to speak of. The communication links between ourselves outside the country and the masses of our people were still too slow and weak to meet the situation such as was posed by the Soweto Uprising.[161]

There was the very real threat that the ANC would be superseded by forces outside of its control. This danger was intensified by a major wave of industrial action across South Africa in August and September 1976.[162] Tambo was one of the few leaders who realized the ANC needed effective propaganda to attract South Africans to the cause and the urgent need for increased attention to political mobilization inside the country. He warned: 'when will they ever understand that you cannot wage a liberation war just with the man and his guns. Who is going to receive them, who is going to feed them, who is going to hide them, why will those people receive them, why will those people feed them?'[163] Once again, it was a warning that was never adequately heeded and the problem continued to impede the progress of the struggle.

However, the ANC moved quickly to exploit the fallout from the Soweto Uprising to its advantage. Facing state repression in the aftermath of the uprising, by 1977 as many as 4,000 people had fled persecution in South Africa.[164] Acting as the first point of contact for many new exiles, cadres in Botswana, Lesotho and Swaziland worked to assimilate the vast majority of these into its ranks, promising either military training or education. In reality many joined the ANC because it was the only option available to them; Anthony Marx argued that 'the flow of exiles to the ANC is a notable example of how material resources, rather than ideas or prestige have determined opposition allegiances'.[165] The ANC had to manage the new influx of recruits carefully and 're-educate' them in the values and ideology of the movement. Nevertheless, the Soweto generation of exiles revitalized the ANC, with a new set of young, dynamic and militant people swelling its ranks.

Conclusion

By 1976, the ANC had made considerable progress during its first 16 years in exile. Indeed, the movement's very survival during the 1960s was in itself an impressive achievement. The ANC had worked hard to establish a global network of support for its struggle, assisted by newly independent and (largely) sympathetic Southern African states, such as Tanzania and Zambia. The wide-ranging nature of its international support was typified by a close and fruitful association with the Soviet Union, which effectively bankrolled the movement during this period, making it the ANC's most important external ally. The relationship with the Soviet Bloc had also played a crucial role in the ANC establishing an alliance of like-minded Southern African liberation movements at the Khartoum Conference, which began to pay effective dividends after 1976. Furthermore, the movement had launched its armed struggle and successfully organized the Morogoro Conference, which had, in part, set about planning for the future. However, it seemed that for every step forward, the ANC was forced to take two steps backward. Many of the hard fought gains were reversed by changes outside its direct control. The most notable example was the ever-shifting relations with host governments in southern Africa such as Tanzania, which, after initial support, later expelled the ANC from the country. Such developments left the ANC in a position of serious weakness, even further from South Africa's borders, with little opportunity for intensifying the struggle against the apartheid state. Moreover, in the early 1970s, South Africa's diplomatic efforts to break its isolation through 'Dialogue' had a negative material and ideological effect on the struggle. This process demonstrated that behind the rhetorical support for the ANC, there was an appetite amongst some African leaders to negotiate with South Africa. These incidents served only to highlight that, despite establishing an impressive support network and having a close affiliation to a number of African governments, the ANC's position in Southern Africa was extremely tenuous. Importantly, decisions made by the ANC during the first half of its exile directly impacted upon its foreign policy options. The most notable was its alliance with the Soviet Union. Although vital for its very survival, the ANC's links to the Soviet Union engendered deep suspicion and hostility amongst many African leaders. With African governments unable to provision the ANC with the necessary financial and material backing required, the movement was subsequently forced to rely ever more heavily upon assistance from Moscow; only serving to accentuate the sense of dislocation between the ANC and the continent.

The course of the ANC's struggle was drastically altered by two regional events over which it had no control. First, the Portuguese decolonization of Angola and Mozambique changed the geopolitical fabric of the region. The white buffer zone had crumbled, and two members of the Khartoum Alliance came to power, establishing Marxist-inspired states that promised unwavering support to the ANC. Secondly, the Soweto Uprising was a dramatic moment and demonstrated a renewed militant opposition to apartheid within South Africa. The ANC quickly took advantage of the uprising in a number of ways, such as assimilating the new highly militant exiles into its structure. The Soweto Uprising was also enormously symbolic and played an important role in shaping international attitudes. For the ANC, the aims and objectives of international civil society such as the Anti-Apartheid Movement (AAM) increasingly became aligned with the movement's goals.[166] Soweto triggered a shift in international opinion, prompting greater awareness about apartheid, reinforced by domestic campaigns to put pressure on countries such as Britain to boycott or apply sanctions against South Africa (though the majority of Western governments ignored this upsurge). By the 1980s, these international campaigns would help to play an important part in the eventual demise of the apartheid regime. It was however a concern for the ANC that events outside of its control or influence were shaping the destiny of the struggle. Nevertheless, the initial efforts of the ANC in exile ensured that it was ideally positioned to exploit these unfolding events, enabling the exiled movement to pursue its foreign policy goals far more effectively after 1976.

CHAPTER 3

FROM EXILE TO LIBERATION, 1976–90

The Late 1970s

Nothing shaped the course of southern Africa's political development more than Portuguese decolonization from Angola and Mozambique. The outcome of the withdrawal had wide-ranging regional and international repercussions. In terms of African liberation it was an undoubted step forward. Not only was decolonization now underway in the region, two Marxist governments had been installed in power, offering previously unattainable opportunities for other liberation movements. The ANC was immediately offered safe haven in both countries, allowing the creation of training camps for Umkhonto we Sizwe (MK), infiltration routes from Mozambique, via Swaziland, into South Africa, as well as increased material and rhetorical support. The development opened up a new chapter in the ANC's liberation struggle. However, the onset of independence was tempered by greater international attention on Southern Africa, especially from the West. Viewing the region through the prism of the Cold War, the rise of two Marxist parties – the MPLA and FRELIMO – was regarded as a serious threat to Western interests. Their unwavering support for African liberation only increased this perceived threat. The ANC was consequently seen as a Soviet-sponsored, communist movement, and steps were taken to halt its progress.[1] The ideological lines were hardening in southern Africa, demonstrated by the civil war raging in Angola between the MPLA, backed by the Eastern Bloc (in particular Cuba) and UNITA, which was supported largely by

South Africa and the United States. The spectre of communism defined the political thinking of the NP government. External intervention in Angola provided South Africa with a degree of international legitimacy and manoeuvrability as a bulwark against communism, and framed Pretoria's subsequent foreign policy. Up until the NP's decision to unban the various liberation movements in 1990, southern Africa was unduly affected by South Africa's projection of power. In the late 1970s, with the perceived threats mounting, the NP government depicted the country as facing a 'Total Onslaught' from communism. Using the Cold War as justification, the apartheid regime acted with impunity against the ANC and the region as a whole, with a focus on the Marxist governments of Angola and Mozambique. With an array of techniques, the South African government used the carrot of economic ties and peaceful coexistence, and the stick of destabilization and violence, in an attempt to intimidate its neighbours into submission through its Total Strategy. As a result of their support of the ANC, Angola and Mozambique bore the brunt of South African destabilization. Indeed, ANC leader and National Executive Committee (NEC) member Matthews Phosa later acknowledged that 'the people of Mozambique paid a supreme price for the struggle of South Africa'.[2]

The ANC's Improved Position in Southern Africa

Following the events in Soweto and the large influx of new recruits, the ANC steadily began to improve its standing in southern Africa, especially compared to that of the early 1970s. The revitalized movement established a regional network of bases and offices, which stretched across the region. Yet, the ANC was never fully able to ascertain the level of support for the struggle from its host governments; this was epitomized by the Zambian state's extremely mixed attitudes towards the ANC in the late 1970s. On the one hand things were very positive, with Ronnie Kasrils noting in 1978 that:

Zambia is not unaffected by the existence of revolutionary governments in Mozambique and Angola and is smack in the front line struggle against Rhodesia and Pretoria, giving us and ZAPU full support. Geopolitically this country is placed at the strategic crossroads of the battle to liberate Southern Africa, and Kaunda is four-square behind us.[3]

During the course of the 1970s, the ANC in Lusaka had managed to transform itself from a beleaguered, disparate community in exile into what was effectively a government-in-waiting. With the consent of Kenneth Kaunda, the membership and administration of the ANC rose rapidly, with around 800 non-combatants stationed in Zambia by 1980, supported largely by Scandinavian aid. However, problems arose as 'Zambian spokespeople continued to pay lip-service to the need for armed struggle while blowing hot and cold on the ANC'.[4] Zambia's reticence to support the struggle fully arose from a number of factors including Kaunda's own shrewd political considerations. Zambia walked a tightrope between supporting African liberation and appeasing the apartheid government, keenly aware of the problems both strategies incurred. The first factor, given the southern African context, was that Kaunda had been secretly seeking détente with South Africa and a political settlement in Rhodesia.[5] The overt presence of the ANC in Lusaka only served to complicate these discussions. Secondly, and far more problematic for the ANC, was that Kaunda was an anti-communist, hence Zambian support for the Angolan nationalist movement UNITA. The ANC's close ties to the Marxist MPLA government, who were fighting UNITA, ensured that there was some official hostility in relations. The Zambian government demanded lists of all ANC members in the country in 1975-6, which the movement suspected would be passed on to South African officials.[6] Furthermore, Kaunda was (largely) a political moderate, eager for peaceful outcomes to the problems in southern Africa; whenever possible he discouraged armed struggle, and stridently insisted that no fighters should be present on Zambian territory. Although Zambia avoided the worst of South African destabilization, it was still vulnerable to South African intervention; thus Kaunda did his utmost to negate any activity that might have attracted the apartheid government's attention. In spite of these issues, the ANC was at least tolerated in Zambia, and its relationship with the government improved significantly during the 1980s.

The ANC was also fortunate that details of South African military involvement in Angola and then the fallout of the Soweto Uprising contributed to a sea change in the political mindset in the region. These events allowed the ANC to improve its relations with a number of sympathetic governments such as Swaziland and Botswana (Malawi was the only country in southern Africa with which it had no direct relations).[7] An indication of this political change came from Lesotho's Prime Minister Chief Jonathan, who altered his views dramatically; according to the *African Communist*, Mozambican independence led him to demand 'an alignment with the anti-apartheid forces, namely the ANC'.[8] The Basotho National Party (BNP) thus established 'closer political relations with the ANC' and 'Prime Minister Jonathan developed an astonishing personal rapport with ANC President Oliver Tambo'.[9] Chief Jonathan's change of heart meant that South African refugees were now permitted to remain in Lesotho, although to avoid reprisals, like Kaunda he insisted that the ANC could not establish military bases there. Another important shift was that the Tanzanian government started to reappraise its position on the ANC; after years of poor relations, Julius Nyerere invited an ANC delegation led by Tambo in 1978. At the meeting, Nyerere pledged to assist the ANC wherever possible, including accommodating guerrillas and using his considerable influence in international forums to back the struggle.[10]

These regional developments were a welcome relief for the ANC, but it was the actions of the MPLA and FRELIMO that were far and away the most significant developments in the struggle. Both governments acted swiftly to honour the Khartoum Alliance; the MPLA granted the ANC military facilities and training opportunities as early as 1976 and a year later an ANC office was opened in Luanda.[11] On the face of it, the MPLA's close affiliation to the ANC was remarkable, given that it was under continuous threat from UNITA and South African military action.[12] However, this support was crucial for the ANC, as it provided added impetus to the struggle. The key aspect was practical military assistance; five camps were established in the north of the country for training, which was conducted by visiting East German, Cuban and Soviet instructors. Further specialist instruction was carried out in the Soviet Union, Cuba, the German Democratic Republic (GDR), North Korea and Bulgaria.[13] By 1978, there were an estimated 1,167 MK fighters abroad, mainly based in Angola.[14] Likewise, FRELIMO enthusiastically supported the ANC and the government allowed numerous cadres to settle in the country after 1975. Although Mozambique offered a transit route for guerrillas through Swaziland into South Africa, the majority of ANC members in the country were not guerrilla fighters. Mozambique instead offered a platform for the ANC to create structures geographically close to South Africa, which facilitated the movement of cadres and information. Various senior ANC figures including Joe Slovo lived in Mozambique, and activists such as Albie Sachs worked at the Universidade Eduardo Mondlana in Maputo.[15] The ANC was provided with housing by FRELIMO, and the movement had worked hard to establish an extensive infrastructure in Mozambique.[16] However, the political dimension of work in Mozambique was rapidly subsumed by military concerns. Activist Nadja Maghezi observed that MK matters started to take precedence over political activities.[17] She argued that this was due to the nature of FRELIMO's support, because 'of the full support of the Mozambican government and people, what would in other areas have had to be hidden or semi-hidden activities could be openly displayed'.[18] In spite of the overt ANC presence, the Mozambican government had to act carefully because of its proximity to South Africa. By the early 1980s, Mozambique bore the full brunt of South African economic and military destabilization, due to its protection of the ANC.

The change in southern African geopolitics was the breakthrough the ANC had been waiting for, and made possible a number of high-profile attacks on South African territory. Termed 'armed propaganda', the ANC was directly attempting to stimulate a People's War against apartheid.[19] According to *Dawn*, acts carried out in the late 1970s included the scattering of pamphlets throughout the country, targeting symbols of apartheid, sabotaging infrastructure and sending parcel bombs.[20] The upsurge in the armed struggle saw 82 such incidents recorded in South Africa between 1977 and 1980.[21] Although armed propaganda did not seriously challenge the military supremacy of South Africa, it marked a new phase in the ANC's struggle. The symbolic impact of MK guerrilla attacks should not be underestimated, as it proved to the world that the movement was actively applying pressure on the apartheid regime. The ANC designated 1979 as the 'Year of the Spear' to represent this new stage in the struggle.[22]

Meanwhile, the ANC also stepped up its international diplomatic offensive against apartheid. In July 1977, the NEC met at Morogoro to discuss the future after Soweto. The discussions concluded that the ANC's international prestige and authority had grown considerably in the aftermath of those events.[23] The report claimed that the ANC's global reputation had been enhanced: by Tambo addressing the UN in October 1976; by the outcome of the Lisbon Conference of 1977 that had recognized the ANC as sole representative of the South African people and by the movement's regular attendance at Frontline States (FLS) meetings.[24] The NEC revealed that the key international objective of the ANC continued to be winning exclusive recognition as the sole representative of the people, declaring that it would be '"fully geared" for this task'.[25] The ANC also started to make useful inroads at the UN after Tambo's speech in 1976. A mandatory arms embargo against South Africa was endorsed by the Western powers in October 1977, and a year later the UN declared an international year against apartheid.[26] The change in attitudes at the UN coincided with developments in the apartheid state. Domestic repression after Soweto was fully underway and South Africa's systematic destabilization of the region, coupled with its testing of nuclear weapons, was regarded by the UN as a major threat to peace. These changing dynamics opened up a space for the ANC to act internationally and mount a campaign against apartheid through the UN.

The ANC was also aided by a series of high-level international meetings with an array of socialist countries including Cuba, the GDR and Vietnam.[27] In 1978, an ANC delegation travelled to Vietnam, to learn from their experiences of successful guerrilla struggle.[28] The trip was particularly significant in that it hardened the resolve of the ANC leadership that victory could be achieved through guerrilla warfare. The ANC had rapidly extended its international network, and was reaping the benefits. However, it must be noted that there was no coherent foreign policy to guide these interactions. If support for the movement, in any form, could be ascertained, then it was accepted without question. The implications of such actions would be felt well into the democratic era.

Therefore, from a position of relative weakness in 1970, the ANC's fortunes had changed successfully and rapidly by the end of the decade. Its foreign policy aims of isolating South Africa, intensifying the guerrilla struggle and garnering international support were all progressing, allowing the ANC 'to make important gains in the international arena'.[29] Yet, despite these successes, the movement was no closer to overthrowing the apartheid regime. As the new decade dawned, the South African state remained relatively unaffected by the international and military activities of the ANC and powerful enough to resist the mounting pressure against it. In fact, the re-energized activities of the ANC prompted a devastating counter-revolutionary strategy from the apartheid state, which affected the whole of southern Africa.

The 1980s

By the late 1970s, the ANC was in a far stronger position than ever before to escalate its international activities, ushering in a new-found sense of optimism within the movement. Throughout the 1980s, the ANC sought to build upon this platform, through a variety of international measures. The new ability to infiltrate guerrilla fighters into South Africa meant a notable upsurge in 'armed propaganda', which spectacularly targeted symbols of apartheid state power such as the Koeberg nuclear facility.[30] The sabotage attacks generated publicity for the ANC at home and abroad, demonstrating its continued opposition to apartheid rule and providing inspiration to the movement and its domestic supporters. Furthermore, following Soweto, the ANC in collaboration with the global Anti-Apartheid Movement (AAM), vigorously lobbied governments and multilateral forums for increased international measures to isolate South Africa, as well as taking steps to mobilize Western public opinion against apartheid. These activities created a groundswell of international public condemnation of apartheid. The mounting pressure ultimately forced several multinational companies and more importantly a number of major banks, to reconsider their ties with South Africa; the decision in 1985 by Chase Manhattan Bank to reduce its operations in South Africa was a major setback to the country's increasingly precarious economy.

The ANC was also able to convene its second consultative conference at Kabwe in Zambia in 1985, where it was able to reassess the struggle and make several important decisions, including an attempt to finally articulate its foreign policy objectives. Other developments that gave the ANC cause for optimism in the 1980s included: the independence of Zimbabwe in 1980, which significantly increased South Africa's exposure to 'black Africa'; the beginning of regular contact with white South African businessmen and intellectuals that set the tone for future negotiations and international recognition of its preconditions for negotiations with Pretoria, presented in the Harare Declaration. The cumulative result was that, by the end of the 1980s, the ANC had firmly established itself as a highly respected government-in-waiting.

However, for all this success, the ANC endured some catastrophic reverses in its fortunes during the 1980s. The programme of 'armed propaganda' prompted a fierce and brutal retaliation from South Africa, whose destabilization targeted not only the ANC but also the whole of southern Africa. These events took place in the context of a shift to the right in the Western international community, especially in the United States and Britain, after the respective elections of Ronald Reagan and Margaret Thatcher. These leaders perceived the world through the lens of the Cold War and 'realpolitik' concerns, with their primary goal being to limit the power and influence of the Soviet Union. Both leaders were hostile to the ANC – branded by Thatcher as a 'terrorist organization' – and its links to the Soviet Union. Although these countries did not condone South Africa's destabilization of the region, they turned a blind eye to its activities in a bid to prevent other Marxist regimes taking power in southern Africa. Indeed, the United States was involved, in consort with South Africa, in the Angolan conflict, and had been supporting UNITA leader Jonas Savimbi, against the MPLA government. South African destabilization severely impinged upon the ANC's operational capacity in the region, forcing host governments seriously to reconsider their support of the movement. Both Mozambique and Swaziland succumbed to Pretoria's acts of aggression, and each eventually signed peace accords with South Africa that stipulated the expulsion of the ANC from their territory. Other regional governments, witnessing the devastating reprisals of the apartheid state, resorted to paying lip service only to the anti-apartheid struggle. The outcome was that the ANC's relations with its southern African allies began to slump from the mid-1980s and its ability to escalate its struggle significantly diminished. By 1989, the ANC was militarily in retreat, as successive southern African states expelled the movement, forcing it to relocate increasingly further away from South Africa.

The decade also saw the formation and rise to prominence of a range of internal opposition groups such as the Congress of South African Trade Unions (COSATU), the United Democratic Front (UDF), and the Zulu Inkatha Freedom Party (IFP). The ANC had an ideological affiliation with the first two (particularly the UDF, which adopted many of the ANC's symbols) offering it a foothold within South Africa.[31] However, it would be wrong to assume the ANC had direct control over these movements or the course of events internally; the emergence of such organizations raised the very real danger that it would be usurped by events outside of its influence or control.[32] According to Gerhart and Glaser, the ANC in the 1980s was a reactive force, 'deploring Pretoria's latest manoeuvres, condemning Western complicity in apartheid's evils, [and] applauding from the sidelines'.[33] The 1980s thus saw both significant gains and setbacks for the ANC, and although it was unbanned in February 1990, that outcome was by no means inevitable.

The ANC Escalates its 'Armed Propaganda'

One of the most important developments in the history of the ANC's struggle in this period was the escalation of 'armed propaganda'. Unlike other struggles in southern Africa, where guerrilla armies had engaged militarily with white minority governments, the ANC resorted to targeting infrastructure and symbols of the apartheid state. In June 1980, the ANC signalled its intentions spectacularly by striking against the SASOL coal to oil facility at Sasolburg. The attack was MK's first major attack within South Africa since the onset of the armed struggle 19 years earlier; the seriously damaged plant was afterwards depicted by *Sechaba* as 'a sea of flame, the fires of freedom'.[34] The attack was an enormous propaganda success and a highly symbolic strike against the apartheid state, whose reliance on producing oil from coal was crucial to the economy. Before the 1979 Iranian Revolution, 90 per cent of South Africa's oil had come from Iran, but Ayatollah Khomeini halted supplies after the shah had been overthrown.[35] The destruction of the SASOL facility demonstrated to the world that the apartheid state was no longer invulnerable and was a huge morale boost to the masses in the townships. The attack marked a new phase in the ANC's armed struggle, with a number of similar sabotages carried out across South Africa. The most noteworthy were: a rocket attack in August 1981 against Voortrekkerhoogte, the South African Defence Force (SADF) head-quarters outside Pretoria; a limpet mine strike against the Koeberg nuclear facility, in December 1982 and a car bomb explosion in Pretoria outside the South African Air Force (SAAF) headquarters in May 1983, which killed 17 and injured over 200.[36] The last of these was the first instance of MK killing civilians, and marked the departure from simply targeting symbols of the apartheid state. The killing of civilians was against official ANC policy, and the incident compelled Tambo to reiterate publicly that the movement did all it could to prevent such eventualities.[37] These deaths caused some international consternation (which downplayed South Africa's repeated and indiscriminate killing of civilians across Southern Africa) and did little to alter Western views about the ANC. The escalation of the armed struggle had at last brought the guerrilla war home to South Africa, with 467 incidents recorded in the period 1980–6.[38] With the mounting number of attacks within South Africa it was increasingly difficult for the apartheid state to deny the growing threat of MK.

The sabotage activities were not only designed to dent the strength of the apartheid state, but also to publicize the ANC's capacity to turn its rhetoric of an armed seizure of power into reality. Senior NEC member Pallo Jordan argued that 'armed propaganda' had two purposes:

> First of all, to register an armed presence and the capacity of the movement to respond to the regime's violence. And then also, apart from that, it was conceived of as being vital in terms of hitting strategic enemy installations, not only for demonstrative of that [sic] but in fact to deliver crippling blows against the enemy. But over and above that, there was the need to build up the confidence of the army we had trained.[39]

Sue Rabkin, a member of the ANC underground, supports Jordan's view that 'armed propaganda' was 'seen as a way of agitating, of doing political work, and [showing] we were there. And that, just on its own, was absolutely crucial because that's what our people needed to hear. It was a very correct decision. It said we are around and capable of blowing up Sasol and Koeberg and wherever.' Furthermore, Rabkin also thought that 'armed propaganda' was a means of coalescing regional support and persuading leaders of the ANC's seriousness: 'the OAU specifically ... were impressed. I mean they had been getting pissed off with the ANC for years.'[40] Subsequently, the upturn in incidents of 'armed propaganda' allowed the ANC to portray itself as a 'credible' fighting force to its domestic and international supporters. The upsurge in action also created a mystique around MK, with guerrillas killed in action venerated as heroes of the struggle.[41]

However, incidents of 'armed propaganda' became less frequent as the decade wore on. Infiltration into South Africa became ever more difficult for MK guerrillas, in part because of the shifting nature of southern

African support towards the ANC. The decrease in the ANC's armed activity directly coincided with South Africa's increasing political and military pressure directed against its neighbours. In response to MK attacks in South Africa the SADF retaliated against the ANC and its allies across southern Africa. The retribution increasingly impeded the progress and organizational capacity of the movement. Although there was a significant upsurge in internal township unrest called for by the ANC from exile via Radio Freedom and its propaganda pamphlets, the violence was never under its direct control. The result was that new forms of protest and organization began to take hold within South Africa, outside of the influence of the ANC. It must be noted that the NP government's strategy of regional aggression and internal oppression had successfully prevented the ANC from establishing a permanent foothold in the country. The continued absence of underground support networks in South Africa meant that infiltrating guerrilla fighters encountered numerous problems, especially in escaping. Estimates of survival rates differ, but they all demonstrate the high price paid by MK operatives. According to Ivan Pillay, the average rate of survival for a guerrilla fighter was around five months; a casualty rate that he later conceded was unacceptably high.[42] ANC exile Garth Strachan, depicted an even more depressing picture, asserting that from 1986 onwards, MK cadres operating out of Zimbabwe suffered nearly a '100 per cent casualty rate [defined as killed or arrested within 24 hours]'.[43] Mac Maharaj was equally critical of the ANC's inability to escalate the struggle, describing attempted infiltrations from Mozambique and Zimbabwe, between 1981 and 1983 as 'military misadventure'.[44] The problem stemmed from a combination of the apartheid regime's regional repression, effective intelligence in the region, security pacts with its neighbours and the ANC's inability to establish fully the internal political dimension of the struggle beyond its 'armed propaganda'. Nevertheless the activities of the ANC in the early 1980s had demonstrated its ability to strike at the heart of the apartheid state. The initial successes of 'armed propaganda' undoubtedly had an enormously positive effect on the psyche of the movement and its international supporters.

South Africa's Destabilization of Southern Africa

To understand fully the evolution of the ANC's foreign policy in the latter stages of its exile, the effects of South African regional destabilization must be taken into account. The various activities of the apartheid state across southern Africa acted as a major impediment to the movement's progress. In the late 1970s, the NP government led by President P. W. Botha portrayed the combined threat of communism and Black Nationalism on its borders as a 'Total Onslaught' against South Africa. The growing fear amongst South African officials about the extent of the threat was reinforced by the election victory of Robert Mugabe's Zimbabwe African National Union (ZANU) in 1980. In order to counteract the onslaught of guerrilla forces, the government devised a comprehensive 'Total Strategy', which utilized all possible political, economic and military resources of the state to defend the nation.[45] The implementation of the 'Total Strategy' as a key tenet of apartheid foreign policy initiated an intensely destructive period in southern African history. Pretoria had originally envisaged the 'Total Strategy' as a mechanism to persuade neighbouring governments to form a 'constellation of states' – an economic and political alliance of southern African countries – encompassing South Africa, the 'independent' Bantustans (the pseudo self-governing homelands within South Africa that were set aside for separate African development)[46] and countries such as Botswana and Swaziland.[47] However, Pretoria's plan was scuppered first by ZANU's election victory in 1980, and then by the subsequent decision of the six so-called Frontline States of Angola, Botswana, Mozambique, Tanzania, Zambia and Zimbabwe, which, together with Lesotho, Swaziland, and Malawi, established the Southern African Development Coordination Conference (SADCC) in April 1980.[48] The purpose of SADCC was to decisively break the region's economic dependence on South Africa, and provide a platform for greater co-operation and development.[49] The formation of SADCC, the rejection of South African overtures and the attempt to decrease regional dependency, were regarded as an affront by Pretoria and did little to diminish the perception of an impending Marxist onslaught. However, South Africa skilfully manipulated the regional interdependencies lingering from the colonial era for its own benefit, for example by destroying infrastructure or blockading trade access, ensuring that SADCC aims were never fully realized.

The onset of the ANC's campaign of 'armed propaganda' was premised as a central element of the 'Total Onslaught', and it sparked a vicious cycle of violent retaliation from South Africa against the movement and its hosts. Under the 'Total Strategy' South Africa completely ignored state sovereignty in the region, and targeted with impunity any country that hosted the ANC. By 1981, the SADF had already violated the sovereignty of seven independent countries.[50] The aim of destabilization was thus to apply pressure on regional governments to cease their support of the ANC, to repel the movement away from South Africa's borders and to diminish the threat of communism, which served as useful pretext for its actions. The first major SADF strike against the ANC occurred in January 1981, when South African commandos targeted its residencies in Matola, near Maputo, killing 12 people.[51] The ANC described this as the moment in which South Africa 'declared war on Africa'.[52] South Africa followed up this raid by invading Lesotho in January 1983, when over 100 commandos and helicopter gunships attacked 12 ANC locations in and around the capital Maseru, killing 42 people.[53] Except for its ongoing military activities in Angola, the incursion into Lesotho was the largest by the SADF into another southern African country.[54] Further raids against the Frontline States and the ANC were conducted throughout the 1980s, such as a SADF commando raid into Botswana in 1985, in a bid to thwart the 'Onslaught'.[55]

However, it was not just overt military incursions that had an effect on the ANC and southern Africa. The apartheid state also utilized a range of covert means in support of its strategy, including kidnappings and assassinations across the region, such as the murders of Joe Gqabi in Harare in 1981 and Ruth First in Maputo in 1982.[56] A major concern for the ANC was that South African security officials were operating against its interests, virtually unimpeded throughout southern Africa.[57] More worryingly, these operations were sometimes carried out in co-operation with regional governments, which had increasingly succumbed to apartheid pressure. For example, both Botswana and Swaziland by the early 1980s monitored, arrested and expelled ANC activists from their territory, which drastically impeded the movement's operational capacity.[58] After the Nkomati Accords were signed in 1984, Mozambique also expelled the ANC – another significant setback in the struggle. South Africa contributed further to regional instability by funding and training two military movements against governments sheltering the ANC: the Mozambican National Resistance (RENAMO) and UNITA. This is not the place to explore the impact of RENAMO or UNITA, but they drastically destabilized Angola and Mozambique, resulting in prolonged civil wars, immense infrastructural damage and economic decline.[59] A further example of Pretoria's impact on the internal affairs of southern Africa was in Lesotho. The prime minister of Lesotho, Chief Jonathan, had become increasingly vocal in his support for the ANC. His outspokenness exasperated South Africa, prompting Pretoria to close the border in 1986. South Africa implemented a total economic blockade of the tiny mountain kingdom, which resulted in a military coup; as a consequence, the military junta that deposed Jonathan also expelled the ANC from Lesotho.[60]

The counter-offensive strategy employed by South Africa severely limited the ANC's room for manoeuvre in southern Africa. Maharaj conceded that 'the enemy devised a strategy where at that moment in our thinking, they forced us off track; they removed this central focus on our thinking which was primarily offensive; they forced us into a mode of retreat and discontinuity of structures'.[61] The destabilization campaign ensured that the movement was on the back foot and the impetus of the struggle was lost. More importantly, the devastating actions of South Africa ensured that southern African support for the ANC was no longer guaranteed, as regional governments sought to protect their interests.

The ANC's Precarious Position in Southern Africa

For the NP government, the sustained violence and economic pressure directed at southern Africa had the desired effect. Although regional leaders remained opposed to apartheid, support for the ANC was far more tenuous. As destabilization took its toll, governments had to make tough choices with regard to the ANC's status in their countries; those closest in proximity to South Africa had least choice in the matter. The result was a haphazard and fluctuating pattern of support across southern Africa for the ANC. In 1983, Robert Cabelly, a former US State Department for African Affairs employee, reported 'that behind the united front of the frontline states, they were all very iffy about the ANC'.[62] This section will examine the status of the ANC across the region.

The ANC's relationship with the Zambian government was complex. Officially, they were extremely close, demonstrated by the movement locating its main base of operations in Lusaka. The ANC had between 2,000 and 4,000 members in the country during the 1980s, which illustrates that Zambian officials were prepared to accept a large, overt presence.[63] Kaunda's strict proviso that no military personnel or bases were allowed to operate in the country was generally heeded by the ANC, although MK guerrillas were permitted to pass through Zambia on the way south. The ANC's position was strengthened further by the fact that Kaunda regularly lobbied internationally against apartheid in various multilateral forums. Yet, despite the very public anti-apartheid stance of Zambia, Kaunda maintained covert links with South Africa, with which he had maintained unofficial relations since the late 1960s.[64] Kaunda had met with NP officials on several occasions since independence and secretly corresponded with Pretoria, reflecting the fact that it was imperative for Zambia to maintain trade links with the apartheid state.[65] Kaunda was nevertheless regarded as a dependable ally by the ANC, ensuring that Lusaka became a vital and secure base of operations for the movement. As the 1980s wore on, Zambia had become a home from home for many within the ANC, reinforced by the increasing numbers of cadres who relocated to Lusaka after their removal from other Frontline States.[66]

The close affinity between the ANC and the governments of Angola and Mozambique, due in part to the Khartoum Alliance, ensured that the movement had two strong regional allies in its struggle. In Angola, bases and offices had been established soon after independence; these provided the ANC with an opportunity to receive military training from foreign instructors, and shelter its fighters in the relative security of the north of the country. Not much is known about official relations, as the current MPLA government is still reticent about opening up its archives, but they were clearly very good, as the following examples will indicate. The close ANC–Angolan relations were demonstrated by joint operations in the civil war, with MK guerrillas tasked to fight alongside the Angolan army in its long-running conflict with UNITA.[67] It is unclear exactly how this arrangement came about, but the ANC leadership committed its military forces to the MPLA's war. The decision to fight alongside the Angolan army was not popular amongst the MK rank and file. It did little to diminish mounting tensions amongst cadres, who were increasingly frustrated by the continuous training, poor conditions and the abuse of leadership, and who certainly felt that efforts should be concentrated on targeting South Africa.[68] The ANC's decision to co-operate militarily with the MPLA triggered a mutiny amongst MK guerrillas in 1984.[69] As a direct consequence of the mutiny, the MPLA intervened, using its soldiers to quell a popular uprising within the ANC.[70] The MPLA clearly collaborated with the ANC leadership against its cadres and it was later reported that it had 'played a very dishonest role [as] ... they began to throttle this popular unrest ... abort[ing] a drive to veer the ANC towards democracy'.[71] It would not be the last time an ally of the ANC acted in such a manner. Despite the mutiny, the close alliance with the MPLA stood firm and MK cadres were still fighting in the war against UNITA in 1987.[72] Mutual assistance would not have occurred without a significant degree of co-operation between the MPLA government and the ANC. More crucially, Angola became a military hub for MK fighters, an obligation no other southern African government could fulfil.

Mozambique was vital to the intensification of the ANC's struggle and the country developed into a highly important sanctuary and staging post. Permitted to operate with relative freedom in the country, and benefiting from its geographical proximity to South Africa, the ANC used Mozambique as a platform from which to escalate its struggle. Mozambique became the key infiltration route for its fighters, via Swaziland, into South Africa, and it is no coincidence that the ANC's freedom to operate there during the early 1980s coincided with the most high-profile acts of 'armed propaganda'. The FRELIMO government was unable to offer much military or financial support, but it turned a blind eye to some of the movement's activities. According to former British Ambassador Ann Grant, FRELIMO 'provided [the ANC] with a safe haven and accommodation; they saw that very much as part of their own struggle'.[73] The ideological affiliation was very close, with regular contact between the two leaders. For example, the Mozambican president, Samora Machel, attended and spoke at an ANC mass rally in Maputo alongside Tambo, in February 1981.[74] Rabkin recalled that 'we [the ANC] loved FRELIMO and FRELIMO loved us'.[75] However, destabilization soon took its toll and FRELIMO could not maintain its support of the ANC. Deon Geldenhuys asserted:

in the case of Mozambique, I think the evidence is clear cut, that South Africa's actions at subverting the regime of Samora Machel, were of such magnitude, that the costs of maintaining the relationship that Mozambique had with the ANC was simply becoming unbearable, simply in terms of the punishment South Africa was meting out.[76]

The cumulative result of South African punishment was that in 1984, Mozambique signed the Nkomati Accords, which will be discussed in the next section. The negotiations proved a serious setback for the ANC, as the Accords stipulated that the movement had to be expelled; its cadres were forced out of the country by the Mozambican military, and its structures dismantled.[77] Although South Africa's devastating destabilization was the primary cause of this expulsion, Rabkin believed that the ANC's own actions had contributed: 'there was almost, I'd say, an abuse of borders ... there was no consideration at that stage ... that this was other people's country ... we blatantly disregarded [government requests] ... We were very arrogant. And we paid the price'.[78] The Accord effectively closed the infiltration route into South Africa, and consequently the effectiveness of the armed struggle diminished. Destabilization was making its mark in southern Africa.

Zimbabwean independence should have been a major boost to the struggle, but lingering hostility between the ANC and the ZANU government meant that relations were strained. The uneasy relationship stemmed from the Khartoum Alliance, which had excluded ZANU and prioritized links with the Zimbabwe African People's Union (ZAPU). As a result, very few ANC leaders, with the notable exception of Thabo Mbeki, had approved of Mugabe's election victory in 1980.[79] The tone was thus set for future relations with Zimbabwe. The legacy of the Khartoum Alliance also meant that Mugabe did not trust the ANC believing that, if there was a ZAPU uprising, the two would unite against his rule.[80] Mugabe's fears were somewhat justified when ZANU and ZAPU came into direct conflict in 1982; arms caches were found at ZAPU properties, along with a number of MK commanders.[81] As a result, relations all but collapsed between the ANC and ZANU. Mugabe ordered that the ANC's fledgling structures in Zimbabwe should be dismantled, and the majority of its cadres removed.[82] On several occasions the Zimbabwean state media openly criticized the ANC and its struggle, which did little to help strained relations.[83] Yet rhetorically, ZANU remained a vocal opponent of the apartheid state; Mugabe still permitted the ANC to have an office in Harare, which was later targeted by a South African military raid in 1986.[84] Although Mugabe tolerated a limited ANC presence, ZANU made life difficult because of suspicions about where the movement's loyalties lay. Geldenhuys points out that, 'Zimbabwe had a fairly good understanding of where the proverbial line in the sand had been drawn ... it had a fair amount of freedom of expression so to speak, lambasting South Africa ... [but] stopped short of overtly supporting the ANC's military wing.'[85] The prevention of any MK activity in Zimbabwe, a potentially crucial infiltration point into South Africa, was enforced by the Zimbabwean army and consequently the country did not experience the same levels of destabilization compared to the rest of Southern Africa.[86]

Swaziland had also served as a useful forward area for the ANC, offering a safe haven for fleeing exiles as well as providing an infiltration route into South Africa. The struggle was assisted by the ANC's historic friendship with the Swazi royal family, which had been represented at the founding of the movement in 1912.[87] Kasrils observed that 'the ANC's Moses Mabhida often visited the King [Sobuza II] from Lusaka and Maputo to clarify our position and to influence Swazi foreign policy. Mabhida ... was always well received.'[88] Swaziland had become an increasingly important military location for the ANC as its guerrillas entered the country from the north, allowing it to escalate its 'armed propaganda'. South African Defence Minister Magnus Malan saw Swaziland as a 'second front' against South Africa due to the steady flow of MK guerrillas from the country.[89] However, Swaziland was dependent on South Africa, and its precarious economic position worsened as the apartheid state pressurized the tiny kingdom. In 1982, in a precursor to the Nkomati Accords, Swaziland signed a secret deal with South Africa, which formalized a political and security arrangement.[90] As an incentive to the Swazis, South Africa had offered a land exchange, promising to return to Swaziland the former parts of the kingdom, Kwanhgwane and Ingwauuma.[91] This comprehensive deal stipulated that the ANC would not be permitted to use Swazi territory whilst South African security forces were able to operate virtually unhindered in the country; in 1986 ANC activist Ebrahim Ebrahim was kidnapped.[92] From 1982 onwards, the Swazi police (according to Kasrils), 'zealously' enforced the deal, rounding up and expelling ANC cadres, including key members such as Bafana Duma and Stanley Mabizela.[93] The ANC was infuriated by the deal as it closed a vital route into South Africa, but it had very few foreign policy options with which to influence Swazi policy.[94] Documentary evidence shows how ANC demands were ignored in exchanges of letters and statements with the Swazi government.[95] One such memorandum provides an insight into how by this stage the ANC regarded itself as the government-in-waiting. The document declared that it would 'have been an advantage both to Swaziland and ourselves, if the government of Swaziland had sought the opinion of the ANC on the question under discussion before entering into negotiations with the Pretoria regime'.[96] The memorandum did little to change Swaziland's position (given the pressure the government was under), but it is an important indication of the ways in which the ANC interacted with regional governments, the strategies it employed to alter their actions towards the movement and South Africa, and its own self perceptions.

The ANC remained on cordial terms with all independent southern African nations, except Malawi, but its official status in the region during the 1980s was precarious. The ANC's political aspirations were broadly supported by regional leaders, who at the very least provided it with their rhetorical backing. However, destabilization and South Africa's enforced pacts had taken their toll on the region, and had significantly diminished the ANC's ability to operate in southern Africa. The gains made by the ANC were in real danger of being reversed by Pretoria's campaign against the region, which was extremely successful in disrupting the ANC. The movement discovered that previously friendly governments were all too willing to dismantle its exile structures and expel its cadres. A limited number of cadres did remain in the Frontline States, but by the mid-1980s 'the best forward areas [were] reeling: Maputo [was] virtually over; Swaziland [was] cut off'.[97] The ANC was obviously disappointed by developments, yet it was fully aware of the situation afflicting southern Africa. E. S. Reddy, former head of the United Nations Centre against Apartheid asserted that 'the ANC understood the difficulties of the host countries and did not complain ... it appreciated that frontline states made enormous sacrifices'.[98] The problems in southern Africa meant that global assistance was crucial to the ongoing struggle. The ANC's multifaceted international network spanning the Eastern Bloc, the AAM and Scandinavian countries came to the fore in fulfilling its foreign policy goals of isolating and ultimately overthrowing apartheid.

The Nkomati Accord

The sustained direct economic, political and military destabilization by South Africa had by 1984 brought Mozambique to its knees. It was increasingly apparent that Mozambique could not withstand South African pressure and something had to give. The direct consequence was that in March 1984, Samora Machel and P. W. Botha met to sign an 'agreement on non-aggression and good neighbourliness' between Mozambique and South Africa, known as the Nkomati Accord.[99] The significance of the Accord was that the ANC was expelled from Mozambique (only ten cadres were allowed to remain in Maputo) in what the movement saw as a betrayal of the struggle. This sense of betrayal within the leadership can be attributed to the fact that before the Accord was signed, the ANC had actually been urging FRELIMO to adopt a more proactive stance towards Pretoria.[100] Such an unrealistic position indicates a certain naivety and insensitivity by the ANC, as its very presence was the reason behind South Africa aggressively targeting Mozambique. When the Nkomati Accord was officially announced there was a sense of shock within the ANC. Vladimir Shubin argues that the movement faced 'a strategic retreat without any prospect of return. What upset them most was the absence of consultation between Frelimo and the ANC.'[101] Joe Slovo, who resided in Mozambique, summed up the effect of Nkomati on the ANC: 'it disastrously impeded the prospects that had existed at the beginning of 1984 to raise our urban and rural combat presence ... it is no secret ... that Mozambique had been crucial to our ongoing efforts'.[102]

The sense of anger and betrayal was reinforced when the ANC's erstwhile ally publicly portrayed the Accord as a victory for the Mozambican people.[103] Not too surprisingly, relations between the ANC and FRELIMO deteriorated quickly after Nkomati. One observer argued that the ANC's reaction to the Accord was 'like a petulant, jilted lover'.[104] However, there was a sense of frustration too as South Africa's aggressive outward strategy was reaping dividends. In the wake of the Mozambican and Swazi agreements, the emerging reality was that the ANC's foreign policy in Southern Africa was unable to influence even some of the smallest nations. Although South Africa swiftly reneged on the terms of the Accord, the damage between FRELIMO and the ANC had been done. Only after the death of Moses Mabhida in March 1986 did relations with Mozambique begin to improve. FRELIMO held a full state funeral in Maputo, at which Machel spoke of 'the indestructible fraternity of the South African and Mozambican peoples, of the profound identity of our peoples' struggle'.[105] The funeral provided an opportunity for the leaders to meet in a 'symbolic reconciliation' and re-establish their personal relationships.[106] The funeral and the events surrounding it were described as the burial not only of a liberation hero, but also of the Nkomati Accord itself.[107] However, the renewed support of FRELIMO did not change the geopolitical reality for the ANC. The lingering threat of apartheid reprisals meant that although a limited presence was re-established in Mozambique, it never hit the heights of the pre-Nkomati period.

The Kabwe Conference, 1985

In June 1985, the ANC held its Second National Consultative Conference in Kabwe, Zambia, the first such meeting since Morogoro 16 years earlier. The conference enabled the most open debate the ANC had ever held in exile, allowing its cadres to air grievances and offer suggestions for the future of the struggle. The conference was preceded by an 18-month preparatory stage that involved all the ANC's structures; documents were circulated worldwide, and 82 submissions were tabled for final deliberation at the conference.[108] This remarkably open and democratic process was something that had been strikingly absent from the ANC and the conference was designed to rectify this. The decision to convene in Zambia reflected concerns in the context of ongoing destabilization in southern Africa, and the ANC's fragile position in the region. It did also reflect the ANC's good relations with Kaunda, who allocated a battalion of the army to defend the conference centre from potential South African attacks.[109] *Sechaba* expressed the ANC's 'deeply felt appreciation of the role of Zambia, under the leadership of Kenneth Kaunda, is playing in our struggle for national and social emancipation'.[110]

At the Kabwe Conference, 250 delegates, representing every branch of the ANC, discussed the submissions, planned for the future, and elected a new National Executive Committee (NEC).[111] During the conference, several key decisions were taken that would shape the rest of the struggle, including: the opening up of its membership to all racial groups; a reaffirmation of the Freedom Charter as an expression of the movement's ideals and aspirations; the dropping of the distinction between 'hard' and 'soft' targets; and the renewed commitment to a 'People's War'.[112] The central theme of the conference became preparation for a People's War and the revolutionary seizure of power.[113] The ANC had of course been pursuing this objective for some time, but Kabwe ensured that it had the full endorsement of the movement. However, given the reality of the situation, this emphasis and focus on the armed struggle had a negative effect on other aspects of the ANC's work, including the crucial task of political mobilization inside South Africa. In 1985, the ANC still did not have the necessary underground network in South Africa to accommodate incoming fighters nor the means to ferment an uprising. The predominance of the external armed struggle continued to take precedence over other matters, undermining the ANC's political activity. A key point to emphasize is that there was limited internal participation in policy formation, including foreign policy within the ANC. The result was that decision making was restricted to a relatively small number of people, all of whom were part of the ANC's exiled political elite. What emerged was a profound disconnect between the internal and external dimensions of the struggle, which persisted from exile into the democratic era, exemplified by the marginalization of activists that remained in South Africa. As a consequence, it allowed exiled cadres, most notably Thabo Mbeki, to dominate the foreign policy direction of the ANC.

The Kabwe Conference did allow the ANC to take the important, yet previously unprecedented, step of discussing what its foreign policy objectives were. The conference set aside time to discuss the 'international situation';[114] however, of far more significance was the publication of the Final Report of the Commission on Foreign Policy.[115] The Report is remarkable because it was the first instance, since the vague outlines of the Freedom Charter written in 1955, that the ANC had attempted to formalize its foreign policy position.[116] The Report affirmed the objective of seizing power by force, emphasizing that 'the ANC pursues the strategic goal of the seizure of political power by the revolutionary forces of our country'.[117] The Report also set out three core objectives that the 'ANC should continue to relentlessly pursue':

1. The total isolation of the white minority regime in South Africa, leading to the imposition of comprehensive and mandatory sanctions under Chapter VII of the Charter of the United Nations.

2. The recognition and support of the ANC as the sole and authentic representative of the overwhelming majority of the people of South Africa.

3. The establishment of bilateral and diplomatic relations between the ANC and governments, as well as with the international democratic forces committed to the establishment of a united, non-racial and democratic South Africa.[118]

In order to fulfil these objectives, the document provided a list of goals including: exposing South African criminality; persuading the world to terminate international links with Pretoria; popularizing the ANC; strengthening ties with African states, the OAU, Frontline States and 'authentic liberation movements'; and consolidating support from both Western and socialist nations.[119] Although the ANC had to some extent been pursuing these objectives throughout its exile, the Report was the first time the movement had articulated its approach to foreign policy. As the decade progressed, the ANC did successfully achieve some of these objectives. The Report was therefore an important start for the ANC in consciously thinking about its foreign policy.

However, these objectives focused on the immediate future and there was little consideration given to a comprehensive strategy for negotiations with Pretoria. During South Africa's transition from apartheid to democracy between 1990 and 1994, the Final Report of the Commission on Foreign Policy and the Freedom Charter formed the entire basis of the ANC's thinking on foreign policy, putting it at a distinct disadvantage in negotiations with the apartheid state. Activist and journalist Howard Barrell scathingly criticized the Kabwe Conference, arguing that 'at the most crucial moment in its history, in the midst of the most serious uprisings in South Africa in which its name was being widely proclaimed as leader of a revolution, the ANC had held a conference and concluded it with no generally agreed formulation of strategy'.[120]

The End of Exile

By 1985, white minority rule in South Africa faced mounting domestic and international pressure to dismantle apartheid. The South African government was confronted by the emergence of popular internal opposition led by new movements such as COSATU and the UDF; rising incidents of township rebellion, in part inspired by MK attacks and the ANC's call to make 'South Africa ungovernable'; rolling industrial action by militant unions; international boycotts and sanctions and an ever worsening debt crisis.[121] As the crisis deepened, it was widely hoped that Botha would initiate sweeping reforms to the system of apartheid to ease the mounting problems.[122] However, in his 'Crossing the Rubicon' speech in August 1985, Botha did the complete opposite, demonstrating his belligerence by castigating his critics at home and abroad.[123] Following the speech, the value of the Rand collapsed and the international community, having widely condemned South Africa, subsequently applied punitive sanctions against Pretoria.[124] It also sparked a renewed upsurge in international protest against apartheid, spearheaded by the AAM. The activities of both the ANC and AAM succeeded in applying pressure on multinational corporations, to cease links with South Africa. The mounting pressure and bad publicity against banks such as Chase Manhattan and Barclays forced them into rethinking their ties with South Africa. The result was that many recalled loans or refused to lend further to South Africa, deepening the isolation and economic crisis of the apartheid state.[125]

The ANC, White South Africans, and the Prospect of Negotiations

Within South Africa there was a growing realization, particularly in the white business community, that apartheid was bad for business. Botha's speech was the tipping point for this community, prompting fears that an ANC victory might destroy capitalism in South Africa.[126] In September 1985, at Kaunda's personal lodge in Zambia, a delegation of high-profile white South African businessmen and journalists, led by Anglo-American chairman Gavin Relly, met with Tambo, Thabo Mbeki, and other ANC leaders.[127] The meeting was not intended to act as a forum for negotiations, but rather to allow the two sides to become acquainted, to discuss the role of violence and the SACP in the ANC's struggle, and to assess the movement's economic policies for South Africa's future.[128] Although there was no tangible outcome from the meeting, it marked the beginning of increased white contact with the ANC. For the ANC to be recognized by such an influential section of the white South African community was a major achievement. Tambo later argued that although business leaders were acting in their own self-interest, their influence served as a useful political lever in South Africa.[129] However, the initial optimism surrounding these talks rapidly dwindled; Botha reinforced his authority in South Africa, the white businessmen who had met with the ANC were publicly castigated, and a wave of particularly violent MK attacks in the country also hardened white public opinion.[130]

Gavin Relly's delegation nevertheless encouraged other prominent white South Africans to visit the ANC in exile. The next key figure to visit the ANC in Lusaka was Fredrik van Zyl Slabbert, the former leader of the Progressive Federal Party (PFP), who was impressed by the movement and its vision for the future of South Africa; after the meeting he declared, 'a path away from violence can be negotiated'.[131] The most high-profile meeting with white South Africans occurred in Senegal, in July 1987. Drawn from academic, business and religious circles, 61 predominantly Afrikaans-speaking South Africans attended the Institute for a Democratic Alternative for South Africa (IDASA) conference in Dakar to meet with the ANC.[132] The delegates discussed amongst other things the evolving situation in South Africa, the armed struggle, and the possibility of a negotiated settlement.[133] *Sechaba* reported that the Dakar meeting had caused nervousness amongst senior South African government officials, and described it as an important 'aspect of the struggle to isolate the apartheid regime'.[134] It was a major success for the ANC's international and domestic legitimacy, illustrating the growing sense that there could be no settlement without its involvement.

After several delegations of whites had met with the ANC in exile, the possibility of negotiations with Pretoria became increasingly imaginable. Some elements within the ANC leadership had accepted that the prospect of a negotiated settlement was ever more likely, although the movement was determined to enter any talks from a position of strength. However, the ANC was not particularly clear on its stance towards negotiations, oscillating between propagandistic calls for the military seizure of power, while privately expressing a desire to enter into talks with the South African government. The ANC had spent its long period in exile working on how to overthrow apartheid, and not what would replace it. The consequence was that the Freedom Charter was its only clear vision for the future. A 1987 ANC intelligence report perceptively argued that the ANC needed to alter its approach, concluding that 'we need to move beyond slogans and propaganda and be clear about the society we are trying to build and how we will do it'.[135] There were elements within the ANC, predominantly around Chris Hani, who remained wedded to their belief in the revolutionary seizure of power, and were stridently opposed to any negotiations.[136] Such views were not surprising, given that the ANC had consistently proclaimed the necessity of the armed struggle and a People's War to defeat apartheid. Although such insurrectionary rhetoric continued, by the late 1980s the ANC's hopes of militarily overthrowing the apartheid regime were swiftly diminishing. South African ascendancy across Southern Africa had taken its toll, and the ANC struggled to escalate the military aspect of its campaign. Rumours abounded about the leadership 'selling out'. Secret negotiations were occurring between the ANC and the NP, but publicly the leadership had to try and allay its supporter's fears.[137] The only way that the ANC could 'sell' negotiations to its cadres was by ignoring the unfolding reality, and emphasizing that any negotiations that did occur were 'attributable to pressure imposed on [Pretoria] by the movement, above all through its armed struggle'.[138] At the Kabwe Conference the ANC had conceded the prospect of negotiating with Pretoria, but thought it unlikely: 'this issue has arisen at this time exactly because of our strength inside the country, the level of our struggle and the crisis confronting the Botha regime. The NEC is however convinced that this regime is not interested in a just solution of the South African question.'[139]

Despite attempts to appease its more militant supporters, the ANC leadership and the South African government had established clandestine channels of communication, which, from 1988, involved a series of talks at Mells Park in England. Mbeki, whose own 'thoughts about [a negotiated] strategy had been up against the romantic juggernaut of "Planning for People's War"', was the main driver of these discussions.[140] These talks were the moment when leaders from both sides realized that there was sufficient common ground to make a political settlement possible. Meanwhile, in 1985, Mandela (while still in prison) decided without the knowledge of the ANC leadership, to begin meeting secretly with NP officials to discuss the future; these meetings continued until his release in 1990.[141] These talks provided one of many building blocks to a peaceful transition to majority rule, demonstrating to the NP that they could do business with the ANC.

The stumbling blocks for the apartheid regime remained the ANC's armed struggle and its links to the Soviet Union.

The New York Accords, Namibian Independence and the Effect on the ANC

The ANC's foreign policy outside southern Africa, primarily directed at Western states, had proved increasingly successful in the late 1980s. Regular meetings with senior politicians, international organizations and journalists, helped spread its message to a wider audience and further isolate South Africa. The ANC thereby ensured that it retained the attention of the international community, firmly establishing its position as the government-in-waiting. However, in a scenario that had become depressingly familiar for the ANC, a new and unexpected series of international events, over which the movement had no control or influence, decisively shaped the end of its exile.

In the early 1980s, the US Assistant Secretary of State for African Affairs, Chester Crocker, had developed a 'linkage' policy to solve the ongoing crisis in southern Africa. This policy, known as Constructive Engagement, tied South Africa's military withdrawal from Angola and future Namibian independence, to Cuba's disengagement from the Angolan conflict.[142] The Crocker proposal provided the basis for talks between the governments of Angola, Cuba and South Africa in 1987. The negotiations culminated in the three sides signing the New York Accords in December 1988; these set a timetable for South African and Cuban troop withdrawals, and for Namibian independence.[143] In November 1989, Namibia held 'free and fair' democratic elections, which the South West Africa People's Organization (SWAPO) won; the result paved the way for the nation's independence in March 1990.[144]

These events had a significant impact on the ANC. One clause of the New York Accords stipulated that each signatory would prohibit the use of its territory for the perpetration of violence against others in Southern Africa; this meant that the MPLA was forced to cease its military assistance to the ANC.[145] In January 1989, with the assistance of the Soviet Air Force, all ANC Angolan camps were vacated and MK cadres were relocated to Uganda, Tanzania and Ethiopia.[146] The New York Accords struck a serious blow to the ANC's military capabilities, paralysing its activities in the region. All means of infiltration had been effectively closed. The expulsion of MK from Angola also had a severe knock-on effect for the ANC's foreign relations, particularly with Zambia. A series of incidents occurred in Lusaka where increasingly frustrated and ill-disciplined ANC and MK members had killed Zambian nationals, naturally infuriating the government.[147] As on other previous occasions in Zambia and elsewhere, Kaunda deployed his military forces to help the ANC security department disarm its own fighters.[148] Kaunda promptly gave the ANC an ultimatum to leave the country, permitting only a skeleton diplomatic mission to remain.[149] The expulsion from Zambia meant that the ANC were yet again moved further away from South Africa, with almost no chance of return. The movement's revolutionary strategy was set back enormously. The development prompted Thula Simpson to observe that as a result 'the infiltration of large numbers of guerrillas was no longer a feasible option ... it was impossible under these circumstances for the ANC to intensify its armed struggle'.[150]

With the armed struggle drastically curtailed, the ANC urgently began to explore avenues for formal negotiations with Pretoria. The accelerating shift towards negotiations reflected the fact that the ANC was not in control of the unfolding events in South Africa. There was a very real danger that the movement would lose its influence over the proceedings. During the Kabwe Conference, the ANC leadership, in discussing the possibility of negotiating with the apartheid regime, stated that 'we cannot be seen to be rejecting a negotiated settlement in principle', but it did however express the pre-condition that 'no negotiations can take place or even be considered until all political prisoners are released'.[151] In the aftermath of the New York Accords, as the international climate drastically shifted, Tambo tasked the ANC to draft a position statement on negotiations that could be endorsed by the international community. The ANC's thinking on negotiations is summarized by the resulting Discussion Paper on the Issue of Negotiations: June 1989. This acknowledged that the changing geopolitical climate was pushing the adversaries towards détente and settlement.[152] It set out the ANC's preconditions for talks with South Africa, later known as the Harare Declaration, after it was endorsed by the OAU in August 1989.[153] The Harare Declaration confirmed the ANC's willingness to embrace negotiations as a method of achieving change in South Africa. Importantly, the Harare Declaration appealed 'to all people of goodwill throughout the world to support this Programme of Action as a necessary measure to secure the earliest liquidation of the apartheid system and the transformation of South Africa.'[154] The ANC's stance generated worldwide consensus in support of the Harare Declaration. This was a major boost for the ANC's foreign policy and international credibility, as its new position was now regarded as a moderate and responsible engine of change.

While external forces were mounting against Pretoria, incremental internal change to apartheid was finally initiated with F. W. de Klerk's accession to the South African presidency in August 1989, following Botha's resignation. De Klerk signalled his willingness to begin implementing reforms, although initially these were limited, rather than fundamental changes. For example, in October 1989, he began to fulfil the conditions of the Harare Declaration by unconditionally releasing eight political prisoners, including Walter Sisulu.[155] The move provided a clear signal that the NP was prepared to begin negotiations with the ANC in a bid to resolve the crisis; however, like the ANC, de Klerk was keen to do so only from a position of strength.[156] The success of the New York Accords had demonstrated an appetite for peaceful negotiations amongst the adversaries in the region. The real engine of change was however the seismic shift in international politics that finally persuaded the South Africans to begin the process of dismantling the system of apartheid.

The successful implementation of the New York Accords by the superpowers, and the subsequent Namibian elections, demonstrated a new international desire for peace in southern Africa, and the possibility for an effective transition in South Africa. Most importantly, the new Soviet leader, Mikhail Gorbachev, announced in 1986 his desire to solve regional conflicts via peaceful political settlement, in order to extricate the Soviet Union from its foreign adventures. The Soviet Union consequently adopted the policy of *perestroika*, signalling a new approach in its foreign policy, and its diminished interest in supporting national liberation movements.[157] The New York Accords demonstrated the rapid shift in Soviet thinking, as 'Gorbachev had almost lost interest in the problems of liberation movements ... and concentrated on contacts with the west'.[158] The subsequent collapse of international communism meant that South Africa's external scapegoat, and ultimately its justification for maintaining apartheid, had been removed.

In the wake of these developments, Pretoria began to forge surprisingly close ties with the Soviet Union/Russian Federation, which would have been unthinkable a matter of months earlier. Naturally this shift in Soviet thinking was regarded as a betrayal by the ANC.[159] These rapid international changes and the demise of global communism naturally had a profound impact on the ANC. Not only did the ANC lose ideological and vital material support from the Eastern Bloc; it also found that, as a consequence, its southern African allies increasingly abandoned their previous commitment to a revolutionary path. As a further consequence, MK had ceased to be a genuine military threat, having been expelled from all the Frontline States. Yet, despite the dramatic international changes, de Klerk's decision to unban the ANC in February 1990 was by no means inevitable. Although talks had been happening, it was as much of a surprise to many in the white establishment as it was to the ANC.[160]

As the decade came to a close, the ANC once again was in a position both of relative strength, but also of serious weakness. The ANC's foreign policy since 1980 had made huge strides in promoting the goals of the movement, firmly establishing itself as an internationally recognized and respected movement. Its preconditions for a negotiated settlement, defined by the Harare Declaration, had been widely endorsed by the international community, paving the way for talks with the South African government. Through its incessant international lobbying, the pressure against Pretoria had reached new heights by the late 1980s. The ANC had thus manoeuvred itself into a position where it was regarded as the government-in-waiting, without which no political settlement in South Africa could be reached. Simultaneously, however, the ANC was confronted with several major crises. South African destabilization and subsequent 'peace' deals meant the ANC's fighting forces were located further away from home than ever before; its cadres were not united in support of negotiations; and its relations with its southern Africa allies were in jeopardy. Even more serious was the loss of support from the Soviet Bloc, putting the organizational capacity of the ANC at risk. Internally, the movement also remained hampered by its inability to effectively organize politically and militarily within South Africa. Despite the close ideological and personal affiliation with domestic movements such as the UDF, the ANC was by no means in control of unfolding events. Indeed, in 1989, the ANC's return to South Africa was still far from certain. Although the movement's organizational problems were increasingly serious, the ANC nevertheless maintained a public façade of power; for example, as late as January 1990, the ANC committed itself to greater internal mobilization and proclaimed that 'the armed struggle continues to be a critical and decisive component of our strategy ... [and MK is] committed to the intensification of our armed offensive'.[161]

Conclusion

During its 30-year exile the ANC had evolved beyond recognition from the movement that had first left South Africa in 1960. Yet, on the verge of its return to South Africa, many questions remained unanswered about the ANC in general and its foreign policy in particular. The context of the Cold War clearly overshadowed its relations with different liberation movements and newly independent countries, which were in turn shaped by South Africa's aggressive response to those nations harbouring the ANC. All of the Frontline States were clearly opposed to apartheid, but this did not necessarily translate into full or enthusiastic support for the ANC. Not only was the ANC unable to count upon the fulsome backing of southern African governments, its official standing in the region was far from certain. In fact, the actions of previously close allies, such as the MPLA and FRELIMO, highlighted the fragility of the ANC's position. The legacy of fraught relations with African governments would doggedly follow the movement into the transition and beyond. The revolutionary zeal of the 1960s was rapidly replaced by more practical economic and political concerns. The emergence of the 'Dialogue Group' in the early 1970s revealed the tensions and fissures in southern African attitudes towards the ANC, which became more pronounced as the 1980s wore on.

The ANC had in 30 years failed to clarify its foreign policy, resulting in a lack of overall coherence for the movement. Ideologically it was certainly influenced by international communism, which brought the ANC into close contact with the Eastern Bloc, and like-minded liberation movements. Without doubt these linkages were invaluable to the progress of the liberation struggle. However, the ANC was a broad church, encompassing many competing ideologies. On the one hand it relied heavily upon the Communist Bloc for its very survival, yet it strenuously appealed to the West for assistance. The divergence of opinion was starkly revealed during the shift towards negotiations, as the ANC was split between moderates led by Tambo and Mbeki, and the revolutionaries represented by Hani and Slovo. Although Tambo was the overall leader of the ANC, whose influence arguably kept the ANC united throughout exile, there were many other important figures in the movement, pursuing ultimately different goals. For example, both Mandela and Mbeki, secretly and against the wishes of the majority of the ANC's cadres, initiated talks with the apartheid regime. This set an important precedent, as during their presidencies, both men frequently ignored the advice and reports of their government advisors and the wishes of the ANC as a whole.

By 1989–90, the apartheid state was under intense pressure from the continuing domestic uprising, and the mounting economic and international forces mounted against it, in part driven by the activities of the ANC abroad. The collapse of international communism marked a decisive moment, and in the rapidly changing international environment de Klerk seized the initiative in an attempt to claim the moral high ground and to prevent the ANC dominating proceedings (and legitimating its reasoning for maintaining the armed struggle). In February 1990, de Klerk made the momentous, yet unexpected decision to release Nelson Mandela from prison, and unban all the liberation movements. The announcement allowed the ANC to return formally to South Africa after 30 years in exile, setting in motion the transition to majority rule. The period of exile was now over, but it ushered in a different set of challenges to confront the ANC, starting with the negotiations concerning the future. However, as the following chapters will demonstrate, the enduring legacies from the ANC's exile past would continue to play a significant role in influencing and shaping its foreign policy.

CHAPTER 4

ANC FOREIGN POLICY DURING SOUTH AFRICA'S TRANSITION: THE SEARCH FOR DIRECTION, 1990–4

The beginning of the 1990s witnessed seismic global changes, triggered by the fall of the Berlin Wall in November 1989. In the aftermath of this historic event, the Soviet Union began to disintegrate and communism as a viable world ideology collapsed, bringing the Cold War to an abrupt end. The effects of the Cold War's sudden demise sent shockwaves around the world. The underpinnings of the bipolar, superpower-dominated, international community, which had been the status quo since the end of World War II, had been removed. The West deemed it a victory for liberal democracy and capitalism, and the US president, George H. W. Bush, heralded the 'prospect of a new world order'.[1] The United States aimed to export the liberal democratic political model and its associated ideals around the world, through organizations such as the World Bank and the International Monetary Fund (IMF), particularly focusing on former Marxist states.[2] It also marked a shift in thinking about international relations with a move away from the old ideological underpinnings of the Cold War, towards a greater focus on multiparty democracy, human rights, and multilateralism.[3]

In southern Africa, where the campaign against white minority rule in the region had been defined and played out against the spectre of superpower rivalry, the collapse of global communism and the end of the

Cold War had an enormous effect. However, despite the sudden transformation, the process of political change was already underway in the region before 1990. The ANC had engaged in secret talks with the apartheid government from the mid-1980s, and pressure from the superpowers had resulted in the negotiated withdrawal of Cuban troops from the Angolan conflict in December 1988, paving the way for Namibian independence in 1990.[4] However, the speed with which the Cold War conflict collapsed, overtaking these gradual steps towards peace, came as a surprise to the main protagonists in South Africa, whose own international outlooks were heavily influenced by Cold War ideology. Each side faced difficulties in coming to terms with the significant political changes of this period. The ANC, however, struggled far more than the NP, due to the loss of its main ideological supporter; this was compounded by the challenge of having to adjust to becoming a legal political entity within South Africa. The formulation of foreign policy against this backdrop was always going to be an arduous process for the ANC. The sudden dissipation of the rhetorical and material support for both the ANC and the apartheid state would deeply affect the thinking and decision-making capabilities of the protagonists during the transition. It was a question of who would adapt fastest to gain the advantage.

Against the backdrop of these swiftly evolving events, South African President F. W. de Klerk recognized a unique opportunity and took steps to seize the political and diplomatic initiative. In his speech to the opening of Parliament on 2 February 1990, the new President announced that, 'the prohibition of the African National Congress, the Pan Africanist Congress, the South African Communist Party and a number of subsidiary organizations is being rescinded'.[5] De Klerk's reforms heralded the beginning of a new era in South African politics. The white minority regime pledged to end formal apartheid, demonstrated a willingness to enter into negotiations with opposition movements such as the ANC, and attempted to re-engage with the international community to end South Africa's isolation. In fact, a sizeable proportion of this groundbreaking speech was dedicated to the matter of foreign relations. De Klerk was fully aware of the momentous worldwide changes occurring, and saw in them an opportunity for South Africa, and especially the white minority, to take advantage.[6] The international justification for apartheid was now obsolete and without the looming fear of communism, the NP took steps to ensure its own survival. In unbanning the political opposition de Klerk attempted to rebrand the NP internationally as reformist; to set the agenda for negotiations from a position of strength; and to begin the process of firmly aligning the country with the global status quo. Even Mandela was taken aback by de Klerk's initiatives, describing it 'as a breathtaking moment, for in one sweeping action he had virtually normalized the situation in South Africa. Our world had changed overnight.'[7]

The unbanning of the liberation movements opened up the political landscape in South Africa, and negotiations about ending apartheid ensued. During the transition period from 1990 to 1994, various stages in the negotiations can be identified. The Groote Schuur Minute in May 1990 started proceedings, when the ANC and the South African government made a 'common commitment towards the resolution of the existing climate of violence and intimidation ... as well as a commitment to stability and to a peaceful process of negotiations'.[8] This was followed by the Pretoria Minute in August, where the two parties reaffirmed their commitment to the Groote Schuur Minute and where, most notably, the ANC pledged to suspend its armed struggle.[9] The negotiation process then went through two incarnations of the Convention for a Democratic South Africa (CODESA), and later the Multiparty Negotiating Process (MPNP), resulting in the Transitional Executive Council (TEC) being formed in November 1993. This led the country through to the democratic elections of April 1994 (see Chapter Five for a deeper discussion of these events). The detailed development of the negotiations will not be covered by this chapter, because there is already a substantial body of literature on this topic, and also because the constitutional process did not involve direct talks about foreign policy.[10]

Before analysing the ANC's foreign policy during the transition, it should be emphasized that de Klerk and the NP were still firmly in control of all aspects of government in South Africa after the unbanning of the liberation movements. They still directed the formulation and implementation of foreign policy during the transition, as South Africa began the process of reintegrating itself with the international community. The ANC thereby found itself excluded from the main thrust of deliberations until the latter stages of the transition period. This development was crucial as it at last enabled the NP to have an important role in dictating the terms of South Africa's future foreign policy engagements. The NP government's early efforts were laid out by the Department of Foreign Affairs (DFA) Director General, Neil Van Heerden's 'New Diplomacy'; one of Van Heerden's key recommendations was for a greater focus on southern Africa. This policy was put into practice through de Klerk's shuttle diplomacy across Africa, Europe and North America.[11] There was a concerted effort by the government to earn a degree of legitimacy for its reforms and an attempt to get international sanctions removed as a 'reward', to boost the South African economy through much needed investment and trade opportunities. Yet, the 'New Diplomacy' initiative was not established in isolation, but rather it was symptomatic of domestic economic changes underway. After the constraints of apartheid policies, the newly 'liberated' economy had swiftly reverted into one that was market driven and outward looking. The search for new markets and economic investment fed directly into the development of the 'New Diplomacy', which witnessed the pursuit of trade relations as an integral aspect of foreign policy; one observer declared that 'the Department of Foreign Affairs' "new diplomacy" is informed by the understanding that the flag will follow the trade'.[12] The overriding emphasis on economic concerns championed by the NP and later maintained by the ANC-led government, is central to explaining many of the failures of post-apartheid South Africa's idealist foreign policies. In every single instance, no matter the circumstances, economic concerns would trump ideology.

The 'New Diplomacy' initiative was just one example of the various tactics employed by the DFA, de Klerk, and the NP government to start the calculated process of realigning South Africa's foreign policy and halting the ANC's progress at home and abroad.[13] These developments posed a serious threat to the ANC; it faced the very real possibility of post-apartheid international relations being pre-determined for them, if as expected it became the governing political party. To make things worse, its main bargaining chip – economic sanctions – was being steadily eroded by a world that was embracing Pretoria far too rapidly for the ANC's liking. In light of this, this chapter will analyse attempts by the NP government to distort and undermine the efforts of the ANC to establish its own independent perspectives on foreign policy. This chapter charts the evolution of the ANC's foreign policy during the transition period and investigates what it envisaged South Africa's future relations with other nations would be like. It will examine how the

ANC's foreign policy developed, from its early pronouncements in various conference resolutions, through to the publication of its final policy document, Foreign Policy in a New Democratic South Africa, issued shortly before it took power in May 1994 as head of a Government of National Unity (GNU). The development of the ANC's foreign policy will also be scrutinized in the context of rapidly changing international and domestic political events.

The ANC and the New International Order: 1990-2

In the immediate aftermath of de Klerk's landmark speech, the newly legal ANC was left in organizational and political disarray. The turmoil the ANC endured after February 1990 resulted in the transition period being described as the 'most difficult time in the history of the South African liberation movement'.[14] Not only did it suddenly have to adjust to its new-found legal status, but it also had the arduous task of repatriating its exiled members from across the world to South Africa, establishing an internal organization within the country and negotiating a politically acceptable end to apartheid, while also combating the international diplomatic offensive that, as mentioned, was being waged by the government. Amongst these competing issues the question of international support and assistance to the negotiation process became a key priority for the movement during the initial stages of the transition. However, the ANC encountered fierce, yet unanticipated, competition for support and legitimacy in the international arena.

While in exile, the ANC's international diplomacy had achieved some considerable successes, especially during the 1980s. The movement was widely fêted in international circles, had strong bilateral relations with some powerful nations, including the Soviet Union, regularly lobbied powerful multilateral organizations such as the UN and Organization of African Unity (OAU), and was backed by the support network of the worldwide Anti-Apartheid Movement (AAM). All of these organizations had played their part in helping to bring about the political and economic isolation of South Africa. By 1990, the ANC had 34 missions worldwide, of which 14 were in Africa, demonstrating the ANC's significant global reach and influence.[15] Following its unbanning, the ANC was riding a wave of international goodwill and support and it believed, perhaps naively, that this would translate into unwavering support for the next stage of its struggle. The unfolding reality came as a shock to the ANC.

Despite its long-running association with the international community the ANC continued to operate without a definitive set of foreign policy positions. The prominent focus of the movement had been on the revolutionary capture of power through a Peoples' War, rather than planning for what it was going to do when they had actually achieved it. James Barber asserts that 'the ANC had been bound together more by what it opposed than a clear picture of what it proposed; it had broad aspirations rather than detailed plans'.[16] In 1990, the main basis of its foreign policy remained the 1955 Freedom Charter and the Report of the Commission on Foreign Policy adopted at the Kabwe Conference in 1985.[17] These documents were far from a sufficient basis for the effective foreign policy of either a liberation movement or an aspiring party of government; they were merely a wish-list of principles. For example, the Freedom Charter's international demands called for 'peace and friendship' and for 'independence and self government' in Africa, which broad statements evidently did not constitute a basis for foreign policy.[18] Both documents contained noble ideals, but there was nothing definitive to guide the movement through the difficulties of the transition period and into power. The lack of a concrete vision for the future was a severe problem for the ANC.

In the twilight of its exile, a significant ANC document had been penned that later became an important barometer for the start of negotiations with the apartheid state. Known as the Harare Declaration, the movement set out its preconditions for negotiations with the NP, and these had been adopted by the OAU Ad Hoc Committee on Southern Africa in 1989.[19] The Declaration was subsequently endorsed by the UN General Assembly as a roadmap for the peaceful resolution of the conflict. The ANC sought the full implementation of these principles before formal talks could begin, urging the international community to apply pressure on the South African government to implement them.

Following his release from jail on 11 February 1990, Mandela began a hectic international schedule of shuttle diplomacy, in order to press home the advantage and ensure the fulfilment of the Harare Declaration. By mid-1992, Mandela had made 16 trips abroad and visited 49 countries.[20] These international visits enabled the ANC to continue to exert political pressure on Western and African governments to maintain sanctions and assist the movement. The ANC leadership believed that sanctions against the apartheid state would force the pace of political change. However, the ANC was at a severe disadvantage in these efforts because it had no overall guiding foreign policy framework that could inform and direct its international efforts. Given the seismic international developments, coupled with its lack of a clear foreign policy direction, the ANC struggled to adapt to the new international situation confronting it. The difficulties were accentuated by the fact that the movement's capacity for theoretical analysis drastically diminished when the Cold War came to an end.[21]

The ANC's National Consultative Conference (NCC) in December 1990 was the first to be held in South Africa for 31 years, and it provided a vital occasion for the movement to reflect on the struggle and the work still to be accomplished. The international community's role in South Africa's transition was high on the ANC's agenda. In the keynote address Mandela was quick to emphasize the role of southern African support to the liberation struggle, declaring: 'the Frontline States bled in equal measure so that we might meet in this manner today. Words cannot express our profound appreciation for the solidarity, succour and support we received and continue to receive from the sister nations of Africa.'[22] He went on to condemn the NP's belligerence during the initial stages of the negotiations and stressed the importance of the international community to the outcome; he stated that the 'continuing pressure from the international community ... remain[s] [a] key factor in compelling the government to honour the agreements reached. These must be maintained!'[23] One of the main points of discussion at the conference was international sanctions against the South African state. Such was the popularity of this policy, the final resolutions demanded that sanctions should be maintained and strengthened. Furthermore, the conference resolved that the ANC should be 'cognisant of the necessity to counteract the growing perception that de Klerk and his government should be rewarded for recent reforms ... [and] we resolve the existing package [of sanctions] be maintained'. It also agreed to appeal 'to the EC, US Congress, EFTA and all other international bodies to postpone any consideration of the issue of sanctions against apartheid South Africa'.[24] Sanctions were regarded as the core weapon in the ANC's arsenal against the NP government.

The demands for continued international sanctions were not however universally supported within the ANC hierarchy. In preparation for the conference, senior ANC leader Thabo Mbeki had written a document advocating the phased withdrawal of international sanctions, but recognizing the militant atmosphere amongst the delegates it was not even tabled for discussion.[25] During his opening speech, President Oliver Tambo pursued a similar line, declaring that 'it is no longer enough for us to repeat the tired slogans. We should, therefore, carefully re-evaluate the advisability of insisting on the retention of sanctions, given the new developments in the country and abroad.'[26] According to Mandela, Tambo's proposal was met with indignation by the delegates. The leaders backed down and the conference subsequently resolved to campaign that sanctions remained in place.[27] In supporting continued sanctions, the ANC's militant cadres had failed to appreciate the enormous and rapidly changing international situation affecting the movement and South Africa. Yet, the grassroots position on sanctions is understandable. The international changes that had shattered the status quo meant that there were real difficulties for many in coming to terms with what had occurred. Many ANC supporters remained wedded to the desire for the revolutionary seizure of power, the very message that the ANC had been espousing as late as January 1990. But a major problem in this regard was that as early as June 1990, six months before the ANC's conference, the EC (European Community) had already eased its sanctions against Pretoria, and was highly unlikely to be re-introducing them.[28] It led one commentator to argue later that 'the ANC's arrogance, as much as its naiveté, blinded it to the fact that the scales were tipped heavily against it'.[29] Yet, it must be recognized that in this early stage of the process, the ANC was at its most democratic. After decades of speaking on behalf of the oppressed masses although in reality being an elite, centralized movement in exile, the ANC had swiftly managed to establish itself in South Africa as a broad-based popular party, uniting under its umbrella structure a wide range of people, including the democratic traditions of the UDF and the Robben Island prisoners.[30] Heeding the popular consensus of the conference delegates, the leadership accepted the resolution as a programme of action.

Immediately after the conference, the ANC held a mass rally at Soccer City in Johannesburg. It was noticeable that Tambo's speech did not explicitly mention the delicate issue of sanctions, but instead chose to reiterate the importance of the international community and southern Africa to the ANC and the future of South African democracy. He concluded:

> One thing we should never forget and shall never forget is the role of the international community in our struggle. Countries far and apart will do everything to aid our struggle ... But you should have seen the international response the last time Nelson toured the world, a journey he is yet to complete. Above all, we have enjoyed solid support from Zambia, Tanzania, Mozambique, Zimbabwe, Angola, Botswana, Namibia and Nigeria. The failure of these countries in anything would have been our failure. They hold our ground, and we are grateful ... The international community have an equal duty, not to relax pressure until the apartheid crime against humanity has been ended.[31]

This speech reveals how important continued international support remained to the ANC's strategic thinking in late 1990. The leadership realized that its efforts to apply pressure on the South African government to reform in a manner acceptable to the ANC still required active international involvement. While there may not have been party-wide consensus on how best to harness this support, the ANC leadership realized it was vital to the process. Chris Landsberg agrees that the international community remained central to the ANC's strategy, arguing the leadership still 'regarded foreign intervention as a key source of influence over an unresponsive and powerful white government'.[32] Tambo's speech also hinted at a sense of disquiet within the ANC hierarchy; without active and decisive support from external sources, there was a real possibility that it would get left behind not only in the negotiations, but also in decisively shaping the future of South Africa.

Meanwhile, as the ANC discussed its options, the South African government had been increasingly successful in developing and renewing friendly links with Africa and the West. Both regions were eager to re-engage with South Africa to take advantage of the new economic opportunities available, and were therefore willing to accept at face value the NP's declared intentions to reform rapidly. The result was a steady easing of South Africa's isolation, undermining many of the ANC's international strategies. Even as the NCC was in session, the EC had lifted its ban on new investments in South Africa, although existing sanction packages remained in place.[33] Landsberg observed that 'the nature of South Africa's diplomacy became captivating ... the ANC was on the defensive, notably on its economic policy, sanctions, and the armed struggle'.[34] In 1989, an internal ANC document had explicitly warned that the movement 'cannot afford to tail behind the regime and allow ourselves to fall into a defensive posture, with the regime maintaining the offensive'.[35] This was however, exactly what was happening. The success of de Klerk's international strategy had wrongfooted the ANC, which was left posturing from the sidelines.

The effectiveness of sanctions as a weapon for the ANC continued to unravel in subsequent months. In February 1991, Mandela angrily threatened to 'turn South Africa upside down' unless the EC maintained its sanctions programme.[36] However, his rhetorical denounciation was to no avail, as the EC unanimously renounced sanctions in April 1991.[37] The US quickly followed suit; President George H. W. Bush lifted sanctions against South Africa in July.[38] These incidents demonstrate the extent to which the ANC had been unable to convince the West of its point of view and how successful de Klerk had been in championing his alternative vision. The shift to an overriding emphasis on economic considerations in the 'new' world order had caught the ANC off guard, leaving it outside the emerging international consensus. One observer later argued that 'the ANC seems to have been oblivious to the fact that the end of the Cold War did not so much herald the demise of the Soviet Union as it symbolized the triumph of neoliberalism. The ANC's continued advocacy of sanctions ... raised eyebrows.'[39]

By July 1991, when the ANC convened its 48th National Conference, the movement's influence over the international community's policies towards South Africa was severely limited; little progress had been made in the negotiations and rumblings of discontent about the pace and direction of change was evident amongst the rank and file. It forced Tambo to stress the need for the movement to maintain its unity in order to finally defeat apartheid. At the conference, the international situation was once again high on the agenda. In the seven months since the NCC, the demands of the ANC's leadership regarding international support had apparently changed little. There were, however, indications that political attitudes were beginning to change within the leadership.

There were many similarities between the ANC's NCC in 1990 and its 48th National Conference. In his opening address, Tambo declared that 'as in the past, our leadership should be exercised both here and abroad. This becomes even more important given the changing face of the international community. We must therefore refocus international attention on the need for continued support.'[40] This point was elaborated by Mandela, who stated that 'the continued support of the international community remains vital for the victory of our cause. We also need further to strengthen our links with the rest of the world.'[41] Furthermore, Mandela demanded that the ANC 'should find ways and means by which to arrest the process of the erosion of sanctions ... [so] we do not lose this weapon'.[42] Although the ANC was evidently still seeking to preserve its external support, it remained wedded to the retention of sanctions as a mechanism for political change. The leadership understood the need for international assistance, but had little idea of how best to proceed in engaging external actors to this end. There was at this point, no clear direction or understanding of how best to implement its demands. The consequence was that the machinery of the NP government retained a distinct advantage over the ANC. There were real structural difficulties for the ANC in the initial stages of the transition; understandably foreign policy matters were not fully discussed because there were more pressing concerns to consider.

The 1991 conference did however provide a forum in which the ANC could begin formulating a plan of action on foreign policy. Mandela pointed out that 'elaboration of policy cannot itself go on forever. We must begin to arrive at firm conclusions about what we would do with the country once we become the governing party.' Furthermore, he argued 'it would be important that we discuss the question of the possible role of the international community'.[43] Following the conference deliberations, a set of 'resolutions on foreign policy' were adopted. These resolutions reaffirmed and built upon the ANC's existing foreign policy statements: the Freedom Charter, the Kabwe Document and the Harare Declaration.

More importantly, the resolutions of the 48th National Conference produced the first ANC foreign policy document that recognized the fundamental global changes that had occurred since 1990, and the enormous impact that these were having on the movement. The resolutions on foreign policy set out five main areas of concern; firstly, sanctions and the need to utilize them as a form of pressure against the NP government. The ANC recognized that it needed to discuss with its external allies how best to utilize sanctions in the changed international environment; the leadership insisted that 'the international community should be urged to listen to the view of the democratic forces and not seek to reward the apartheid regime'.[44] The second and third areas covered the mobilization of international anti-apartheid forces and the ANC's dire need of financial and material assistance. The document highlighted the perceived importance of the AAM, not only in providing moral and material assistance to the ANC, but also in encouraging the international community to fulfil its 'obligations' towards South Africa's transition. The conference resolved that 'the world anti-apartheid movement should prepare adequately for an important post-apartheid role', underlining the ANC's expectations and optimism regarding future external assistance.[45] The significance of regional and international co-operation was also identified; resolutions hinting towards future developments, set out how the ANC hoped actively to promote human rights, democracy and African solidarity, and, as the future government of South Africa, the importance of working with multilateral organizations such as the OAU.[46] In keeping with developments within the ANC, the final subsection called for the National Executive Committee (NEC) to ensure wider democratic participation in foreign policy discussions amongst the movement's members and that sub-committees should be established to help guide these discussions.[47] As the resolutions indicate, the ANC had taken the first tentative steps towards developing an overt framework for its foreign policy. Existing demands such as sanctions and international assistance had been elaborated upon, while dominant international discourses of the time, such as human rights and weapon controls, were incorporated into the document.

Whilst this process was unfolding, a diplomatic battle between the ANC and NP was raging over relations with other African states. Throughout its exile, the ANC had relied heavily upon African support in order to wage its struggle; it simply assumed that these relationships would endure. However, this was a fundamental misreading of events by the leadership, as longstanding allies had already begun to distance themselves from the movement. The ANC had been on the retreat in southern Africa in the 1980s, as successive Frontline States were forced by apartheid pressure to expel its cadres. Behind the façade of African unity, relations with erstwhile allies were starting to crack. To make matters worse, the ANC was left reeling by the election defeat of its long-standing ally and benefactor, the Zambian president, Kenneth Kaunda; in November 1991, his United National Independence Party (UNIP) lost to the Movement for Multiparty Democracy (MMD) in the country's first multiparty elections since 1968.[48] The ANC's ideological stalwart had been democratically voted out of office, which effectively severed its ties with the Zambian state. It was a sign of wider political change on the continent; between 1990 and mid-1991, for the first time in post-colonial African history, three presidents lost power through democratic elections.[49]

The strained relations between the ANC and continental powers during this period were exacerbated by the efforts of the NP government to develop closer ties with African states. During the apartheid era, South Africa had repeatedly attempted to lure the continent into its embrace through a series of initiatives such as the Dialogue programme of the early 1970s and its plans for a constellation of states in southern Africa. After 1990, the NP renewed and intensified these efforts, illustrated by de Klerk's numerous visits across the continent to establish ties with a range of African leaders. The 'New Diplomacy' had emphasized the importance of Africa and by reaching out to the continent de Klerk fulfilled three objectives. The first was to gain legitimacy for the NP and the South African state; the second was to appease economic demands for new markets and investment; thirdly, de Klerk's diplomacy also proved an ideal opportunity to undermine the ANC's continental alliance network.

For example in June 1991, de Klerk made an historic visit to Kenya to meet President Daniel arap Moi, to discuss greater economic collaboration; de Klerk emphatically declared that there was now a 'new wind of change blowing across Africa'.[50] Although the creation of formal economic ties with African states had become a pressing concern for South Africa, it was far more important for the rest of the continent. De Klerk's claim was supported when the government published its trade links with the continent in December 1991. They revealed that it had business links with 'nearly every country on the continent' despite the extensive sanctions campaign against Pretoria; exports to Africa had grown by 40 per cent in 1989 and another 22 per cent in 1990.[51]

The figures indicated an overall shift in attitudes, where African governments were prioritizing economic self-interest over matters of ideology. More importantly for African leaders, relations with Pretoria no longer had to be kept secret. It was increasingly acceptable to do business with South Africa. As such, this was a serious setback for the ANC. The data indicated that after the ANC was unbanned many of its allies regarded the struggle as being over – the movement was free and de Klerk was implementing reforms (albeit in a limited fashion). While the struggle to end apartheid clearly had not ended in 1990, it was, however, hardly surprising that African states would put their economies before international solidarity. It must be remembered that many governments had supported the ANC in an attempt to isolate the apartheid regime at great financial and material loss; after 1990 they rushed to take advantage of the new possibilities South Africa afforded.

A further setback for the ANC's strategy occurred in April 1992 when de Klerk visited Nigeria. Nigeria, one of Africa's largest and most politically significant countries, had been publicly hostile to apartheid rule, but this meeting began a new chapter in bilateral relations and so 'was a tremendous breakthrough for Pretoria's Africa strategy'.[52] In fact, Nigerian President Ibrahim Babangida, the then chairman of the OAU, welcomed de Klerk with open arms, declaring: 'we are delighted that we have at last found someone in South Africa with whom we can do business'.[53] The *Financial Times* observed that the Nigerian visit marked 'South Africa's final reconciliation with the rest of Africa, from which it has been so long estranged. No African door can remain closed to Mr de Klerk, now that Nigeria has welcomed him back'.[54] The acceptance by Nigeria was an indication of the new political and economic reality sweeping the continent, prompting other African states to follow suit.

The Nigeria visit naturally infuriated the ANC, further limiting its policy options. The ANC's perceived 'natural' support base was being rapidly eroded, with little it could do to rectify the situation. Although African states clearly continued to support the movement, they were no longer confined to the international dictates of the Cold War. Mandela had publicly criticized Babangida for establishing diplomatic contacts with South Africa, but was rebuked by the Nigerians and told 'that they would "not be dictated to by anyone's business but our own"'.[55] At this point it appeared that de Klerk's initiatives had achieved the desired aim of reaching out to the continent. Despite the ANC establishing new foreign policy guidelines, and mounting a concerted effort to counteract Pretoria's diplomatic offensive, little had been achieved. In fact, the ANC's hard-won international recognition and diplomatic successes attained during exile were being all too rapidly undermined.

The turning point for the ANC and the transition process occurred in June 1992. A domestic incident sparked international furore (much akin to previous apartheid atrocities), marking the beginning of the end for de Klerk's successful diplomatic offensive. The Boipatong Massacre left over 40 people dead after Inkatha members, actively assisted by South African security forces, attacked township dwellers, an event 'which set a new standard of South African atrocity'.[56] De Klerk was blamed for official complicity in the massacre.[57] The massacre prompted the ANC to walk out of the CODESA negotiations in protest and begin a campaign 'of rolling mass action' to coerce de Klerk into genuine reform.[58] Internationally, this was the turning point for the movement's foreign policy, as it proved the 'ideal opportunity for the ANC to reactivate the diplomatic support of the international community'.[59] The international community, horrified by the incident, was unwilling to allow South Africa to descend into a spiral of violence, nor was it willing to accept the whites' continued domination of the levers of political power. Steven Freidman argued that 'the sense of crisis [Boipatong] engendered ... triggered international involvement in the transition'.[60] The outcome was greater international intervention in the transition process and more pressure being applied to force both sides to the negotiating table.

This new urgency in multilateral engagement became clear when, in August 1992, the UN Security Council unanimously approved a resolution to send international observers to oversee the negotiations in South Africa. The Commonwealth also agreed to send an observer team.[61] The arrival of the UN mission was a hailed as a victory by the ANC, as its strategy had been to advocate a greater degree of external intervention. These decisions also demonstrated to both sides that the international community was closely watching the transition process and was willing to play an active role in the negotiations, to achieve a democratic outcome. Although international opinion alone did not change the situation in South Africa, it certainly contributed to creating a political climate more conducive to negotiations.

As will be addressed more fully in Chapter Five, negotiations resumed in September 1992, when a Record of Understanding was signed between the ANC and NP. According to Mandela, the 'agreement set the mould for all negotiations that followed ... we were now aligned on the basic framework that would take the country into a democratic future'.[62] Although still facing challenges on a number of fronts, the resumption of negotiations (the outcome of which was by no means certain) provided the ANC the necessary space to begin the serious process of shaping its future foreign policy. While foreign policy deliberations were still not paramount in ANC thinking, there was a clearer realization that a formal position must be agreed upon to guide the movement in office once the elections had occurred.

Formalizing a Foreign Policy Perspective: 1993–4

While the transition process predominantly focused on the negotiations to end apartheid and bring democracy to South Africa, behind the scenes the ANC was forced to address a range of issues, including its foreign policy. As already established, the ANC had only really begun to consider scenarios for a state-based foreign policy during its 48th National Conference. However, once substantive negotiations with the NP resumed in September 1992, the opportunity for the ANC to start the process of policy formulation arose. In these latter stages of the transition the ANC began to develop a greater sense of the direction and substance of its policies and this found concrete expression in a number of documents. The clearest example, Foreign Policy in a New Democratic South Africa, was published in the run-up to the elections in April 1994 and was the culmination of extensive preparatory work. It set the tone for a new, human rights centred, international vision for South Africa.

Work on this process was conducted by the ANC Foreign Policy Working Group, which had begun meeting a year after the movement's return to South Africa. Members of this group included, amongst others, Peter Vale, Rob Davies, Gary van Staden, Alan Hirsch, the brothers Aziz and Essop Pahad, Thabo Mbeki, Welile Nhlapo, Sankie Mthembu and Stanley Mabizela.[63] Although Mbeki was officially a member of this group, he was not a regular attendee of its meetings, but when he did attend, the attitude of its other ANC members was deferential towards his opinions on foreign policy (the theme of deference within the movement, and the increased centralization of ANC foreign policy thinking that this indicated, will be returned to in due course).[64]

The respect afforded to Mbeki by the ANC is none too surprising given the influence he wielded over foreign policy during the 1980s. It also neatly demonstrates the level of continuity within the ANC's decision-making structures throughout this period, including the predominance of individuals from exile. The Foreign Policy Working Group met on several occasions to discuss future policy and to draft a working policy document for the ANC. An early indication of the thinking and direction of the ANC Working Group's deliberations after Boipatong can be found in the draft document entitled, 'A New Foreign Policy for South Africa: a Discussion Document'.[65] The document, primarily written by academic Peter Vale, elaborates upon the proposals outlined in the Resolutions on Foreign Policy agreed at the 48th National Conference.

The document set the tone for the ANC's new vision. The drastic global changes and the resultant evolving forms of state interaction were described as being a positive step forward for the international community, although the document did point to the 'intense uncertainty' worldwide, and warned of potential dangers of Western triumphalism in the new world order.[66] The document recommended that the ANC should exploit this new era in international relations, especially by focusing on human rights; it expressed the belief 'that South Africa should become a beacon for, a champion of, the international crusade for the values associated with this noble goal'.[67] The proposals marked the beginning of a brief period when the central focus of the ANC's foreign policy approach was human rights and its promotion. The document also set out the principles that would guide ANC foreign policy in the future: a preoccupation with human rights; a belief in global solidarity; a belief that justice and democracy should be the basis of its international relations; a desire for international peace and the importance of Africa.[68]

The draft elaborated upon each principle in turn. For example, an explicit commitment was made to working closely within multilateral organizations like the UN and the Southern African Development Community (SADC) to pursue aims such as disarmament, human rights and economic development. The unique nature of the ANC's liberation struggle, which had resulted in interactions with countries from across the globe, straddling the Cold War divide, was treated as a major advantage for the 'new' South Africa. The document asserted that because the world stood at 'this new international crossroads' the movement's past experiences allowed it to fully 'understand how to

manage international relations ... where worlds may clash'.[69] This
vision illustrated the ANC's confidence in post-apartheid South Africa's
ability to become a fully-fledged and active member of the international
community. Having overcome injustice and inequality via a negotiated
transition, it would act as an example to the wider world.

The focus on Africa was informed by the ANC's earlier public pledges
and was heavily emphasized because 'our destiny is intertwined with
theirs; our peoples belong with each other'.[70] This theme was one that
the Working Group was keen to stress, and nine pages of the document
were devoted to the question of future interactions with the continent.
The main aim was to prevent Africa's growing international marginalization, and to strive for equitable, mutually beneficial relations, and
greater regional integration.[71] This principle was designed to recognize
African assistance and suffering during the liberation struggle, as well as
an attempt to appease fears of South Africa's continued domination of
the continent (see Chapters Six and Seven for this in practice). Vale now
recalls there was a consensus amongst members of the Working Group to
stress the importance of southern Africa, because 'there was a large sense
of optimism that we could transform Southern Africa, in a kind of
positive way ... [and to act as] restitution that we had to pay these
people back for everything they'd done for us'.[72]

There was, however, an element of self-interest to these proposals,
much akin to the initiatives being concurrently espoused by the NP. The
ANC, as the assumed future governing party, was keen to promote
stable, democratic nations in Africa, which it hoped would then develop
economically. If achieved, businesses would be able to take advantage of
these opportunities and increase South Africa's trade links with the
continent. Furthermore, it would help make southern Africa an
attractive location for global investment. This would in turn boost the
economy of South Africa, and enable the ANC to quicken the pace of
domestic development and change.

The draft discussion document was modified several times before
being published in a substantively identical form in October 1993 as,
'Foreign Policy in a New Democratic South Africa: A Discussion
Paper'.[73] The document clearly indicates how the ANC's thinking on
foreign policy had evolved since 1991. The core message was one of
democracy, human rights and the primacy of Africa. This was the most
explicit statement of foreign policy intent the ANC had ever produced,

offering a powerful indication of the influences on the movement and the policies that it hoped to pursue once in government

'Foreign Policy in a New Democratic South Africa', is very much a product of its time. Primarily, it reflects the ANC's vision of the world from the perspective of its own perceived moral struggle for democracy, and the broad consensus of the early 1990s that the global community would unite to bring about democracy, prosperity and human rights for all.[74] The document is rather celebratory in nature, rejoicing in the end of the Cold War and the emerging, new world vision. It is clear that the ANC Working Committee had embraced many aspects of the new trends in international thinking. It was envisaged that once in power, an ANC-led South Africa would play a significant role in the new multilateral world. The Working Group was also optimistic about the ways in which the international community would assist the country. Thabo Mbeki insisted that the world had a special responsibility to the country that 'entails the obligation of the international community to assist the people of South Africa to effect the transformation'.[75] This was a theme to which he would later return as President.

Foreign Policy in a New Democratic South Africa was the most definitive statement of intent on foreign policy produced by the ANC during the transition, but it was overshadowed by an article in the prestigious journal *Foreign Affairs*. Published in late 1993 under the name of Nelson Mandela, the article 'South Africa's future foreign policy' set out in detail what the country's foreign relations under an ANC government would entail.[76] The article summarized the document, 'Foreign Policy in a New Democratic South Africa', in a form more accessible to a wider international audience. The main points made in the article were the widely publicized six pillars of the ANC's foreign policy: human rights; the promotion of democracy; justice and respect for international law; primacy of peace initiatives through non-violent means; the importance of Africa and economic development through regional and economic co-operation.[77] The article reaffirmed the focus on 'unity and closer co-operation' with Africa, and declared that a 'democratic South Africa will . . . resist any pressure or temptation to pursue its own interests at the expense of the sub-continent'.[78] The article also publicized the decision to make human rights a central tenet of future foreign policy. 'Mandela' argued that a human rights based approach to South Africa's future foreign policy, 'will be the light that guides our foreign affairs'.[79] Despite the idealistic underpinnings of the article, it did express more pragmatic tendencies in reference to economic priorities. The need for foreign investment to alleviate inequalities and improve education, skills and opportunities is strongly emphasized in the article, but there was also an astute awareness that foreign intervention would not be a quick solution to South Africa's problems.[80]

The article has been widely identified as the benchmark for what South Africa's new, moral foreign policy would constitute, as well as displaying the personal beliefs of Mandela. However, this article was not actually written by Nelson Mandela, who had no involvement in its creation. In fact the ANC had very little input into it. The *Foreign Affairs* article was written mainly by Peter Vale, who constructed its intellectual argument, while various experts (Gary van Staden, Alan Hirsch and Rob Davies) contributed to specific sections of it.[81] However, the ANC leadership did edit and approve the final piece, illustrated by its willingness to allow Mandela's name to be publicly associated with the principles it espoused. Interestingly, there was originally a section about Burma (officially known as Myanmar) which would have given concrete emphasis to the democratic and human rights sections of the article, but it was removed from the final published version. Vale recalls that senior ANC member 'Kader Asmal read the paper and exorcised bits of it. Particularly, exorcised the bit about Burma that was in it, and he took out the reference to Aung San Suu Kyi.'[82] Perhaps, even in the process of endorsing the primacy of human rights to its foreign policy, some ANC leaders realized that it would not be possible to implement this policy in every case; in this instance it chose to avoid publicly criticizing the Burmese Junta before taking power. Given what occurred to South Africa's promotion of human rights after 1994, this is a plausible explanation.

In fact, two prominent members of the ANC Foreign Policy Working Group have expressed their doubts about there ever being a widespread consensus on human rights within the ANC leadership. Alan Hirsch argues that 'there was tension between those who preferred human rights to be the fundamental basis of foreign policy (most of the participants) and those who believed that this was not realistic ... As I recall, the main opponents to the "unrealistic" view were Thabo Mbeki and myself.'[83] Furthermore, Vale recalls:

I never thought that there was a commitment on the human rights. I always thought that there was a real worry by some people, let's call them the group around Thabo [Mbeki], that the new human rights thing was quite dangerous. And that's why it reverted very quickly to a national interest centred approach. In fact, when I think about it now, the human rights dimension was carried by very few of us. But we were extremely influential because we were writing the document.[84]

These testimonies bring into doubt, first, the ANC's control over the process of foreign policy formulation and, second, the extent of the leadership's commitment to its well-publicized human rights inspired foreign policy. It is a position also supported by Mbeki's biographer Mark Gevisser. He documented Mbeki's doubts about the pursuit of human rights, believing that Mbeki thought that 'while such high-minded principles might befit a liberation movement, they were entirely impractical for the government of an emerging power, struggling to re-enter the global economy'.[85] Gevisser's, Hirsch's and Vale's sentiments are illuminating, and offer an explanation for the root causes of some of post-apartheid South Africa's more contradictory policies. What emerges is that Mbeki and his confidants had serious misgivings about the ANC's new public foreign policy direction, even as it was being written. It begs the question, why would the ANC leadership commit itself to the centrality of human rights in its foreign policy if it did not genuinely believe in pursuing it?

There are several explanations for this. One is that the ANC had historically declared the primacy of human rights in the Freedom Charter, and throughout its exile had emphasized the moral nature of its struggle against apartheid. As the Freedom Charter had been the movement's enduring vision during exile, its leaders could not simply abandon this longstanding principle in the run-up to the first democratic elections, especially because of the popularity of such sentiments. It must also be kept in mind that in the early 1990s, human rights discourse was in the ascendency, both internationally and domestically. For example, in the South African constitution, which the ANC had a key role in creating, human rights are given a prominent position.[86] It would have been contradictory of the ANC if it had pursued a policy of human rights at home, but ignored it abroad.

Furthermore, during exile and reaffirmed during the transition, the ANC had emphasized that the 'people' of South Africa would have a say in governing a democratic country, a principle enshrined in the Freedom Charter. By including a group of South African experts in the task of foreign policy creation, in collaboration with the movement, it allowed the ANC tenuously to fulfil this longstanding objective. It did however mean that the ANC leadership was not entirely in control of the process of policy formulation. As Hirsch and Vale point out, only a few people within the Foreign Policy Working Group had promoted this principle. However, because they were the key advocates of such a principle, and more importantly had been tasked with writing the document, ultimately their opinion held sway. It meant that senior ANC leaders such as Mbeki had little influence or control over the policy being adopted in their name. This is somewhat surprising as Hirsch recalls that 'the most influential participant was Thabo Mbeki, but I am not sure that he always held sway'.[87] The outcome was that the human rights aspect of foreign policy was, in many respects, imposed upon the wider movement. Although some of the movement's leaders may not have fully agreed with the document, they could not easily be seen to oppose the prevailing sentiment.

However, the acceptance of human rights as part of its broader foreign policy can also be seen as the ANC leadership cynically exploiting the Western international community. They were fully aware that its commitment to such a noble ideal would bring valuable plaudits to the movement and the 'new' South Africa. It is worth bearing in mind that Mbeki was a wily and experienced international politician, skilled at manipulating politicians from either side of the Cold War divide to the ANC's advantage. More importantly, in exile, Mbeki had been regarded by Western diplomats as the moderate, 'acceptable face' of the ANC and someone they could do business with. Mbeki may well have agreed to adopt the human rights aspects for immediate political gain, but in the long run he never actually intended to maintain such policies once in power. What can be observed from this episode is that, while the ANC leadership may not have been fully supportive of the notion of human rights as a central element of its foreign policy, it was willing to submit itself to the consensus view, and take a bold step in this new direction.

This process does, however, raise important questions about the true nature of the ANC in exile, its democratic credentials, and the extent to which human rights was fully endorsed within the movement. What is clear is that Thabo Mbeki and his allies were not in favour of human rights as a guiding principle for foreign policy. This was to have serious implications for the foreign policy of the ANC after 1994. What becomes apparent is that on the eve of the elections, there was already an emerging tension in the ANC's foreign policy between pragmatism and idealism. Although it was publicly willing to pursue this moral stance internationally, the ANC leadership had also expressed a need for a pragmatic approach to foreign policy. The contradictions and inconsistencies that emerged in the ANC-led government's foreign policy after 1994 were already evident by the end of the transition.

As South Africa's Future Foreign Policy was being drafted and published, South Africa had moved rapidly towards a democratic future. In November 1993, the interim South African constitution was approved by delegates to the multiparty conference.[88] As part of the transition, the Transitional Executive Council (TEC) was established in December, to ensure the effective administration of South Africa until the elections; it effectively governed the country from December 1993 until April 1994.[89] The TEC consisted of six sub councils that were created to help oversee various state structures, one of which was the Sub Council on Foreign Affairs (SCFA). The SCFA played a vital, but little studied or understood role in shaping the future foreign policy of the new South Africa. The activities, findings, and recommendations of the SCFA will be fully explored in Chapter Five, which will also illustrate how the Sub Council influenced the ANC's own foreign policy perspectives.

Conclusion

The TEC provided the mechanism for a peaceful transition from apartheid to democracy, and the process involved the ANC working closely with various political organizations in the SCFA. However, there were concerns about the extent of the continuity between the 'old' and the 'new' in South Africa that occurred because of the transition process. It has been argued that the unique changes in the international community, the economic leverage of whites and the reconciliatory approach of the ANC, meant that 'few ruling groups have ever wriggled themselves out of a deadly predicament more elegantly'.[90] For some observers, the new ANC-led government's foreign policy was criticized for being too closely connected with and reflective of the old illegitimate order. In many respects this is a fair point. Beneath the gloss of human rights, the ANC's new foreign policy closely resembled that proposed by the NP, with its underlying focus on Africa and economic interest. The outcome was that on the surface there was little obvious change between the new and old governments or their foreign policies. This should not come as too much of a surprise. Both the ANC and the NP were profoundly shaped by the international circumstances in the post-Cold War era, and each was forced to react rapidly to the changed environment in which they found themselves. In the early 1990s, there was only one dominant narrative on foreign policy. Given the international focus on the transition and its outcomes there was in reality never going to be much 'official' deviance from the status quo. Chapter Five will explore more fully the extent to which the old order, in close co-operation with the international community, 'captured' aspects of the 'new' South Africa's foreign policy. The revelation that Mandela did not write nor contribute to the *Foreign Affairs* article to which the ANC put his name, and that other foreign policy documents had largely been created outside of the control of the ANC leadership, raises a number of important questions. Do these public announcements really represent the 'true' nature of ANC foreign policy and did the ANC leadership (let alone its membership) ever 'own' its foreign policy?

While the ANC may have 'succumbed' to the dominant international narrative of the time in its foreign policy positions, it did not mean that the movement had fully embraced these ideals. What can be clearly ascertained is that aspects of the ANC's ideological foundations, shaped indelibly by its experiences of exile, did not simply disappear as apartheid crumbled and the Cold War ended. It would be folly to think otherwise. Important continuities from exile and the transition process manifested themselves in the democratic era, including: the structures of the ANC and the way in which it operated as a movement; the role and influence of individuals from exile over decision making; a commitment to anti-imperialism; and its problematic relationship with many of its allies. When placed aside the normative ideas of the international community that had been 'enforced' during the transition, these historic legacies were always likely to generate tensions. The ANC could not escape its history, which continued to inform the movement once in political power.

Nevertheless, one of the most remarkable aspects of the transition is the extent to which the ANC successfully adapted, at least superficially, to the immense global changes. After its initial problems in coming to terms with the situation that faced it in 1990, the ANC's foreign policy gradually evolved throughout the transition. By April 1994, certain aspects of foreign policy may have mirrored the NP's initiatives, but these were essentially pragmatic decisions. It would have been foolhardy for the ANC to have pursued anything radically outside the international mainstream. However, the transition did witness the ANC making some bold and distinctive assertions in its foreign policy. Most notable was its focus on human rights, which became the central tenet of its foreign policy. No matter who created it, what may have occurred to this policy after the ANC took power and what might be seen in hindsight as its naiveté, this was a noble ideal for the movement to officially pursue, and one that few others would have dared to embrace. By embarking on this policy the ANC showed that it was willing to lead South Africa into a new era under the guiding light of a bold, human rights foreign policy. The challenge the ANC faced was how best to implement its new foreign policy ideals in an unforgiving world.

CHAPTER 5

THE SUB COUNCIL ON FOREIGN AFFAIRS OF THE TRANSITIONAL EXECUTIVE COUNCIL: THE EFFECTS ON THE ANC'S POST-APARTHEID SOUTH AFRICAN FOREIGN POLICY

The formation of the Transitional Executive Council (TEC), a key component of South Africa's transition to majority rule, was the clearest signal that a negotiated end to apartheid could be achieved. Months of intricate negotiations between the apartheid government and the different political parties culminated in the TEC being established. Enacted in law by State President F. W. de Klerk on 27 October 1993, the Transitional Executive Council Act was passed 'with a view to promoting the preparation for and transition to a democratic order in South Africa'.[1] The cross-party TEC, made up of the 19 political parties involved in the negotiation process (with the notable exceptions of the Freedom Alliance and the PAC), was tasked to lead South Africa through until the elections set for April 1994. The main focus of the TEC was on managing South Africa's domestic transition to democratic rule. It nonetheless had a vital role in the future direction of South Africa's foreign policy. This chapter will explore how the TEC, and more importantly the activities of its Sub Council on Foreign Affairs (SCFA), played a decisive but historically marginalized part in shaping the country's international relations in the context of the 'new world order'. The outcome of the SCFA process was also important, as it saw the co-option of a number of senior ANC leaders to a specific way of thinking, and simultaneously negated and undermined the movement's embryonic vision for a post-apartheid foreign policy.

In the histories of South Africa's transition a number of key themes have been covered in considerable depth, such as the intrigues within the negotiation process, the violence that ravaged many parts of the country, and the clash of ideas between the NP and the ANC. However, the same cannot be said of the TEC, nor especially of the activities of its composite sub councils. Despite playing a significant role during the latter stages of the transition, the TEC and the SCFA have been largely neglected. There are a number of possible explanations why they have been overlooked or omitted from the narrative. It is important to recall the importance of South Africa's transition, both domestically and internationally. The term 'miraculous' has frequently been used to describe this momentous event in South African history, an indication of the dominant interpretation of the transition. As the negotiations unfolded and the elections loomed, the attention of the media and the academic world was on the dramatic domestic political transformation underway. The *Financial Times* described the process in South Africa as 'one of the most extraordinary political transformations of the twentieth century'.[2] Whilst it is evident that many important people, including politicians, civil servants, journalists, and academics in South Africa and abroad were well aware of the SCFA and its activities during the transition, in the excitement of the election period and with the inauguration of the new government, it would appear that most of the important work of the sub council went unnoticed and has since been forgotten. Furthermore, because the TEC lasted for only five months, its short lifespan may have been equated to an apparent lack of importance, given its brief of managing the transition.

Nevertheless, what makes this glaring omission even more surprising is that the SCFA had profound ramifications for South African foreign policy after April 1994. The previous chapter illustrated that during the four years of South Africa's transition, the ANC had never been in full control of the creation of its foreign policy. Even as the transition process was coming to a close, senior figures were already expressing doubts about the new-look, human rights inspired vision created by the ANC Working Group. The profound disconnection between the movement's official policy and the evolving opinions of its leaders was remarkable, and an indication of what would later transpire in government. Against this backdrop, the activities of the SCFA significantly affected the course of the new ANC-led government's foreign policy. While being extremely important, it is in many ways an untold story. This chapter will therefore explore the ways in which the SCFA played a considerable role in transforming, influencing and directing the post-apartheid government's policy choices.

The Multiparty Negotiation Process and the Transitional Executive Council

Before a thorough analysis of the SCFA can be undertaken, it is necessary to provide some context behind the formation of the TEC and its sub councils. South Africa's transition went through a number of convoluted and evolutionary phases before the April 1994 elections. In December 1991, the negotiation process in South Africa had been embodied by the Convention for a Democratic South Africa (CODESA). However, by May 1992, CODESA had broken down, in part due to the intransigence of the various political parties, and also because of their widely differing visions for the future of South Africa. The Boipatong Massacre on 17 June 1992, 'precipitated the irreversible collapse of the Codesa talks' bringing South Africa's transitionary talks to an abrupt halt.[3] However, both the NP and the ANC faced domestic, and more importantly, international pressures to resume negotiations. In August 1992, bilateral talks resumed between the two parties, represented by Roelf Meyer, Minister of Constitutional Development, and Cyril Ramaphosa, Secretary General of the ANC. The meetings were designed to remove outstanding obstacles towards the resumption of negotiations; these talks culminated in the Record of Understanding, signed on 26 September 1992.[4] There were several vital aspects to the Record of Understanding. Primarily, it provided a binding agreement for a constitution to be drafted and adopted and, secondly, established that a transitional interim government (along with various accompanying structures) would be created to oversee the transition.[5] This agreement between the NP and the ANC was 'a turning point in political negotiations. It set broad terms for the negotiated transition from which subsequent talks never departed.'[6]

The Record of Understanding consequently facilitated another round of formal negotiations, resulting in the formation of the Multiparty Negotiating Process (MPNP). The MPNP was a mechanism designed to bring together the previously bitterly opposed parties, and signs were positive that a compromise would be reached to bring about a democratic solution. On 5–6 March 1993, a multiparty planning conference took place at the World Trade Centre, in Kempton Park, where the parties were tasked with setting a date for the resumption of formal negotiations.[7] Appreciating the need for swift and decisive action to overcome the impasse, the delegates agreed that the MPNP would convene on 1 April 1993.[8] Between April and November 1993, delegates to the MPNP debated and finalized issues that ranged from plans for the South African constitution to arrangements for the future elections. The MPNP was supported in its task by various technical committees and commissions, which 'was a fundamental departure from the structuring of the Codesa process: its importance cannot be overstated'.[9] A key lesson from CODESA was that large gatherings of politically opposed parties could never hope to reach agreements, or even compromises. Therefore, the new setup was organized in such a way that the MPNP comprised a range of small working groups that discussed specifically assigned issues; as a consequence the decision-making process was simplified.[10] This was a crucial development, as the successful model of establishing smaller working groups provided the entire basis and justification for the formation of the TEC and the SCFA. These recommendations were subsequently presented to the Negotiating Committee of the MPNP for further debate, and then later to the plenary for ratification. The Technical Committee on the Transitional Executive Council agreed to the proposals, marking the creation of the TEC.

The First Report of the Technical Committee on the Transitional Executive Council of the MPNP, from May 1993, set out the justification for such a process in South Africa. It suggested that there was a need for transparency, legitimacy and stability in order to foster free and fair elections and inspire international confidence in the electoral process.[11] Following the Boipatong massacre, the MPNP was fully aware that the eyes of the world were monitoring events in

South Africa. Appreciating the ever-deepening role of the international community in the process, its recommendations were in part an effort to appease any lingering fears and to instil confidence in the negotiations. The Technical Committee proposed that as part of the TEC there should be several sub councils, each of which was 'to be a small and effective working group' that would engage with issues on a daily basis.[12] Another key proposal was that 'the Transitional Executive Council shall be constituted with executive powers to facilitate, in conjunction with existing legislative and executive structures, the transition to a democratic order', with the primary aim of levelling the political playing field between all the parties involved in the MPNP before April 1994.[13] Furthermore, the report identified several key questions that would require further investigation, predominantly regarding the power that the TEC would wield.[14] The report however, did not provide any significant detail concerning the exact nature of what the TEC or the sub councils would entail, the details of which were left up to future discussion. Even at this early stage in the proceedings, the negotiators regarded the creation of sub councils as a crucial mechanism to ensure a peaceful and successful transition.

Between May and October 1993, members of the MPNP met to resolve the outstanding questions posed in the First Report of the Technical Committee and to add further detail to the tentative points raised. In doing so, they laid the groundwork for what would later become the TEC. These recommendations subsequently were enshrined in law when de Klerk signed the TEC Act in October 1993. The 42-page TEC Act outlined the purposes, role and objectives of the TEC, and more importantly for this chapter, its sub councils.[15]

The Formation and Significance of the Transitional Executive Council

The TEC had no precedent in history and was an innovative way of attempting to resolve the political crisis in South Africa. The TEC was even more remarkable in the way in which it successfully bound the political parties towards the common goal of a peaceful and democratic transition. The transitional body was composed of the TEC, a smaller Management Committee, and eight sub councils. Each of the political parties that had adhered to the MPNP principles were permitted two representatives on the TEC in order to prevent the process being dominated by the NP or the ANC; especially as they had been the main players behind the return to the negotiating table.[16] The Management Committee was to provide oversight of the process and was composed of members from the TEC; this body would meet before general meetings of the entire TEC to set the agenda and review the activities of the eight sub councils.

The uniqueness of the TEC was reinforced by the sub council structure. The eight sub councils that constituted the process and mirrored the departments of an elected government were: Regional and Local Government and Traditional Authorities; Law and Order; Stability and Security; Defence; Finance; Foreign Affairs; the Status of Women; and Intelligence.[17] Each sub council, depending on its brief, consisted of six or eight members nominated by their respective parties, ranging from apartheid-era politicians to African liberation activists; the breadth of representation aimed to address the racial and political divisions in South Africa. In order to maintain equality and balance, no party was allowed to have more than one member on each sub council.[18] Informed by the previous experiences of the MPNP, these small sub councils were regarded as the best way of reaching a broad consensus. The process was also aided by the technical knowledge of government and the international community. The sub councils liaised closely with the relevant government departments, providing the members with access to the expertise and opinions of the civil servants. The close co-operation between the SCFA and the Department of Foreign Affairs (DFA) proved crucial to the transition process in this area, and to post-apartheid South African foreign policy.

During its lifespan, the TEC and the sub councils were bestowed with significant legislative powers, which impacted on the day-to-day activities of the government, its civil servants and departments. First, there was a supervisory role assigned to the TEC to 'ensure that no government or administration exercises any of its powers in such a way as to advantage or prejudice any political party'.[19] There still remained a fear that the NP would attempt to subvert the process for its own gain. This role assigned to the TEC the ability to implement and enforce the stated goal of levelling the political playing field before the elections. More importantly the TEC had been granted the authority to override and block any government activity. The TEC Act stated:

Each Government and administration shall keep the Council informed of and shall provide it with copies of all of its proposed legislation, including regulations, by-laws and other subordinate legislation, which have a bearing on the objects of the Council. If the Council or the subcouncil concerned has reason to believe that any proposed legislation of any Government or administration is likely to have an adverse effect on the attainment of the objects of the Council, it may, after affording the Government or administration concerned an opportunity to make representations to the Council or the subcouncil concerned, and subject to the other provisions of this Act, direct that Government or administration in writing not to proceed with the legislation concerned, and that Government or administration shall, subject to section 23, comply with such direction.[20]

The clause ensured that, even though the NP was still technically in control of the bureaucratic machinery of South Africa, its decision-making was subject to the approval of the TEC structures. Any government department that wanted to accomplish a specific task, even as seemingly minor as sending delegates to a conference, would have to seek the approval of the TEC or the appropriate sub council before it could be implemented.[21] A former senior civil servant in the DFA, former diplomat, and liaison officer to the SCFA, Tom Wheeler recalled that 'it was very important to get their [SCFA] endorsement for anything that the Department wanted to do ... the government continued, subject to endorsement'.[22] Indeed, in certain circumstances the activities, influence, and power of government could effectively be overridden by the TEC. According to Ivor Sarakinsky, the SCFA was able to prevent the NP from 'projecting its interests abroad as those of the country'.[23] *The Star* newspaper, in its analysis of the TEC and its role during the transition, noted at the time that 'on paper, the TEC, and sub councils do, therefore, have powers that could be significant and will be binding'.[24] The ability to oversee government departments and prevent unfavourable legislation being passed was an extremely powerful tool for the TEC. In effect, it became the de facto government during the last five months before the elections in April 1994.

In the new-found spirit of co-operation, there were minimal protests from the NP about the overall direction and aims of the process, demonstrated by its willingness to cede its authority as South Africa's government. This was crucial in ensuring a smooth transition to democracy, particularly demonstrating the goodwill of the governing party to the other political parties involved in the negotiations. The powers of the TEC had a significant bearing on the actions of the SCFA and on South Africa's future foreign policy. An important caveat is that the SCFA did not have a mandate to formulate foreign policy itself; it was only a bridge to future policy formulation by the Government of National Unity (GNU).[25] Nevertheless the SCFA was highly influential. The DFA fully appreciated the influence it could wield and chose, out of necessity, to work closely with the sub council in order to advance its own agenda. To influence the decision making of the SCFA, the DFA did its utmost to control and direct the activities of the sub council and therefore South African foreign policy. This chapter will elaborate on this aspect of the SCFA in greater depth.

The Sub Council on Foreign Affairs

The TEC Act defined the remit of the SCFA to attain the broadest possible consensus on matters affecting South African international interests. To do so, the sub council was tasked with discussing and securing appropriate agreements with the international community that would benefit the incoming democratic government, and provide it with the necessary information to act as a basis for its initial forays into international affairs. The SCFA's activities culminated in May 1994 with a set of proposals, recommendations and agreements for the new government. In part, the SCFA's activities were designed to enable the new administration to 'hit the ground running'. The mandate of the SCFA set out in the TEC Act was as follows:

> The Council shall, for the purpose of attaining its objects, through its Subcouncil on Foreign Affairs, in regard to foreign policy liaise, monitor, make recommendations and, where it is considered necessary, assist with a view to –
>
> (a) achieving progressively the broadest possible consensus on matters affecting South Africa's international interests, particularly its long-term interests;

(b) securing appropriate agreements with the international community regarding the contribution that community could make to the peaceful transition to democracy in South Africa;

(c) in consultation with the Subcouncil on Finance, securing such international assistance as the Subcouncil considers necessary in order to address the socio-economic needs of the people as a whole and not to serve the interests of one or other political party;

(d) ensuring that any foreign policy initiative benefits the country as a whole and not one or other political party; and

(e) promoting such international relations, including trade, finance, culture and sport relations, as in the opinion of the Subcouncil will benefit the country as a whole.[26]

The emphasis on ensuring that foreign policy benefited the national interest of South Africa, not individuals or political parties, reflected the fact that, even at this late stage in the transition, there was still widespread concern that one of the political parties would manipulate the TEC for its own interests. These concerns were well-founded as the process was indeed subverted not, indeed, by a political party, but instead by a government department, namely the DFA.[27] The mandate also specifically identified the financial relations that the sub council could promote via its activities. With the Western international community's primary focus now on economic relations, pursuing such links became a vital component of the SCFA's work.

The individual members who were nominated to the SCFA were John Barratt (Democratic Party), Aziz Pahad (ANC), Leon Wessels (National Party), Stella Sigcau (Cape Traditional Leaders), Godfrey Hetisani (Ximoko Progressive Party), and Ossie Gannie (National People's Party).[28] The choice of candidates for the SCFA is intriguing in itself. All the members of the sub council were representatives of their respective political parties except Barratt. Despite being nominated by the Democratic Party, Barratt was not actually a member. As the national director of the South African Institute of International Affairs (SAIIA) and an expert on foreign affairs, his candidacy turned on his technocratic knowledge, whilst the others had been selected for party political reasons. Nevertheless, both Pahad (Department of International Affairs in exile and member of the ANC's Foreign Policy Working Group) and Wessels (former Foreign Affairs deputy minister) had significant foreign policy experience. It did mean there was an imbalance within the group, as those nominated by the major parties had technical know-how of foreign affairs, while the others members had little or no knowledge. The sub council met regularly, both in South Africa and abroad, with the chairmanship of meetings rotating amongst the six members on an alphabetical basis in order to avoid accusations of political or racial bias. To ensure the decision-making process remained fair, all agreements endorsed by the SCFA had to be reached through the votes of its members, with each resolution requiring a two-thirds majority to be approved.[29]

The first meeting of the SCFA took place in Cape Town on 22 December 1993, and was attended by all six members. The sub council also extended an invitation to the South African Foreign Minister Pik Botha, the DFA's Director General Rusty Evans and its three deputy Director Generals, Jeremy Shearer, Derek Auret and Albert Van Niekerk.[30] The roll call of high-ranking attendees from the DFA at the meeting provides an early indication of how seriously the Department regarded the activities of the SCFA. The discussions were held in a 'positive and relaxed atmosphere' in which those present outlined the tasks of the SCFA.[31] Given that the sub council and the DFA would be working together during the process, the meeting was also an opportunity for the civil servants to clarify how the relationship between the department, the TEC and the SCFA would work in practice.[32]

Foreign Minister Botha addressed the assembled members during a working lunch, where he expanded on many of the themes that were outlined in the TEC Act. Botha insisted that the country's 'international relations should be apolitical and that we should have a non-partisan foreign policy', adding that 'in the field of foreign relations we should not allow internal political differences to weaken the solidarity'.[33] Although an idealistic sentiment, it was a particularly asinine comment by the foreign minister, given what would later transpire during the process. Indeed, foreign policy by its very nature is political, and the interests of the DFA were certainly not apolitical. Botha also instructed the sub council to subsume its political differences so as to benefit the whole country and not those of one party. In doing so, they were instructed to relegate 'their party political aspirations to the background'.[34] Apparently, the SCFA members achieved this with considerable and surprising ease. This interpretation of harmonious working relations is supported by Tom Wheeler, who suggests that the TEC process allowed DFA officials and the members of the sub council, who came from diverse political and social backgrounds, to engage with one another on both a professional and a social level. It meant that, in Wheeler's words, 'they weren't sort of a strange bunch of people who were ... a threat to us'.[35] The growing co-operation between members enabled the DFA and SCFA to make significant progress with the task in hand.

The strength of this emerging relationship was powerfully demonstrated in Singapore during one of the SCFA's many foreign visits, on which it was accompanied by DFA officials. During the trip, all the delegates embarked on a cruise around Singapore harbour, which ended in a shared evening of karaoke.[36] A report of the visit to Singapore detailed the events of the evening's entertainment, claiming that those present, had through the power of song, 'set about nation building'.[37] Although, a slightly exaggerated claim, it reveals the growing personal ties that were being forged during the short period of the SCFA's existence. Furthermore, it is an indication of how the members of the sub council and the DFA had indeed been able to put aside their political differences for a common cause. The close working relationship developed into a social relationship, and in due course they became 'drinking partners'.[38] Having previously approached each other with political caution, within a few months of working and extensive travelling together, they discovered significant common ground. According to Wheeler, this particularly paid off in the case of Aziz Pahad, who was appointed as Deputy Minister of the Department after the elections.[39] The sub council provided an important mechanism for integrating the old and new administrations. The outcome was that Pahad already knew many of the people serving him (such as the Director General, Rusty Evans), and the internal workings of the DFA. Pahad's role in the SCFA also enabled him to begin work in his new position immediately, as he was already informed on the issues at hand concerning South Africa's foreign policy options.

As previously noted from the opening meeting, senior DFA officials had taken a keen and pro-active interest in the activities of the SCFA.

Moreover, the report of the meeting describes the DFA's presentation to the SCFA by the Director General, Rusty Evans, who set out the department's ongoing initiatives during the transition, such as the 'New Diplomacy'. Furthermore, the DFA had put in place a liaison officer for the sub council; Evans also offered the SCFA free use of its offices and conference facilities in the Union Building.[40] The DFA had all the necessary facilities, knowledge, contacts and experience to initiate the members of the SCFA into the world of foreign relations. By providing such extensive assistance to the process, the DFA was fulfilling the mandate of the TEC and adhering to the recommendations of Pik Botha. In fact, Wheeler believed that 'it was an interactive process . . . There was no hostility mutually between us; we worked very well with them . . . And so it was useful to the old government until the change came, to have this body that would legitimise what they were doing.'[41] The idea that the DFA would try to use the TEC as a vehicle to approve their work is an important concept to keep in mind.

Although the DFA was compelled to act in accordance with the TEC, the department did its utmost to influence the findings and recommendations of the SCFA. The DFA's foreign policy since 1990 had gone through several phases, with the main focus on breaking South Africa's isolation, exploiting new economic markets, and reintegrating the country back into the international community. The NP and the DFA in tandem had been extremely successful in improving South Africa's international standing, especially through its wholehearted embrace of fashionable neo-liberal ideals. Deon Geldenhuys recalls Pik Botha arguing at this time that 'as far as foreign policy is concerned, South Africa, or at least the out-going government, more or less handed the world on a platter to the ANC'.[42]

The notion that the SCFA's final recommendations were designed to benefit the whole nation and not the interests of one political entity was an important idea. Yet, what made the SCFA so powerful was that it could nullify the nascent policy formulations of both the ANC and the NP, and set the tone for South Africa's international affairs. Importantly, the sub council was empowered to reach agreements and set policy frameworks with other countries and multilateral organizations for the democratic administration. As a consequence, it would be virtually impossible for the incoming GNU to rescind any such agreements without severely damaging South Africa's international reputation.

Despite Pik Botha's appeal for the process to be apolitical, there were obviously vested interests in the final outcome. The ANC did not want to be hamstrung by decisions it could not alter, and the NP/DFA were unwilling to sacrifice its efforts at aligning and reintegrating South Africa with the neo-liberal, Western-dominated international community. Recognizing the authority of the sub council to decisively shape the future, the DFA did its utmost to monitor and influence its activities, in accordance with its own international perspectives. The following section explores how the DFA went about achieving this aim.

The Department of Foreign Affairs and its Influence Over the SCFA

In order to fulfil their mandate, the SCFA members set about reviewing the options available for South Africa's future foreign policy. There were, however, major challenges in meeting this objective. Primarily, the sheer scale of the task was staggering. The SCFA had to pass judgement on a wide range of issues, including regional political concerns in every corner of the globe, trade agreements, and South Africa's reintegration into multilateral organizations like SADC or the Commonwealth.[43] The second problem was one of time. The SCFA had only five months to complete its review and put in place recommendations for the GNU. A further difficulty was the degree of foreign policy experience of the SCFA members, with only Barratt, Wessels and Pahad with previous working knowledge of foreign affairs. Whilst these three were extremely knowledgeable on foreign policy issues, the same could not be said of the others. In order that these three did not dominate proceedings, the other members of the SCFA required substantial assistance in rapidly raising their proficiency in international relations to an adequate standard, especially within such a tight deadline. In light of this, the SCFA faced a daunting undertaking.

The issues were not insurmountable, but could have seriously impinged upon the impact and quality of the SCFA's work. The DFA positioned itself as the solution to these problems. The department and its civil servants had all the necessary tools to formulate and conduct foreign policy, and were therefore in the ideal position to assist the SCFA. Through a range of means, including organizing conferences and foreign visits, providing access to the international community and supplying detailed reports and policy positions, the DFA provided substantial support to the process. In fact, the DFA's influence is remarkable. The department organized many aspects of the SCFA's activities during its lifespan, providing the DFA with an extraordinary degree of control over the whole process and, ultimately, the 'new' South Africa's foreign policy.

An important early concession for the DFA was successfully securing the right to observe all the activities of the sub council. Director General Rusty Evans ensured from the very start of the process that at every single working meeting of the SCFA at least one member of DFA staff would be present during the deliberations.[44] The exact role of the civil servants at the SCFA's meetings remains unclear, but it can be safely assumed that the minute details of the discussions were relayed back to senior DFA officials. However, the active participation of the DFA did not go unnoticed by the TEC. In a memorandum from March 1994, the TEC's Management Committee took the sub council to task about this relationship stating: 'we also note that the Department of Foreign Affairs attends all the meetings of the Sub Council. We are of the view that this is against the spirit of the Act [Transitional Executive Council Act]. We are therefore of the view that the Department should attend the meeting only when summoned.'[45] The memorandum signalled the genuine unease regarding the role and conduct of the DFA in the process. However, it is striking that the TEC was unable to prevent the DFA's continued participation in the activities of the sub council. The protest from the Management Committee was simply ignored, as the minutes of all the SCFA's subsequent meetings right through until the election indicate that DFA staff continued to be present.[46] What the memorandum does aptly demonstrate is that there were justifiable concerns about the sub council's independence and the DFA's interference.

A key way in which the DFA influenced the thinking of the SCFA was through the flow and provision of information. The SCFA members regularly requested information and advice from the DFA on a wide spectrum of foreign policy matters to assist them in reaching definitive conclusions. The DFA was eager to oblige, and did so in a variety of formats, particularly through meetings, reports and policy documents.[47] Given the immense scope of foreign policy, the sub council could not possibly have been expected to acquire extensive insights into the various strands that constitute international affairs. To circumvent this issue, the specific area desks of the DFA commissioned reports from their civil servants and ambassadors, which detailed the problems, policy options and their recommendations for South African foreign policy. One illustration is an in-depth report entitled 'The Directorate: Africa Multilateral'.[48] The dossier, created by the African and Middle East Desk of the DFA, analysed what the country's foreign policy towards the continent should entail after 1994. In doing so, it proceeded to categorize every nation on the continent, describing the nature and content of current relations, proposed future relations, the importance of that country to South Africa and a recommended approach.[49] The main focus of this report was the southern Africa region, which correlated with the dominant foreign policy thinking of all the key South African protagonists at this time. As a means of familiarization with the intricacies of South Africa's foreign relations, and more importantly those of its neighbours, this report was of immense potential value to the SCFA. The reports and documents created by the DFA covered an array of issues and were clearly useful tools for the members of the sub council, as they neatly synthesized often complex issues and provided them with important details and policy options.

Despite the obvious benefits of the DFA's provision of information, there was an ulterior motive. As the DFA created the documentation, they were clearly in control of the flow and content of information sent to the sub council. This is not to claim that the SCFA's members did not have access to other sources of information concerning foreign policy, but what was provided by the DFA was the most influential component. Wheeler describes the various DFA reports as having been drafted by 'the appropriate desks in the Department, perhaps at the request of the TEC, or perhaps to guide the way the TEC thought'.[50] Wheeler is quite explicit in revealing exactly what the DFA was trying to achieve during the TEC process. The creation and use of the documentation by the DFA enabled civil servants to highlight the areas of concern that they deemed as most important to South Africa, while having the power to diminish the significance of other options. By creating reports such as the one mentioned above, they could provide the 'appropriate' information to the sub council members, in order to influence their decision making. Although the sub councils were supposed to be independent bodies, free from the old government structures, the process was being manipulated by the civil servants of the DFA. The result was that the international outlook of the SCFA closely resembled that of the department.

As part of its remit, the SCFA embarked upon a series of overseas trips to meet with various individuals and organizations. In order to provide the sub council with the greatest possible opportunity to broaden their foreign policy perspectives, its members were subject to a gruelling schedule of meetings, presentations and visits during the five months of its existence. Governments, politicians and organizations from across the world enthusiastically sought to be seen playing their part in South Africa's miraculous transition.[51] During three separate trips the SCFA, accompanied by civil servants from the DFA, were in 1994 sent to: 1) New York, Washington and London, 4–12 February; 2) Nairobi and Addis Ababa, 18–22 February; and 3) Paris, Brussels, The Hague, Geneva, Singapore, Kula Lumpur, Seoul and Tokyo, 16 March–2 April.[52] All the trips were meticulously organized by the DFA, which had set up meetings with South African ambassadors, high-ranking politicians from some of the world's most powerful nations, and representatives of multilateral organizations. The international visits had several purposes, which to varying degrees, and in different ways, benefited the DFA, the sub council, and the wider international community. More importantly for South Africa, the meetings abroad provided the opportunity to inform a broad spectrum of global leaders about the evolving situation in the country, and how the international community's continued support would enhance the positive steps already being made. By providing assurances in person about the progress being made, such meetings also instilled confidence in these important stakeholders.

While the international trips played a vital role during the five months of the SCFA, the idea for them originated from rather more pragmatic intentions. As soon as the formation of the TEC had been announced, the DFA's Director General, Evans, arranged a high-level meeting of his senior officials. It transpires that he was less than enthusiastic about the prospect of the SCFA dictating the future course of South Africa's foreign policy. Wheeler recalls that, as soon as the implementation of the sub councils was announced, Evans brought the DFA's chief directors together to discuss the situation:

> we are now stuck with this TEC business, and we need to keep
> them out of our hair, I think what we should do is take them on a

> tour of the world ... It was to keep them out of our way, so we could get on with our business. It was a misreading of how things were going to develop, but that was ... how he [Evans] saw it.[53]

Despite initial disquiet amongst the Department's senior officials, the foreign trips proved extremely beneficial to them and the SCFA. As well as being an opportunity for meeting the international community, the overseas visits gave the sub council an insight into the day-to-day workings of the DFA. During the three visits, the SCFA met a wide spectrum of South Africa's ambassadors, as well as participating in a number of planning conferences. For example, during the SCFA's visit to New York in February 1994, its members met with the ambassador, V. R. W. Steward, while in the same month they participated in a Foreign Affairs Planning Conference in Nairobi.[54] The SCFA's meetings with the DFA's overseas staff usually took the form of short presentations from the chief directors of the appropriate desks on specific topics, followed by round-table discussions to facilitate decision making.[55] Such occasions ensured that the SCFA was fully briefed 'on current and important issues' that were of significance to South Africa by people actively engaged in pursing foreign policy objectives.[56]

At some of the DFA-arranged meetings and conferences, the ANC's external heads of missions were also invited, giving them the opportunity to meet with DFA officials; they allowed the civil servants to offer the ANC representatives their perspectives on foreign policy concerns directly. The SCFA documents claim that the Planning Conference held in Nairobi 'was the first opportunity ever for the ANC Representatives to jointly meet with their counterparts in South Africa'.[57] Likewise the tours of Europe and Asia provided similar opportunities for the SCFA, ANC and DFA operatives to work together.[58] These played a crucial role in the assimilation process. By bringing the different parties together, it provided occasions for the representatives to put aside their differences, and discuss South Africa's future. However, the meetings that involved the former liberation movements were not always welcomed by apartheid-era civil servants, who still viewed the ANC through the prism of the Cold War. Indeed, the ANC's involvement caused some apprehension within the DFA. In several internal DFA documents from early 1994, concerns are expressed about the ANC's role, because 'the ANC will, subject to developments, be prominently represented on the

SCFR [the document incorrectly refers to the SCFA as the Sub Council on Foreign Relations] mission. This raises questions regarding whether the ANC and/or PAC representatives are to be acknowledged or accommodated in any way, including socially, before or during the mission's visit.'[59] A few days later, DFA officials in New York requested 'guidance, as noted in previous communications, on the handling of the ANC representation in New York, both prior to and during the visit'.[60] These misgivings indicate that old habits die hard, with some officials having not yet come to terms with the imminent election of the ANC. Even at such a late stage in the transition, members of the old apartheid-era bureaucracy were apparently resistant to change and distrustful of the aspirations of the liberation movements, questioning their right to full participation in international negotiations. However, other documents indicate that such attitudes were not widespread. Instead, the ANC was encouraged to play a full and constructive role in the various planning conferences and individual meetings.[61]

Another important aspect of the overseas trips is that they gave the DFA an opportunity to introduce the South African delegation to the international community. During the course of the three foreign tours the SCFA met a wide range of people and international organizations including the UN secretary general, the EC, the OAU, the World Health Organization, and various presidents and foreign ministers.[62] In doing so, the SCFA and, to a lesser extent, the ANC, were given the chance to have discussions with some of the world's most senior and influential politicians, whose personal views could shape the relationship between their government or organization and South Africa. One example of such a high-level meeting was during the SCFA's visit to New York, where they met the UN Secretary General Boutros Boutros Ghali to discuss South Africa's future relations with the organization.[63] Another was during the European leg of the tour, when the SCFA held discussions with Dr Ergon Klepsch, the president of the European Parliament.[64] These two instances indicate the importance of South Africa's transition to the international community, but also the DFA's careful administration of meetings between the sub council and these powerful figures.

The SCFA was given unprecedented access to key figures, enabling them to question, discuss and learn about the benefits of conducting a foreign policy that interacted in an advantageous fashion with multilateral organizations such as the UN. It was also an opportunity to establish closer working relations that would be invaluable to the new South African government. For international representatives, it was a chance to meet the SCFA for the first time. It allowed them to inform the sub council about their roles and activities, and how they expected South Africa to contribute to their organization and/or to the international community once re-admission had been granted. For example, during a working lunch, UN officials in New York informed the SCFA that 'the foreign policy of the Government of National Unity will be closely monitored by the world'.[65] It would not be the last warning the SCFA would be served about the content and vision of post-apartheid foreign policy.

The control the DFA had over the whole process ensured that it was in a position to dictate the itinerary of the sub council. For example, the department had the ability to select the people and organizations it wished the SCFA to meet. This control over the schedule meant that the DFA could filter the options available to the sub council, selecting only those it deemed as 'appropriate'. Relations with major nations and organizations had already been deemed as vital to South Africa's future; without the political and economic support of the West the new government would face severe policy limitations. The DFA therefore exposed the sub council members to the global community who in turn emphasized the importance of adherence to the international mainstream. During the three international visits, the DFA introduced the SCFA to the global economic and political powers (with the exceptions of Kenya, Ethiopia and the OAU) all of which held similar neo-liberal views. It guaranteed that the SCFA were exposed exclusively to a particular international outlook. Of course this was an era of enormous global change. The demise of the Soviet Union had seen socialist and left-wing political views losing much of their potency in the mindset of international elites since 1990. In the emerging new world order, the SCFA were not entertained with alternative notions during the tours. The visits also witnessed the SCFA being warned in person by the world's leading political powers; nothing should be done to oppose the international consensus.

The degree of the DFA's control can also be seen by analysing the composition and length of the various legs of the international tour. For the most part, the three visits were spent in the United States, Europe, and Asia. To briefly illustrate this point the SCFA had opportunities to meet various branches of the UN, the US State Department, EU member states, and representatives of the Japanese, Korean, and Malaysian governments. These destinations were, according to the SCFA in a document addressed to the TEC's Management Committee, regarded as 'of paramount importance ... [and] will contribute to the revival of the South African economy more significantly than any other grouping'.[66] By visiting major world economies, the sub council was pragmatically fulfilling the important objective of attracting capital investment to South Africa. It is a clear demonstration of the new international thinking of the time, and the overriding significance of economic concerns. Yet, in order to maximize the rewards from these economic ties, it was paramount that the 'new' South Africa conformed to a specific set of international criteria. In setting the sub council's agenda, the DFA could ensure that this message of conformity was conveyed to the SCFA by the global elites; the content and language of sub council documents indicate that they had become very much attuned to the principles of the new global status quo.

Given the dominant focus on meeting multilateral organizations and important trading nations, the sub council's itinerary woefully neglected Africa. During three trips abroad, only five days in total were spent on the continent.[67] The main purpose of the African leg of the tour 'was to promote current and future effective management of South Africa's relations with Africa ... by analysing tends, identifying objectives, opportunities and coordinating policy with regard to normalizing relations'.[68] The painful and very recent legacies of apartheid's outward-looking policies were a serious issue for many of South Africa's neighbours. There may have been an 'official' normalization of relations, but in reality an underlying suspicion of South African influence and power on the continent continued, as the ANC-led government could attest to. During the trip, the delegation met with Kenyan President Daniel arap Moi, Ethiopian President Meles Zenawi, and also the Secretary General of the OAU Dr Salim Salim.[69] The meetings provided a much-needed opportunity to discuss future South African–Africa relations with some of the continent's most influential people. However, the scant time dedicated to the continent is somewhat surprising, as the DFA, NP and the ANC in their foreign policy announcements had all stressed the paramount importance of Africa to South African interests.

Despite the rhetoric concerning the continent's significance to South Africa's future, Africa was largely ignored by the sub council's activities. This may have been due to the DFA's lack of organizational presence on the continent after years of isolation, or a lack of time in the tight schedule of the TEC, but it might equally suggest that Africa was deemed not to have the necessary capacity to assist post-apartheid South Africa. In the new world order, the continent's lack of economic development and power meant that the SCFA focused its attentions upon the major trading nations, which could aid the democratic transition in the country and provide much-needed investment. Yet, the SCFA's dominant focus on Western nations was arguably to the detriment of South Africa and Africa. After 1994, the new ANC-led government made strident efforts to work more closely with the continent, especially southern Africa, but these policies had in the main not been aided by the sub council's work. In fact, when compared to the expectations of Southern African governments about Pretoria's future role in the region, the neglect by the SCFA seems startling.[70] A question then is how important were African concerns to the new, democratic South Africa?

As previously discussed, the international community had taken considerable interest in South Africa's transition to democracy for a host of altruistic and pragmatic reasons. Preceding the establishment of the TEC, the ANC had begun to formulate its own set of foreign policy positions, outlining its vision for South Africa. Although there were many similarities with the NP/DFA's 'New Diplomacy', there was an underlying fear within the international community that the former liberation movement would adopt a more revolutionary position, placing South Africa on the fringes of the international consensus. However, the perceived radicalism of the ANC could be partially negated by the recommendations of the sub council. The SCFA was in a prime position to have the decisive say on the 'new' South Africa's foreign policy. Recognizing the power and influence wielded by the SCFA, the Western international community deployed a range of tactics to convince the South Africans to align their recommendations with mainstream international thinking. There is little doubt that concerted efforts were made by the international community to influence and dictate the results of the transition process. Chris Landsberg asserts 'that world opinion – and the need to accommodate it – formed a constant backdrop to the thinking of domestic negotiators'.[71] Although the point has been made before, it is worth reiterating; the end of the Cold War and the rapid changes in international thinking played a constant and crucial backdrop to developments in South Africa. David Ginsburg argued that 'we should not underestimate the extent to which the South African transition was shaped precisely by the fact that it gathered momentum just when alternative visions of democracy were becoming discredited by experiences in the Eastern bloc ... Nothing could have played more into the hands of those Western powers anxious to shape the outcome of the transition.'[72] With few other genuine alternatives, it is of little surprise that the SCFA recommendations closely resembled the perspectives of the Western international community.

To ensure the compliance of South Africa, the SCFA members were regularly cautioned by diplomats about straying from the status quo. One of the clearest examples of such a warning occurred during a meeting between the deputy director general of the DFA and the ambassador of the Russian Federation E. P. Goussarov on 11 April 1994, only a matter of weeks before the election. In a confidential memorandum to the SCFA, there is an explicit warning to South Africa to opt for continuity in its foreign relations:

> [the ambassador] added that it was essential for South Africa to demonstrate to the world that it could be relied upon as a solid partner, not only now but in the future. Continuity of foreign policy, in substance if not in style, was the very cornerstone of interstate relations. He could not emphasise too clearly the importance the world would attach to an unambiguous demonstration of reliability and continuity.[73]

As a record of an official meeting between the two nations, the content of the document is unequivocal in its message to South Africa, with its stress on 'continuity' and 'substance'. In effect the Russian ambassador was informing South Africa that it could change the way in which it presented foreign policy to the world, but not the content or direction. For the DFA, this was unambiguous support for the approach it had been pursuing from a powerful member of the UN Security Council. What makes such a conservative message even more striking is that the former Soviet Union (now the Russian Federation) had been the key supporter of the ANC during its exile; this transformation in approach towards

South Africa was remarkable.[74] In a short period of time, Russia had performed a dramatic about-turn, moving away from championing global communism to supporting free market capitalism. Russia had offered a plain and simple message to the sub council. If South Africa failed to adhere to the dominant international thinking of the time, then the global community would not provide the financial and developmental assistance the country so desperately needed.

The Russian Federation was not alone in this; there was a concerted international effort under way to influence post-apartheid foreign policy. A similar warning can be found in another memorandum from the DFA to the SCFA that analysed South African and Greek relations. In October 1993, the Greek socialist PASOK party won a 'surprise' landslide electoral victory; the document expressed a sense of horror at a new socialist government taking power, 'which sent shockwaves through Europe'.[75] The memorandum emphasized that 'the general feeling within the EC community was clearly not in favour of Greece ... [which] according to all expectations, would follow a ... foreign policy, that would not be acceptable to the country's other European partners'.[76] Given the events of the early 1990s, the surprise at the election of a socialist government in Europe is palpable. The memorandum pulls no punches, asserting that the EC mistrusted Greek intentions, and emphasizes the fear that the socialist government would pursue a deviant foreign policy compared to the rest of Europe. It was a none too subtle warning to the SCFA. If South Africa adopted a foreign policy 'unacceptable' to the West, then it would suffer the consequences. The two examples of diplomatic intervention in the SCFA process demonstrate how measures were taken that 'enabled foreign govern-ments to influence the ... negotiating process directly'.[77] The SCFA had been sent clear signals. There must be no major re-alignment in South Africa's foreign policy that might damage political and economic relations with the West. It was rather effective blackmail.

An intriguing feature of the sub council's activities is that the policy positions and recommendations were accepted with minimal fuss by all the political parties involved. A report noted that:

it had seemed self-evident beforehand that ... there would be vast areas of disagreement about a future foreign policy orientation for South Africa. There was nothing of the kind. Instead, common goals emerged, a common reality was perceived and agreement was reached on methods of achieving the desired goals. Ideological differences appeared to be almost completely absent.[78]

Yet the ANC's position during the SCFA process is striking. While the TEC was in progress, the ANC's Working Group had been finalizing its own foreign policy positions, which had emphasized the importance of human rights concerns. A key member of the Working Group was Aziz Pahad, who also happened to be the ANC's representative on the SCFA. Although each political party was permitted only one member in any of the TEC sub councils, it would have been expected that the ANC would have tried to influence proceedings more, in an attempt to align them closer to its ideals. This did not transpire, and indeed quite the opposite happened. In many respects the transition brought the different parties closer together; James Barber observed that through the extensive negotiations there was 'an increasing convergence of views ... The change came gradually, perhaps unconsciously, as with increasing contact and the search for support the ANC absorbed more Western views and outlooks.'[79] While this convergence of opinion might be true, it still leaves several important questions unanswered. In Pahad, the ANC had the perfect conduit to try and align SCFA recommendations with those of the movement, but it did not occur. Why? Furthermore, the final SCFA proposals effectively set the terms of engagement for the incoming government, which Pahad agreed to without any notable dissent, even though they were out of sync with those of the wider ANC and its supporters. Had the ANC leadership pragmatically started to abandon its own newly formulated foreign policy positions even before the end of the transition?

The ANC's acceptance of the SCFA recommendations as the initial basis of the democratic South Africa's foreign engagements must be viewed in an entirely pragmatic light. The movement was fully aware of the international interest in the outcome of the transition and, through Pahad's role in the SCFA, would have been alert to the dangers of straying from the status quo. Although the ANC's headline policies were idealistic, the fact remained that there was also a strong realist streak running through them, particularly given the emphasis on economic relations. By accepting the sub council's proposals, the leadership had not moved too far from the pragmatic aspects of its new foreign policy.

Furthermore, it must be reiterated that the inclusion (or imposition if you will) of human rights as the central pillar of ANC foreign policy was by no means popular within the leadership. Notable differences in opinion had emerged and there were serious misgivings about human rights. In the ANC's Working Group, the opposition to this policy strand was led by Thabo Mbeki and supported by his close confident Aziz Pahad. In light of Pahad's opposition to the ANC's own policy, there was very little prospect that he would have been advocating it through the SCFA. This is a clear example of the gap between the wishes of the ANC elite, the party and those of its support base. Finally, the initial adherence to the SCFA recommendations by the ANC-led government was because there was no real alternative. Without Western support, many of the transformative goals of the ANC would have been short-lived. This is not to claim that the ANC agreed with every aspect of the SCFA recommendations, political expediency made adherence the necessary course of action for the new government. In the long run, leaders such as Mbeki had little intention of maintaining them.

Conclusion

When the GNU was inaugurated on 10 May 1994, the work of the TEC Sub Council on Foreign Affairs came to an end. In five months the sub council had held 21 meetings covering a range of issues such as South Africa's membership of the Commonwealth, the country's development status and the transfer of Walvis Bay to Namibia; had met 13 foreign visiting delegations to South Africa; while on official visits abroad, had held meetings with senior international diplomats and had participated in four regional planning conferences.[80] The meetings, agreements and copious recommendations by the SCFA enabled the new government to begin an informed process of rapidly reintegrating South Africa back into the international community.[81] This act of re-engagement has to be viewed as one of the key successes of the ANC-led government's foreign policy after 1994. In the following months and years South Africa became a member of almost every important international organization open to it, ranging from the Commonwealth to the Non-Aligned Movement. South Africa's reassertion on the world stage began almost immediately with readmission into the OAU in May 1994. This process would not have occurred so smoothly or quickly without the tireless activities and recommendations of the Sub Council on Foreign Affairs.

However, this chapter and Chapter Four, question the extent to which the ANC-led GNU's foreign policy immediately after the elections, can be regarded as truly its own. During the lifespan of the SCFA the available evidence points towards the overarching influence of the DFA and the Western international community. In 1993, Rusty Evans had argued that South Africa could not afford to be out of step with the international thinking of major Western nations, and would be forced to operate within the strict parameters determined for them.[82] The DFA, with the endorsement and active participation of the international community, did its utmost to direct and shape the thinking of the SCFA's final recommendations for the GNU. This process could be described as one of 'domesticating' the former liberation movements.[83] Indeed, Wheeler has argued that, although senior figures in the ANC had represented the movement abroad, they had no government experience and thus had to be 'acculturated into a different way of doing business'.[84] The DFA and the Western international community pursued prevalent shared norms in foreign affairs, and were unwilling to allow South Africa to deviate from this path. They were particularly concerned that a post-apartheid South Africa, led by former liberation activists, might act in a similar fashion to dissident countries such as Cuba or Libya in multilateral forums. The SCFA process provided the perfect opportunity to demonstrate the great benefits that conformity would bring to the country, but was also a means of warning South African's political elites about the dangers of pursuing a 'radical' foreign policy. If South Africa acted like Cuba, then the vast groundswell of popular international support for its transition would swiftly dissipate. The SCFA became a way of schooling the former liberation movements in the established means and practices of international diplomacy and of imbuing them with the normative ideals of the time. It could be put in even stronger terms. For the DFA and the international community, the SCFA process was a way of disciplining the country's upcoming political elite into an acceptable approach to foreign policy. The SCFA also provides an example of how entrenched elite interests influenced the new South Africa's foreign policy to its own benefit, constituting a specific manifestation and demonstration of the characteristics of a transition process, which Patrick Bond, based on Samuel Huntington's thesis, has referred to as an 'elite pact'.[85] What can therefore be seen is how the 'new' South African foreign policy was partially 'captured' by elements of the old regime and the international community.

It is crucial to emphasize that the sub council did not actually make policy. It was however, instrumental in laying the foundations for post-apartheid South African foreign policy. The findings presented to the TEC would ultimately be used to inform the new government's foreign policy. Yet, the importance of the SCFA to South Africa's foreign relations was highlighted retrospectively in the DFA's 1996 Green Paper, entitled South African Foreign Policy: Discussion Document, which asserted that:

> the Subcouncil therefore became actively and effectively involved in the conduct of South Africa's international relations, as regards not only policy matters but also the creation of the new Department of Foreign Affairs, budgetary matters, senior personnel appointments, the opening of new missions abroad and other management matters of medium or long term importance.[86]

During the first few years of ANC rule in South Africa, the GNU accepted the vast majority of the SCFA's recommendations, with its foreign policy following many of the key tenets the sub council had proposed.[87]

Therefore, not only had the ANC's foreign policy positions been created outside its direct control, but so too had those of the 'new' South Africa it would be governing, following the SCFA's work. It must be stressed that the international community's concern for South Africa was not simply one of benevolence, but based on self-interest. Foreign state actors tend not to intervene unless they can see a benefit to themselves. The SCFA provided an opportunity to 'capture' South African foreign policy (and at the very least the economic components) even if the results did not correspond with the broader aspirations of the ANC as a party nor those of the majority of the population. In light of these revelations, it is therefore worth considering whether the positions adopted by the new government were really reflective of its own international agenda, or those of the officials of the DFA.

The evidence offers some explanations as to why post-apartheid South Africa's foreign policy has been criticized for lacking direction under the

ANC. The combination of a foreign policy vision not entirely of its own creation and with the nation's international position largely pre-determined by the SCFA, meant the new government's initial policy options were limited. After 1994, the ANC-led government found itself implementing a foreign policy that was not truly its own, and one that it could not immediately refine nor reject for fear of alienating important international backers. It was only much later when Mbeki began to assert greater control over foreign policy, particularly after the NP left the GNU in 1996, did South Africa's international positions begin to move away from those formulated by the SCFA. Yet, the picture was complicated further by the historic legacies of exile and the ideological incoherences already at large within the ANC: human rights based idealists, neo-liberal capitalists, revolutionaries and Africanists, were all jostling for position within the movement. It is hardly surprising that the ANC in government struggled to contain all of the contradictory elements within the party. This caused numerous problems for foreign policy after May 1994, as the ANC elite was unable to placate the demands of all the organizations' supporters. The following chapters will explore how these frequently ignored historical legacies came to play their part in shaping the direction of the ANC's foreign policy during the presidencies of Mandela and Mbeki.

CHAPTER 6

IDEALISM VERSUS REALISM? THE CONTESTED NATURE OF SOUTH AFRICAN FOREIGN POLICY, 1994–6

One of the more challenging questions concerning post-apartheid South Africa has been the struggle to identify the composition and nature of the nation's foreign policy. The ANC-led Government of National Unity (GNU) came to power in May 1994 equipped with an ambitious set of foreign policy principles that would provide a framework for the country's interactions with the international community. However, critics were soon questioning the nature and direction that foreign policy was taking under the ANC-led GNU. South Africa's foreign policy has been variously described as being poorly planned, inconsistently implemented, and unrealistically idealistic.[1] The cartoon, 'Great Unsolved Mysteries', by South African satirist Zapiro printed in 1995, neatly encapsulated the confusion surrounding the country's international perspectives in the mid-1990s. The cartoon depicts the puzzled ANC Minister of Foreign Affairs, Alfred Nzo, carrying a briefcase emblazoned with 'Nzzzzo' (the malicious, but not entirely inaccurate, nickname given to him because of his habit of falling asleep in meetings) and a question mark above his head labelled 'South African Foreign Policy'.[2] Indeed, this issue would pose many problems for the ANC leadership, the Department of Foreign Affairs (DFA), the international community and South African observers – what exactly was the 'new' South Africa's foreign policy?

There already exists a substantial literature on the economic policies of post-apartheid South Africa, which will not be repeated here.[3] Although this discussion will not address the ANC's domestic economic policies in detail, these had undoubted implications for its emerging foreign policy. The Reconstruction and Development Programme (RDP) and, later, the Growth, Employment and Redistribution (GEAR) strategy were important aspects of South Africa's interactions with the West, which, in tune with the recommendations of the Sub Council on Foreign Affairs (SCFA) aimed (among other things) to make the country more attractive to international business.[4] These economic policies would have a significant effect on South Africa's interactions with the rest of Africa. Freed from the constraints imposed by the apartheid state, South African business expanded rapidly northwards across the continent. While proving extremely beneficial to the nation's economy, aggressive outward investments were not always welcomed by the recipients.[5] The implementation of new economic policies such as GEAR was subsequently criticized by some observers as involving unconsidered acceptance of Western neo-liberal policies. Mark Gevisser suggested that the 'implementation of GEAR was a "culmination" of the systematic pursuit of the ANC leaders by Western Diplomats and big business, and [represented] the liberation movement's "moral surrender"'.[6] As argued, this 'surrender' to external interests had also been seen in certain aspects of South African foreign policy. Through the SCFA process and the transition more widely, certain members of the ANC leadership were influenced into adopting conservative, Western-inspired policies. Throughout Mandela's presidency, the ANC led-government paid close attention to Western demands, something that later exposed deep-seated divisions within the party as a whole. Yet, implementing a comparatively liberal economic policy undeniably played an important role in transforming South Africa's fortunes, as the country sought Western endorsement for its efforts.

An important development that would considerably impact upon the formulation and implementation of South African foreign policy, was the deepening centralization of decision making and Mandela's personal influence over the process. Evidently, it would be incorrect to attribute the foreign policy of modern South Africa to only one person given the multitude of actors involved in the process. However, throughout Mandela's and later Mbeki's presidencies the inputs from the ANC as a party, from government committees and the civil servants of the DFA, were increasingly circumvented or simply ignored. The centralization of foreign policy within the upper echelons of the ANC became ever more noticeable and was to have a profound effect on the content and direction of South Africa's international affairs. It would certainly have a major role in the unfolding 'inconsistencies' that emerged so soon after May 1994. The theme of the centralization of the ANC and its decision-making structures will be revisited in the following chapters.

Nelson Mandela's inauguration as South African president on 10 May 1994, as head of an ANC-led GNU, was a moment of great international significance. Against the backdrop of enormous global expectation, South Africa had successfully emerged from the transition from apartheid to multiparty democracy in a relatively peaceful fashion. The success of this process could be gauged by the fact that heads of state from across the world arrived to be part of this historic occasion. South Africa's achievement was rightly lauded by the international community. Nonetheless, precisely because of the manner in which South Africa had effected change, there were high hopes at home and abroad (from very diverse viewpoints) about what the ANC-led government could achieve as an emerging actor on the international stage. An indication of the international expectations regarding South Africa's role comes from two high-ranking American politicians. The former US ambassador to South Africa, Princeton Lyman wrote an article in 1996, entitled 'South Africa's promise'; and President Bill Clinton's secretary of state, Warren Christopher declared 'I see very few countries with greater potential to shape the twenty-first century than the new South Africa.'[7] It was a mantle that South Africa's new leaders were eager to fulfil, but one which placed a considerable burden on the fledgling democracy.

The process of creating a 'new' foreign policy had been far from simple. The ANC's official foreign policy positions in the early 1990s were developed largely by academics and liberal advisors, who had settled on a headline grabbing human rights inspired vision. However, this vision was partly vitiated by the concurrent activities of the SCFA. The sub council had dictated many of the terms of engagement for the incoming government's immediate relations with the international community before the elections had even taken place.[8] These contradictory outcomes meant that, on entering office, the ANC-led government was already confronted by a number of constraints and contested aims. Add to the matrix the historic continuities of exile and these constraints would ultimately have a significant role in shaping South African foreign policy during Mandela's presidency. Importantly, the SCFA had laid the groundwork for a number of treaties and policy positions which the ANC-led government could not realistically have reneged on, for fear of losing international credibility. Through the process the DFA and the Western-dominated international community had attempted to 'domesticate' the ANC into the world of global politics, imbuing it with many of the hegemonic norms of the time, such as neo-liberalism. The SCFA had facilitated the partial capture of the 'new' by the entrenched interests of the dominant international order, as well as remnants of the out-going apartheid regime. Leading DFA officials and the international community had influenced a small group of ANC leaders into accepting a Western-inspired position. In doing so, the Western world appeared to have ensured that South Africa would uphold the international status quo by pursuing a largely liberal foreign policy. The Western powers were therefore prepared to place a great deal of faith in the new ANC-led government, believing that South Africa would engage with the wider world according to these principles.

Now this was a significant development because the ANC had been, and remained, a far from monolithic organization. Even in exile, the ANC had been a 'broad church', encompassing various ideological perspectives ranging from Marxism to bourgeois nationalism. During the transition period the characteristics of the ANC changed enormously as a large number of different people joined the newly legalized party. Yet, the transition primarily involved a relatively narrow process of negotiations between the leaders of the ANC and the NP, whose deliberations formulated changes in all areas of government policy. The end of CODESA and the formation of the MPNP streamlined negotiations into smaller working groups and sub councils; however, this simultaneously removed the vast majority of people from the process, leaving many disillusioned that their ideals had been undermined. The 'miracle' of the transition can therefore be best described as an elite pact.[9] Nonetheless, due to the way the ANC was organized and structured, this small elite (which itself was not unified) was unable to contain all of the contradictory elements that resided within the wider party. The Western world believed it had secured South Africa's membership of a liberal orthodoxy, but would often be left surprised by some of the actions of Mandela's government that contradicted its expectations. In the words of Tony Leon, the leader of the opposition from 1999, South African 'policy lurched between high-minded principle and the lowest common dominator of Third World struggle solidarity'.[10] The failure to meet the expectations of its diverse constituents was to have a damaging effect upon how South Africa was viewed.

The external constraints imposed on the ANC were compounded by the party's own ideals, which included a commitment to remain friendly with all nations, to reward revolutionary allies from its period in exile and to pursue a human rights based foreign policy. These points alone immediately demonstrate the evident contradictions in the ANC's foreign policy perspectives; publicly acclaiming the centrality of human rights, while maintaining links with liberation allies now presiding over authoritarian governments would inevitably create opposing pressures. Some policies could therefore not be reconciled with others, and these contradictions would subsequently contribute to the emergent problems in the new South Africa's foreign policy.

Foreign Policy After the Elections

The new government wasted no time in implementing many of the foreign policy recommendations set out in the final report of the SCFA.[11] The SCFA had concluded that the country required a flexible but principled approach to foreign policy, arguing that 'the world has a perception of South Africa and expectations of what it can offer. It is therefore incumbent upon the democratic South Africa to define a policy that will inter alia respond partly to the challenge.'[12] Central to the sub council's recommendations was that South Africa apply for membership of various multilateral forums as quickly as possible, so the country could begin to participate actively in international affairs.[13] The new government turned its attentions to this task immediately. The first major foreign policy decision was an application to join the Organization of African Unity (OAU) on 20 May 1994, which was formally accepted by its Secretary General Dr Salim Salim three days later.[14] After the raising of the South African flag at the OAU headquarters in Addis Ababa on 'Africa Day', the country became an officially recognized member.[15] This swift foreign policy initiative both symbolically and practically laid down a statement of intent. At the OAU heads of state meeting in June 1994, Mandela announced: 'we have entered this eminent African organization and rejoined the African community of nations inspired by the desire to join hands with all the countries of our continent as equal partners'.[16] Deputy Foreign Minister Pahad described the decision to join the OAU as one that demonstrated South Africa's commitment to the continent and as an opportunity to 'contribute to the role that Africa can play in world politics'.[17]

South Africa swiftly built upon its entry to the OAU by applying for membership of a whole range of other multilateral organizations. By early August, South Africa had in quick succession joined the Non-Aligned Movement (NAM), the Group of 77 (an intergovernmental caucus of developing nations at the UN), retaken its seat at the UN and rejoined the Commonwealth.[18] These decisions were important early steps for the ANC-led government. Not only did they make practical sense for South Africa, they also provided an opportunity for the ANC to affirm its commitment to working closely and positively with the international community. The decision to request membership of these organizations symbolized an important break with the apartheid past. No longer would South Africa be an isolated state. Instead, under the ANC, it aimed to have a significant and constructive global impact. Within a few months of democratic rule, South Africa was well on its way to becoming a fully-fledged, dedicated and extremely active member of the international community.

During the first few months of democratic rule, South African leaders had regularly taken to emphasizing the importance of international actors to the country. Appreciating the great lengths to which many had gone in the struggle to overthrow apartheid, the ANC was keen to pay its respects. On 24 May 1994, during his speech at the opening of Parliament, Mandela asserted the importance of the international community to South Africa, declaring that the nation's people were now truly 'citizens of the world'.[19] Mandela informed parliament about the key principles that would guide the 'new' South Africa's foreign policy, emphasizing his government's commitment to human rights and continental peace processes then underway in Angola, Mozambique and Rwanda.[20] These themes would be replicated in numerous other speeches at various international forums, in which ANC leaders committed the country to a role of service and duty to the world.

Foreign Minister Nzo later built upon Mandela's message, by setting out his vision to parliament in August 1994. Nzo repeatedly expressed gratitude for the global efforts to help South Africa overcome its problems, stressing that 'South Africa is indebted to the international community'.[21] However, the continual expression of gratitude from the ANC-led government after the elections was a clear rewriting of the historical record. Whilst millions of ordinary people from across the globe had indeed campaigned against apartheid, Western governments had generally not assisted the ANC and, in fact, had actively helped to extend the lifespan of the NP government.[22] The policy of actively forgetting the realities of the past and thanking the international community for its assistance was a clever political manoeuvre. Ann Grant, the former British High Commissioner to South Africa, argued that 'Mandela's big trick of course was to exaggerate the extent to which people in the West had supported the anti-apartheid struggle, and that was a very good tactic'.[23] By including the world in its 'miracle' transition, the ANC hoped that the resultant goodwill would translate into sustained assistance. Moreover, Nzo also addressed the themes of human rights, economic development, and African co-operation, which were all seen as being of central importance to the country's future. The foreign minister committed his government to close co-operation with international organizations, stressing consultation and consensual decision making.[24] This he hoped would be exemplified by the country's relations with Southern Africa, in which 'South Africa will not prescribe the nature or form of regional co-operation but will consult with our neighbours as equal partners'.[25] Again, this was an attempt by the ANC to forge a new path distinct from that of the apartheid regime. The commitment to consensus-building was seen as a necessary mechanism to avoid accusations of domination over other countries. It was however, an approach that would later lead to condemnation and criticism of the ANC-led government for sacrificing its principles. This would be most starkly exemplified during Mbeki's presidency and his response to the crisis in Zimbabwe.

The ANC as a political party was also keen to be seen repaying the support of its southern African allies for the suffering the region had endured at the hands of the apartheid regime. Therefore the new strategy placed great emphasis on the importance of Africa. Senior ANC official, the then Minister of Water Affairs and Forestry, Kader Asmal, expressed the widely held view 'that post-apartheid South Africa would owe its regional neighbours compensation for the devastation it had wreaked'.[26] The notion of a debt of gratitude was prevalent within the new government after 1994, but there was no consensus of how it could be adequately fulfilled. Furthermore, there was a growing tension between the distinctions of the ANC as party and government; what became increasingly noticeable was that the ANC-led government was taking measures that benefited the party and not the interests of South Africa. For example, Mandela repeatedly visited African heads of state to pay his respects and to thank them for their contributions to the ANC's liberation struggles.[27] It provided an opportunity for the ANC-led government to rewrite its notoriously poor relations with the continent and reiterate the differences with its predecessor. South Africa insisted that it could now play a positive role on the continent by engaging constructively and innovatively, based on mutual co-operation.[28] Nzo highlighted these new concerns by arguing that 'the normalization of relations with Africa ... [was] a priority of the new government'.[29] Government ministers were acutely aware that stability and democracy across Africa was crucial to South African development: 'central to our thinking is that we in the Republic of South Africa cannot be an island of prosperity, surrounded by a sea of poverty and deprivation'.[30] The ANC-led government's concerns for its neighbours were thus borne out of liberation solidarity and realist economic thinking.

However, these new-found intentions inspired a mix of fear and expectation amongst its southern African neighbours. The ANC actively sought to avoid accusations of dominating its neighbours, and the leadership regularly had to appease these concerns. Wary of the destructive violence of destabilization in southern Africa, the ANC was certainly conscious of the limitations the country's recent history imposed. Mandela stressed: 'we are largely inhibited by the legacy of apartheid ... we need to think very carefully as to what we do because however justified ... we may be accused of merely carrying on the policy of a government which we sharply criticized'.[31] At a meeting of African heads of state in Tunis, Mandela asserted: 'it will never happen again that our country should seek to dominate another through force of arms, economic might or subversion'; the objective was instead for 'the creation of a South Africa that would be a good neighbour and an equal partner with all the countries of our continent, one which would use its abilities and potentials to help advance the common struggle'.[32] This was a noble idea, but one that created difficulties when South Africa's interests were threatened. The tensions were eased slightly by South Africa's accession to Southern African Development Community (SADC), which helped to reinforce the ANC's commitment to the region. Nzo also tried to dispel any lingering suspicions about South African intentions, arguing that 'it would be a pity if co-operation and progress were to fall victim to unfound fears of South African domination. Such fears are not a good formula for growth ... [we are] one player amongst many. We harbour no desire to be the dominant partner. We entertain no illusion of becoming the regional benefactor – because such capacity we do not possess.'[33] Statements by senior ANC leaders demonstrated that the 'new' South African government was extremely aware of its uncertain position in the region, conscious of its regional responsibilities, but equally cautious of the adverse reactions that this might provoke. It left the government with a serious dilemma on how best to approach southern Africa. The provision of assistance to southern Africa became a thorny issue for the new government. Following years of sustained destabilization at the hands of apartheid, many states expected South Africa to be the continent's saviour, magically alleviating many of the economic and political woes. The West also wanted Pretoria, as the continental powerhouse, to adopt the mantle of regional power but South African officials quickly put a dampener on these 'unrealistic' expectations.[34] Rusty Evans, Director General of the DFA declared: 'of course they (African countries) have expectations ... of course, in their misery, they look at South Africa as something that might suddenly bring relief of sorts. At the same time there is a sense of realism. The South African delegation has been warning against expecting too much.'[35] Indeed, the South African government's coffers were empty, and the focus was very much upon spending limited funds on domestic transformation. Without financial aid, a troubling question for the ANC was how to solve its own poor relations with its erstwhile southern African allies, which, by the late 1980s and early 1990s, had soured considerably. Despite this pressing concern, within a month of the elections, the ANC made it abundantly clear that direct financial compensation requested by regional governments would not be forthcoming. Instead South Africa 'would enter joint projects aimed at developing the region'.[36] The ANC-led government thereby signalled a cautious approach to the region, willing to assist in mutual economic and political development, but without an overtly interventionist approach. Yet, in spite of its efforts the ANC failed to fully overcome the suspicions and expectations of its neighbours. This would ultimately inhibit South Africa's room for manoeuvre in its policy making concerning southern Africa.

In the months immediately after the elections, South Africa's foreign policy remained largely rhetorical. The nation was still finding its feet internationally, urgent domestic problems needed to be addressed and the DFA lacked the capacity to deal effectively with all the demands placed upon it. The start of a new era in South African diplomacy was understandably slow to get off the ground. However, to avoid criticisms of inaction, the ANC-led government did make some early tentative steps in engaging with southern African governments. One of the first problems that confronted the new government was the escalating tensions in the mountain kingdom of Lesotho. The Lesotho military was in a state of near revolt in 1994, resulting in the assassination of the deputy prime minister and sparking a constitutional crisis.[37] South Africa adopted an active role in the multilateral commission that investigated the Lesotho Defence Force and made recommendations to ease the tensions.[38] In consort with Botswana and Zimbabwe, South Africa attended and hosted several meetings and helped broker an agreement in September 1994.[39] The mediation effort was hailed as a victory for democracy and stability in the region. The crisis allowed South Africa to demonstrate clearly its commitment and credentials to the promotion of stability and democracy through peaceful negotiation.

One of the new government's more eye-catching and surprising acts in demonstrating its commitment to the region occurred in December 1994, when South Africa cancelled Namibia's R 800 million debts.[40]

Discussions about such a proposal had been under consideration since the April elections. In a meeting with the Namibian president, Sam Nujoma, at Upington airport, Mandela announced, 'SWAPO and the ANC have been allies in the struggle for decades. We do not think that it is morally correct for us to call upon the SWAPO government to pay a debt of this nature.'[41] Despite the DFA previously insisting that financial aid would not be forthcoming, the government made a rather abrupt policy U-turn. The announcement came as a welcome reprieve for Namibia, a country crippled by economic underdevelopment.[42] The debt cancellation served as a perfect opportunity for the ANC to publicly repay one of its liberation allies. However, this was a pertinent example of the ANC in government making decisions that were in its own interests, rather than that of the state. It was an early indication of how the president's personality came to dominate decision making and the evident discontent between government departments and the upper echelons of the ANC.

A 'Foreign Policy Perspective in a Democratic South Africa': The ANC Sets Out its Post-election Vision

Throughout the latter stages of the transition, the formulation of a new foreign policy had been addressed by both the ANC and the SCFA. The outcome of these deliberations provided a set of recommendations and overarching principles for the new democratic government. In short, these amounted to an idealistic wish-list of how it was hoped South Africa would engage with the wider world. The result was that for the first seven months of ANC-led rule, foreign policy was largely conducted at the behest of its leaders, or on the basis of the aforementioned principles. The first formal, post-election document produced by the ANC (as a party) concerning foreign policy was 'Foreign Policy Perspective in a Democratic South Africa'.[43] However, barring the addition of an introduction describing the post-Cold War world, the document was virtually identical to the October 1993 publication 'Foreign Policy in a New Democratic South Africa: A Discussion Paper'.[44] The publication of 'Foreign Policy Perspective', nevertheless provided an opportunity for the ANC to reiterate its core principles governing foreign policy interactions; echoing the Freedom Charter, it emphatically declared that 'foreign policy belongs to South Africa's people'.[45] This bold statement did not reflect the unfolding reality, which in fact saw policy making in South Africa being increasingly confined to a small number of people within the ANC hierarchy. The development did little for earlier ideas of a peoples' democracy in South Africa.

The new document emphasized seven core principles that were to guide South African foreign policy. These had been previously publicized several times, most prominently in the ghost-written Mandela article in the blue-ribbon journal *Foreign Affairs* (although the article lists only six principles; the final point on the list below is an addition) as well as in the October 1993 discussion paper, and through various speeches by ANC leaders. The principles were:

> A belief in, and preoccupation with, Human Rights which extends beyond the political, embracing the economic, social and environmental;
> A belief that just and lasting solutions to the problems of human kind can only come through the promotion of Democracy, worldwide;
> A belief that Justice and International Law should guide the relations between nations;
> A belief that international peace is the goal to which all nations should strive. Where this breaks down, internationally-agreed peaceful mechanisms to solve conflicts should be resorted to;
> A belief that our foreign policy should reflect the interests of the continent of Africa;
> A belief that South Africa's economic development depends on growing regional and international economic co-operation in an independent world;
> A belief that our foreign relations must mirror our deep commitment to the consolidation of a democratic South Africa.[46]

The clear message was of a party dedicated to issues of human rights, peace, economic growth, democracy, and the primacy of the African continent. The importance of two key principles, human rights and the importance of Africa, will be assessed in greater depth.

In 1994, human rights were made the cornerstone of the ANC's post-apartheid foreign policy vision. Despite some misgivings within the leadership, it was an issue that Mandela and other party leaders regularly promoted. In the words of the 'Foreign Policy Perspective in a Democratic South Africa' document, this was because, 'the world dare not relinquish the commitment to Human Rights ... Our Struggle to end apartheid was a global one and we believe that a change has enhanced the necessity for a worldwide Human Rights campaign. South Africa should and must play a central role in this campaign.'[47] The ANC also rejected claims that human rights pledges would be only symbolic: 'in our efforts to canonise human rights in our international relations, we regard them as far more than this'.[48] Setting South Africa on such a bold path was a courageous statement of intent by the ANC. Based on its own experiences, the party saw the pursuit of human rights as an ideal basis for its foreign policy in the 'new world order'.

Yet, the centrality of human rights and the almost missionary zeal of the ANC in promoting it demonstrated a degree of naiveté concerning its foreign policy. The ANC asserted that 'we shall not be selective, nor, indeed be afraid to raise human rights violations with countries where our own and other interests might be negatively affected. South Africa's experience, we believe, shows how damaging policy can be when issues of principle are sacrificed to economic and political expediency.'[49] This was certainly a noble position and, if the government had stuck to this principle, then the country would truly have been an agent for change. Indeed, given South Africa's successful transition, it was probably the only country that could have realistically pursued such a goal in the 1990s. The country, its president and the ANC, were all held in such high esteem by the global community that they might just have been able to enact such a policy. However, the inconsistent implementation of this policy and indeed its inherent problems meant that this clear statement of intent would later come to haunt the ANC. Although the pursuit of human rights would cause a number of dilemmas for the ANC-led government, its predicament was not unique in international relations. For example, US President Jimmy Carter in the 1970s and British Prime Minister Tony Blair in the late 1990s, had both committed their respective governments to moral and human rights based foreign policies.[50] Ultimately, despite their best intentions, both powerful leaders struggled to live up to their lofty principles, illustrating the difficulties of implementing such ideals. The overwhelming 'realist' view of the world meant that ideological concerns were frequently subsumed by other issues, especially economic ones. For an emerging nation such as South Africa, it was always going to be a challenge to encourage international change, particularly if two of the world's most influential countries could not succeed.

The second main aspect of 'Foreign Policy Perspective in a Democratic South Africa' was Africa. It was at the forefront of the ANC's efforts because 'a democratic South Africa's future is inextricably intertwined with that of Africa', and furthermore, because 'the region sustained us during our struggle ... Southern Africa is, therefore, a pillar upon which South Africa's foreign policy rests'.[51] The document declares: 'we dedicate our foreign policy to helping to ensure that Africa's peoples are not forgotten or ignored by humankind'.[52] The premise was that the South African government would aim to enhance regional and continental unity by creating a balanced, more co-operative approach to trade and development. Furthermore, by working in multilateral forums such as the OAU, South Africa could also pursue the goals of peace, stability and democracy. It was a principle informed by the recommendations of the SCFA, and the experiences of the ANC in exile. Without peace and stability in Africa, the aim of rapid economic development would not be fulfilled in the manner that South Africa required for its own envisaged domestic transformation. The emphasis on Africa thus made perfect sense for the ANC, but was a decision influenced by both altruistic and material motivations. However, the ANC's understanding of its African partners was clearly lacking, and it quickly became apparent that South Africa was actually very unlike other states on the continent.

As has been discussed previously, most of the 'Foreign Policy Perspective' document had been drafted during the transition, at a time when the pressures and realities of power had not yet tested the viability of its principles. It is perhaps surprising then that the ANC did not modify the document after seven months in power. It might have reasonably been expected that after its initial international forays a period of contemplation and reflection would have occurred. However, the ANC optimistically believed that its seven principles could be achieved and asserted that there was widespread domestic and international support for its initiatives. The new introduction claimed that 'our policies and programmes have, by and large, been accepted by the international community as realistic and the endeavour to transform South Africa into a truly free, prosperous and non-racial society has been acclaimed ... The world is literally bending backwards to make us a success story.'[53] The wider world may have paid close attention to the transformation of South Africa, but it was hoping for very specific outcomes from the ANC-led government. The goodwill of the international community endured well into Mbeki's presidency, but it was increasingly tinged with a growing exasperation at the actions of the ANC.

With no other foreign policy statement in place, this document acted as the framework for the ANC's first tentative foreign policy steps in government. But, the 'Foreign Policy Perspective' document was not a foreign policy in the truest sense of the term. Although it successfully helped smooth South Africa's entrance into the international community, it did not provide definitive guidance. For example, the document did not at any point define what South Africa's national interests were. As foreign policy is normally considered an extension of domestic priorities, it is usually necessary to identify what the national interests of the country are. This is something the ANC consistently failed to do. Furthermore, there was no indication of how the South African government would be able to achieve or even implement the ANC's highly ambitious goals. The result was that South Africa did not have a definitive foreign policy by the end of 1994 to guide its international interactions. This was to prove crucial.

South Africa and the Nigerian Crisis

The first major diplomatic issue for the new ANC-led government was its confrontation with the military dictatorship of Nigerian president, Sani Abacha. In 1993, Abacha had assumed power by dissolving democratic institutions, ousting civilian rulers and replacing them with military personnel, while clamping down on domestic dissent.[54] Nigeria therefore provided the first real test case for South Africa's well-publicized democratic, human rights and African-focused foreign policy. Nigeria was a particularly interesting country for the ANC-led government to stake its foreign policy principles on. Despite Nigeria's domestic instability, it remained an extremely powerful country and one that many African states regarded as a natural leader; it had been an active supporter of the ANC during the liberation struggle, providing training and financial assistance and was the largest contributor to the OAU, providing a third of its budget.[55] With its huge oil reserves, Nigeria was a major economic power and a country with which South Africa would have realistically expected to have established close links. However, as the ANC had so clearly stated, South Africa 'would not be selective' when dealing with human rights abuses and acts that violated democracy. For the declaration to have any meaning the ANC-led government was compelled to take action. The subsequent responses of South Africa, the Nigerian government and the international community between 1994 and 1996 resulted in a complete breakdown of relations, commonly known as the Nigerian Crisis.

The South African government initially adopted a 'quiet diplomatic' stance towards Nigeria, encouraging and prompting Abacha to reform his style of government, release political opponents and initiate democratic elections.[56] However, Abacha was an autocratic leader who did not conform to international norms, and in fact openly defied them.[57] Moreover, it must be noted that the issues with which the South African government were confronting Nigeria – human rights abuses and demands for democracy – are not 'traditional' foreign policy concerns. In this regard traditional foreign policy making is largely based on the 'realist' world view that informs the international system. South Africa found it difficult to implement its 'idealistic' vision for foreign policy (and attract others to support its goals), because the pursuit of human rights falls outside the scope of common concerns such as national interests. More importantly, the notions of state sovereignty and non-intervention are two factors that underpin the current international community. A central dilemma was that South Africa did not have the instruments in place to force Nigeria to comply with its demands. Nigeria was economically powerful enough to resist any South African sanctions or coercion. Furthermore, South Africa could not realistically have engaged Nigeria militarily, not only because of the distance, but also because of its belief in non-intervention. Leading South African politicians such as Mandela, Mbeki and Nzo all made visits to Abuja during mid to late 1995 to discuss their concerns; the South Africans claimed they were making progress, 'because we are certain that the Nigerian government is sensitive to the concerns we and many other people have raised with regards to clemency'.[58] Although South Africa repeatedly engaged Abacha and his government in quiet bilateral talks, no concrete gains were ever achieved because they possessed neither the incentives nor the means to encourage Nigeria to act differently.

Matters came to a head in November 1995 when Nigerian activist Ken Saro-Wiwa and nine others were executed at the time of the Commonwealth heads of state meeting in New Zealand. Mandela was genuinely shocked, as he believed that he had persuaded Abacha to alter his stance. The president furiously condemned the execution and 'the callous disregard of efforts by the South African and other African governments to lend assistance in the restoration of democracy'.[59] Nigeria was immediately suspended from the Commonwealth and Mandela personally pushed for greater punitive punishment, including an international oil embargo and diplomatic isolation. To force the issue, Mandela made personal phone calls to the US and UK governments to demand immediate implementation of these measures.[60] At Mandela's insistence, South Africa withdrew its high commissioner in protest, and convened a regional meeting of SADC heads of state to formulate a cohesive plan of action against Nigeria.[61] Mandela became increasingly belligerent in his personal attacks against Abacha, describing him as 'a corrupt dictator in charge of an illegitimate and barbaric regime'.[62] President Mandela also demanded African unity behind international sanctions to isolate Nigeria in a show of disgust. It was a highly principled stand by the South African government, but unfortunately its efforts were in isolation.

South Africa's diplomatic efforts came to nothing. Instead it was the ANC-led government that was forced to back down and apologize, with Foreign Minister Nzo subsequently insisting that 'we have never intended to humiliate or destabilize' Nigeria.[63] Mandela had failed to convince Abacha to soften his stance, and found that South Africa was being lambasted for its approach. Comprehensive sanctions against any government require widespread international support, which was not forthcoming, leaving South Africa diplomatically isolated. Despite its strident efforts, South Africa was accused by Nigerian civil society of being too weak in its actions; Nigerian poet laureate Wole Soyinka accused the government of 'appeasement and compared the strategy of quiet diplomacy to the notorious strategy of constructive engagement adopted by the Thatcher and Reagan administrations in dealing with apartheid'.[64] In hindsight, this statement is grossly unfair, as there was little else South Africa could have done. In fact, South Africa took the strongest stand of any nation, and was promptly pilloried for it. What this does demonstrate is that, regardless of South Africa's best efforts, many Africans expected far more. Certainly, the two stages of South Africa's approach, quiet diplomacy followed by over-stated individual condemnation, proved wholly inadequate in altering the Nigerian president's errant behaviour.

More damaging for South African initiatives, was that Mandela failed to unite the continent in condemnation of Nigeria. The OAU's inaction was described by *The Star's* foreign editor, Dale Lautenbach, as a 'disgraceful silence'; only four heads of state attended the emergency SADC meeting, leaving Mandela 'without the regional solidarity he was seeking'.[65] The SADC meeting agreed to defer any decision to the Commonwealth Ministerial Action Group, meaning that by December 1995, South Africa had surrendered its bilateral efforts towards Nigeria, in favour of collective measures.[66] These failures damaged South Africa's prestige, indicating that it lacked the ability to wield decisive influence in Africa. Matters were worsened by the barrage of hostility from Nigeria. Abacha openly ridiculed Mandela, arguing that 'probably because . . . of being incarcerated for 27 years, he cannot understand the complexity of modern diplomacy'.[67] He also cited the history of Nigerian support for the South African struggle, stating: 'I cannot understand . . . why [they] . . . are behaving the way they did. These were the same people for whom we have made a lot of sacrifices in order to ensure freedom.'[68] Abacha even described South Africa as a 'traitor' on the continent for having an overtly Western-centred approach.[69] These insults were rather too close to home for the ANC's liking. The new South African government had been desperate not to damage relations with Africa, nor arouse resentment or suspicion. Despite the wrongdoings of the Nigerian government, it was the South Africans who attracted enormous hostility for their moral stand. The continent had largely rejected Mandela's efforts to pursue a human rights vision. Moreover, South Africa had broken with unwritten diplomatic tradition by publicly attacking Nigeria. It was a mistake that the ANC-led government and Thabo Mbeki in particular, endeavoured to avoid in the future.

Some do consider Mandela's stand against Abacha as one of the greatest achievements of his presidency.[70] *The Star's* foreign editor argued that Mandela's active defence of his principles was a bold and courageous move 'because South Africa has chosen the "right way" ... we cannot imagine that others should not see the light'.[71] However, notwithstanding the merits of the ANC-led government's bold stance, its handling of the crisis was an abject failure of its foreign policy. It was clear that quiet diplomatic talks had no substance and South Africa lacked any sort of bargaining tool. It was also evident that there was no co-ordinated diplomatic approach towards Nigeria, with the DFA failing to brief Mandela properly.[72] The *Mail and Guardian* exposed that neither Nzo nor Mbeki had done anything substantial to resolve the situation, keeping out of the public eye and leaving Deputy Foreign Minister Pahad to pick up the pieces.[73] It was also revealed that the South African high commissioner to Nigeria, George Nene, had failed to follow his instructions to keep in regular contact with opposition groups in the country, thus limiting the quality of South African intelligence.[74]

It would not be an overstatement to suggest that, even at this early stage of the administration, the Nigerian Crisis was a seminal moment in the ANC-led government's nascent foreign policy. It was the moment that the ANC learnt hard lessons about the nature of foreign policy in Africa and the wider international community. It undoubtedly shaped the ANC's approach to future events. Primarily, there was a realization that a more discerning approach would be required. In the wake of the crisis, the ANC officially stuck to the human rights vision, but realized it would need to approach its implementation in different ways, primarily through multilateral forums and consensus building. South Africa increasingly turned to institutions such as the UN and SADC to promote its international agenda. The ANC also realized the need to rethink its emphasis on the term 'human rights' in order to avoid similar diplomatic disasters. Pahad later argued that 'the ANC had not fully elaborated on its human rights policy – possibly due to inexperience in government'.[75] Pahad explained the government's naiveté of approach by its inexperience: 'we had to learn by doing. We were new.'[76] Another key lesson was the stark appreciation that the international community's rhetoric about defending human rights and democracy were often ignored (as were Mandela's calls for sanctions and diplomatic restrictions on Nigeria) no matter how obvious the abuses. During the transition the DFA and SCFA had noted that economic considerations would be more influential on policy than ideology, and the crisis in Nigeria reinforced this position.[77]

The most significant and enduring lesson of the Nigerian crisis was in its revelations about African attitudes towards South Africa. Despite the ANC's efforts at forging closer relations with African governments, the reality was that after 30 years in exile it did not truly understand the continent, its leaders or their priorities. This was an important historic legacy of the struggle given the ANC's reliance on external backers such as the Soviet Union. Once in government, the ANC's tensions with continental leaders persisted. In turn, much of Africa remained suspicious of South Africa. A *Star* editorial argued that 'we fail to understand the power politics of Africa', and that the OAU's silence on Nigeria 'reflects the reality of the sum of African states'.[78] The ANC wanted to reform Africa and the international community's perceptions of the continent, yet these initiatives were clearly unwelcome. South African foreign policy makers were confronted by 'the dilemma of pursuing goals which clash so fundamentally with many of the practises and customs of African politics'.[79] South African foreign policy aims were not aligned with the rest of the continent, and were consequently rejected by the very leaders the ANC was seeking to work with. South Africa was ostracized on the continent for breaking the 'unwritten rule, the gentleman's agreement, that African leaders don't criticise each other in public'.[80] Since the end of colonial rule, it had come to be understood that African states did not condemn one another publicly; rather they closed ranks against external threats. Already regarded with a degree of suspicion, South Africa had openly broken the solidarity rule.[81] From this moment onwards the ANC-led government was far less willing to stick its head above the parapet and take initiatives on human rights alone. South Africa sought consensus with others before taking action where possible. The message to the ANC had been clear, 'that you dare not stand alone, don't swim against the tide in Africa'.[82] This was to be the most important lesson the ANC took from the Nigeria Crisis, and one that would profoundly influence its future.

The Emerging Inconsistencies in South African Foreign Policy

Even before the Nigerian Crisis, there was already mounting concern amongst academics and observers about the inconsistencies in South African foreign policy. These views only hardened further during Mandela's presidency. The ANC-led government found itself caught between the competing strands of its foreign policy, including its own ideological principles, the lack of consensus within the party, the centralization of decision making, the Western-orientated recommendations of the SCFA and the expectations of the international community. Trying to fulfil or even match these strands resulted in an inconsistent approach to international affairs. These problems were accentuated by the ANC's seven principles, which were inherently contradictory, and were not in accord with the realities of the world around them. Importantly, it demonstrated the way in which the ANC's past influenced its decision making in office.

An issue that plagued the ANC was the need to be seen repaying its debts to former allies that had sustained the liberation struggle. In the fight against apartheid most of the Western world had not supported the ANC; in fact the movement had been labelled as a terrorist organization by British Prime Minister Margaret Thatcher and US President Ronald Reagan.[83] Lacking Western assistance, the ANC had turned to the Eastern Bloc and to various authoritarian states for support, putting them further at odds with the major economic powers. After the Cold War had ended, the bulk of the ANC's former liberation allies, such as the USSR, the German Democratic Republic (GDR) and Poland had ceased to be communist regimes. They had instead embraced democracy and neo-liberal economics. A small number of former communist and radical nations did manage to survive the upheaval of the early 1990s, becoming ostracized from the much larger and interconnected capitalist world. The ANC-led government's emerging ties with socialist or rogue nations did, however, increasingly concern Western governments. The SCFA process had committed the South African government to a specific manner of interacting with the international community, but the ANC were not sticking to the script. At Mandela's inauguration, there was already evidence of the 'new' South Africa's diplomatic ties with the ANC's former allies as powerful Western leaders found themselves sharing the stage with dictators past and present, including revolutionaries such as Yasser Arafat, Muammar al-Gaddafi and Fidel Castro.[84]

South Africa's links with nations on the fringes of the international community such as Cuba, Libya and North Korea were epitomized by the establishment of diplomatic missions soon after the elections.[85] In the new international order, with foreign policy increasingly linked to trade, these countries had almost nothing to offer South Africa economically or politically, although Cuba had sent much-needed doctors to rural health clinics.[86] However, these ties were in the eyes of some critics, 'purely symbolic, nostalgic and ideological'.[87] They simply provided a means for the ANC as a party to thank its former allies. These links increasingly put South Africa at odds with Western governments. In response, Mandela took a thinly veiled swipe at the West by insisting 'that we never forget our friends who were with us when we were all alone, when some of the countries, with whom we now have developed special relations, were on the side of the enemy, giving them resources to enable the apartheid regime to continue the repression'.[88] Yet, this stance presented a major strategic problem for the ANC-led government. The West, upon which South Africa relied most heavily for trade and aid, became ever more critical of the ANC's insistence on entertaining isolated nations; there was a belief that South Africa was offering these regimes a degree of international legitimacy. Mandela was publicly chastized on several occasions for this development. The United States in particular was angered by South Africa's diplomatic ties to Cuba and Libya. There was some expectation that South Africa would conform to Western norms, as set-out by the SCFA process, but in cultivating these other relationships, the ANC-led government was doing exactly the opposite. However, the more South Africa's international relations were criticized, the more insistent Mandela became on retaining them; these developments led to a growing sense of unease amongst many observers.[89] On one occasion, when questioned about South Africa's relations with Libya, Mandela reacted furiously, claiming that 'those who feel we should have no relations with Gadaffi, have no morals. Those who feel irritated by our friendship with President Gadaffi can go jump in the pool.'[90] Yet, despite Mandela's firm stance, the international community did nothing to coerce South Africa to change its diplomatic position. However, it did reflect the increasing confusion about what South Africa actually stood for internationally.

The emerging links with former ANC allies were also informed by an initial desire to make South Africa a non-aligned country, but with a particular focus on developing world interests. This was often labelled by the ANC as playing a bridge-building role between the developed and developing world. As part of this stance, the ANC committed itself to the self-determination of oppressed peoples, which in turn potentially meant supporting national liberation movements. As the ruling party of a powerful nation, this certainly caused consternation. In the context that 'one person's terrorist, is another's freedom fighter', the ANC was establishing contact with groups regarded by other governments as terrorists. The ANC argued that establishing links with rebel movements provided a means of opening a channel of communication, so that a peaceful solution could be negotiated. Nonetheless, a number of governments simply saw a powerful African nation undermining their sovereignty by consorting with its enemies. Several examples neatly illustrate this point.

The continuation of fraught relations with southern African governments was an unresolved issue for the ANC, and the example of Angola encapsulates these tensions. Throughout the exile liberation struggle, the ANC had been closely allied to the People's Movement for the Liberation of Angola (MPLA) government, which had provided bases, training, and support. The civil war in Angola had been raging since Portuguese decolonization in 1975, and the MPLA (and at times the ANC) had fought against the rival guerrilla movement, the National Union for the Total Independence of Angola (UNITA). After South Africa's own independence, the ANC-led government committed itself to assisting the Angolan peace process. The strategy that was adopted meant establishing contact with UNITA to bring them to the negotiating table. By aiding the evolving peace process in Angola, the ANC-led government hoped to not only win the favour of an erstwhile ally, but also to secure peace and stability in southern Africa. However, the ANC's decision to initiate talks with UNITA infuriated the Angola government, who regarded the move as a betrayal of liberation solidarity. The Angolans would have much preferred destroying UNITA militarily to beginning talks. Already declining relations between the ANC and the MPLA were exacerbated by the South Africans' decision to talk to the rebel leader Jonas Savimbi. The incident was just the tip of the iceberg in an ongoing diplomatic spat. After 1994, the MPLA had been piqued by the ANC decision not to fully acknowledge its role in the liberation struggle of South Africa, and southern Africa more widely. Undeniably the Angolan contribution was particularly significant, so it appeared strange that the ANC had failed to recognize their role. Previously, during the transition period, the ANC had failed to 'tip off the Angolans when they knew that the SADF was trying to provide logistical support for UNITA during the 1992 electoral registration campaign, and that the SADF tried to use their presence in Angola at this time to spy on Angolan forces, which cannot have helped to develop mutual trust'.[91] This was a move that did not endear the ANC to the MPLA government. Furthermore, the new South African government was politically embarrassed when in February 1995 it was uncovered that it had continued to sell weapons to UNITA, contravening an arms agreement signed the year before.[92] The litany of problems lengthened when Mandela chose to cancel Namibia's debts, without offering anything equivalent to the Angolans. The ANC's attempts at ingratiating themselves in the Angolan peace process by negotiating with both sides seriously backfired. The ANC-led government's previous actions did little to ease the tensions with the MPLA, which remained extremely poor well into Jacob Zuma's presidency over a decade later.

A second pertinent example was the ANC's stance concerning the Western Sahara, the former Spanish colony in west Africa. In 1975, Spain ceded two-thirds of the territory to Morocco, which occupied the region, despite it being claimed as a homeland by the Saharawi people. The Saharawi, represented by the Popular Front for the Liberation of Saguia el-Hamra and Rio de Oro (POLISARIO) had fought a guerrilla war operating out of neighbouring Algeria until 1991, where it claimed to be the 'country's' government in exile.[93] Despite the 1991 ceasefire, negotiations had reached a stalemate, and the UN became involved in mediation efforts. The apartheid regime had forged close ties with Morocco, while the ANC in exile had established relations with POLISARIO. Furthermore, the ANC had previously agreed to recognize the independence of Western Sahara when it had gained office. After the 1994 elections, the new South African government pledged to maintain links with both Morocco and POLISARIO as part of its non-aligned foreign policy strategy, with the ANC allegedly receiving financial donations from both sides.[94]

However, President Mandela, who had offered a written promise to officially recognize the state of Western Sahara, subsequently reneged on this commitment. Instead he chose to delay the decision until the UN had made clear its stance on official recognition of the Western Sahara.[95] POLISARIO leaders were furious with Mandela, believing that the financial donations of the Moroccan government had influenced the decision.[96] The indecision of the ANC-led government was compounded by the fact that the Western Sahara was a full member of the OAU, which prompted senior ANC NEC member Jeremy Cronin to observe that 'we are absolutely alone in this regard among all Southern African states, even Malawi has recently accorded recognition'.[97] Although the issue of the Western Sahara had not been satisfactorily rectified, the ANC-led government continued to maintain close links with both sides. This decision sparked a mini-crisis as the Moroccan government, very similarly to the MPLA, took exception to South African talks with POLISARIO.[98] Mandela was forced to call the Moroccan king, in order to bring Foreign Minister 'Nzo's recent North African trip back from the brink of disaster'.[99] The ANC had once again tried to work with two mutually opposed parties, and had resulted in offending both. This did little to enhance its already battered reputation on the continent.

A final and better-known example of South Africa's efforts to pursue a non-aligned foreign policy strategy was in its relations with the People's Republic of China (PRC) and the Republic of China (ROC), more commonly referred to as Taiwan. Apartheid South Africa had established close links and strong economic ties with Taiwan, a similarly isolated country. Given the importance of Taiwan to the South African economy, the ANC-led government was obviously keen to maintain these diplomatic ties. However, this strategy quickly ran into problems. South Africa had naturally sought to establish ties with the PRC, as it was a fast-growing economy, a member of the UN Security Council, and a powerful developing nation. South Africa's strategy towards the two countries was complicated because the PRC did (and still does) not recognize the sovereignty of Taiwan; the communist government categorically refused to establish formal ties with South Africa if the latter pursued dual recognition: the so-called 'Two China's Policy'. It was thought that Mandela's moral authority and charisma would overcome this obstacle, but Beijing stood firm.

Instead, they in turn vigorously lobbied the South African government into ending its official recognition of Taiwan. Mandela refused to submit to the political pressure and made clear that he had 'no intention of ending ties with Taiwan' to achieve diplomatic ties with the PRC.[100] To try and ease the situation and win over mounting South African doubts, the Taiwanese government provided large financial donations to both the state and the ANC.[101] The dilemma for the ANC-led government was that, on the one hand it wished to retain links with an important economic partner and supporter of the party, but on the other hand it needed to recognize the PRC, one of the world's largest and most powerful countries. Ultimately, economic and realpolitik considerations won the day. In a later interview, Pahad admitted that 'it was inevitable that South Africa would follow the one-China policy in the end and join the rest of the world – but money "spoke"'.[102] The 'Two Chinas Policy' formally ended in November 1996, and Mandela publicly announced that South Africa would establish official links with the PRC by the start of 1998. It was a perfectly understandable 'realist' course of action for South Africa to take, bringing the nation into line with the international community and providing vital trade access to China's burgeoning economy. It did, however, contradict the ANC government's earlier statements about dual recognition, and its policy of non-alignment. The abandonment of this policy marked the moment when the ANC-led government realized that such an approach to foreign policy was not entirely feasible. This aspect of the country's foreign policy soon ceased to exist, demonstrating 'that reputation and moral authority achieve little when States interests are at stake'.[103] The recognition of the PRC was a clear indication that the economic imperatives of South Africa's foreign policy were far more important than idealism.

An important contradiction that soon emerged in the ANC-led government's foreign policy was between the non-aligned position it had adopted initially and the equally important principle of human rights. How could South Africa possibly maintain friendly relations with all, when a sizeable minority regularly abused human rights? How was it possible to have close relations with countries which are non-democratic, when South Africa was committed to promoting global democracy? Long before South Africa reproached Nigeria for its abuses of human rights and democracy, the ANC had been trying to square this circle without much luck. The ANC's allies in places like North Korea, Sudan, Libya, and Indonesia were constantly infringing upon human rights and democratic rights. In this regard the legacy of the ANC's Cold War engagement with any government or organization able to offer support was an important continuity into the democratic era. It did mean that South Africa's lofty and well-publicized principles were being regularly undermined by its own policy actions. It was easy for the West to start criticizing South Africa's for its approach, because it was falling far short of its own ideals. As discussed previously, these ideals were further undermined when economics entered the equation. Numerous states had given money to the ANC (both as a liberation movement and a post-apartheid political party) as well as to the South African state. After the elections, Mandela met on several occasions with President Suharto of Indonesia, even though the country was occupying East Timor. It was revealed that, notwithstanding human rights abuses in East Timor, he had accepted substantial donations from Indonesia.[104] Moreover, Taiwan donated large sums of money to the government, with R 35 million going towards the ANC's election campaign, and a further R 141 million towards a demobilization centre for the South African National Defence Force (SANDF).[105] Mandela had to deny publicly that these were not bribes, but the correlation between financial donations and South Africa's continued diplomatic recognition was striking. It appeared that South Africa was happy to downplay its principles in return for a donation to the party or a favourable trade deal. This drew a number of criticisms. Tony Leon, leader of the opposition Democratic Party (DP), argued that 'our whole foreign policy is based on the electoral debts of the ANC ... There is a porous wall between party and state in this regard.' Leon alleged that South African 'foreign policy is largely for hire ... if you make a substantial donation to the ANC you get special foreign policy considerations'.[106]

The new government also continued to undermine its own principles over the sale of arms. During the country's isolation, the apartheid regime had developed one of the most successful domestic arms industries in the world and, despite strict sanctions, had become a major exporter. In Armaments Corporation of South Africa (ARMSCOR), the post-apartheid state had inherited a profitable nationalized industry, which employed many skilled people and was one of the country's biggest export earners. After the election, there had been high hopes amongst some domestic observers that South Africa would end, or at least vastly diminish, its status as a major arms exporter. However, on discovering the extent of ARMSCOR's economic importance, the new government delayed addressing this difficult question. This was entirely understandable, given ARMSCOR's status and the economic imperatives for South Africa at the time. However, it posed several serious dilemmas for the ANC. Foremost, how could they promote human rights whilst selling sophisticated weaponry? This quandary was complicated by revelations that the ANC-led government had sold weapons to Yemen, a UN-prohibited weapons destination, providing a major embarrassment for the new administration. A report into the arms trade noted that, 'the incident had severe consequences for South Africa's international image and was a slap in the face to South Africa's emerging foreign policy'.[107] In response, the ANC established the South African National Conventional Arms Control Committee (NCACC) in August 1995. This was a Cabinet-appointed committee designed to regulate and exercise control over the country's arms sales. It meant the government would have full control and knowledge of where South African arms were being exported to. Additionally, as part of the overhaul of South African arms sales, the Cameron Commission was established by President Mandela to thoroughly investigate the issue. Mandela had emphasized the importance of the issue, insisting:

> our morality as a democratic government dictates that we have to act in accordance with internationally acceptable norms and standards ... In our approach to the sale of arms, we are resolved to act responsibly. Arms are for the purpose of defending the sovereignty and territorial integrity of a country; not to undermine any considerations of humanity nor to suppress the legitimate aspirations of any community.[108]

The key recommendation of the Cameron Commission Report published in 1995, was that South Africa should not sell 'arms to repressive and authoritarian regimes'.[109] This was a perfectly reasonable recommendation and one endorsed by the ANC-led government. South Africa soon emerged as a vocal proponent of disarmament and became signatories to numerous treaties such as the 1995 Non-Proliferation Treaty (NPT).

Yet, despite the new stricter government regulations, there remained an evident gap between rhetoric and practice. While maintaining strict accordance with international arms protocols, from 1994 onwards, the South Africa government knowingly sold weapons to numerous nations that had dubious human rights records, were involved in ongoing conflicts or were undemocratic. It became evident that the Arms Control Committee had ignored human rights concerns as it 'completely abandoned any serious attempt to only supply relatively decent countries with arms'.[110] What made matters worse, was that as the ANC-led government became increasingly centralized, the party elite would clearly have known what was going on. For example, there were arms deals involving sales to Rwanda (before and after the genocide) and Uganda, both of which later invaded Zaire in 1997. In the same period, arms were also sold to Turkey, Indonesia, Algeria, Congo-Brazzaville and Angola.[111] It led the Commonwealth Human Rights Initiative to declare that the 'disturbing record of arms sales since April 1994 has fed the perception, domestically and internationally, that the ANC Government's foreign policy is haphazard and that South Africa has failed to become a restrained and responsible arms trader'.[112] This was a damning indictment, and further evidence that South Africa's foreign policy principles were being undermined by its own actions. A more worrying tendency was that the ANC-led government remained unable to implement its vision in practice, even when regulations were introduced. It is another excellent example of how the ideals of human rights and democracy were rapidly being sidelined by the ANC-led government in favour of economic concerns.

Conclusion

The ANC came to power on a wave of euphoria, with extremely high expectations of what it could achieve internationally. The ANC-led government threw itself into reintegrating South Africa back into the international community, and did so with rigour and enthusiasm. This commitment was informed both by its own perceptions, and the recommendations set out by the SCFA. The result was that after the elections, there were many clear demonstrations of the ANC-led government pro-actively engaging with the international community. Despite South Africa's enthusiasm, many problems arose in its foreign policy. The new government's room for manoeuvre had been constrained by the SCFA process, which had pre-determined its foreign policy interactions along a largely pro-Western path. Yet, the outcomes of the transition clashed with the ANC's idealistic principles, the party's own interests, and also those of its allies. The tensions between the divergent positions developed during the negotiations of the ANC's Foreign Policy Working Group and the SCFA; the attitudes of the international community towards South Africa; and the influence of the ANC's exiled past were problems that continued to afflict foreign policy under Mandela's stewardship.

This chapter has illustrated how the lofty principles of the ANC were steadily undermined. Once in government, the ANC continued to act as if it was a liberation movement. In power, the ANC was surprised to find its foreign policy being roundly criticized from many different quarters. It had also become abundantly clear that the positions of the ruling party were being blurred, undermining South Africa's national interests. Former ANC MP Andrew Feinstein argued that the 'narrow interests of the party are not necessarily in South Africa's national interest ... there has been a combination of national interests and narrow political party interests'.[113] This problem is a theme that will be returned to in the following chapters. Although maintaining relations with allies such as North Korea or selling arms to Indonesia may have been a means of the ANC recognizing and rewarding support for its liberation struggle and boosting its developing world credentials, they offered South Africa little in terms of national interest, particularly given the new-found emphasis on economic relations. Indeed, such ties only generated widespread opposition. The ANC-led government was also criticized by the international community, which was often left confused by the way that South African foreign policy oscillated between different, often contradictory positions. In the West, this stemmed from the mistaken belief that through the SCFA process they had 'captured' South African foreign policy. They were consequently surprised when the government took actions contrary to expectations. Meanwhile, in the process of pursuing its principles, the South Africa government managed to damage relations almost irreparably with former liberation allies such as the MPLA, which it was simultaneously trying to appease. The *Mail and Guardian* rightly argued in 1995 'that we have no coherent foreign policy; we have no firm attitude to human rights abuses in other countries; instead we have an ad hoc series of responses to world events based on Mandela's prestige, his reluctance to become too involved in international affairs, and his party's need for cash'.[114] The following chapter will therefore assess how South Africa's diplomatic strategies under President Mandela began to change and the profound effect this had on the trajectory of the country's foreign policy.

CHAPTER 7

THE CHANGING NATURE OF SOUTH AFRICAN FOREIGN POLICY

The initial implementation of foreign policy in the 'new' South Africa had been a steep learning curve for all involved in the ANC-led Government of National Unity (GNU). Although some notable successes were achieved in foreign policy, the opening years of Mandela's presidency were mired by accusations of repeated diplomatic failures. In a short space of time, the ANC had reneged several times on its stated desire to pursue a human rights based policy, endured harsh domestic and international criticism for its links to dissident nations, and markedly failed to convince Africa of its guiding principles. Stung by the widespread criticism of its actions, and recognizing that the country still lacked a definitive vision for foreign policy, the ANC, the DFA and the GNU all sought to rectify this. In the wake of the Nigerian Crisis, 1996 proved to be a watershed year for South African foreign policy. It marked the beginning of a systematic review of foreign policy, in which key documents were produced by both the DFA and the ANC, namely: the 'South African Foreign Policy Discussion Document'; 'Developing a Strategic Perspective on South African Foreign Policy' and the 'White Paper on South African Participation in International Peace Missions'. Two significant events in 1996 would also have a significant effect on how the ANC would henceforth interact with the international community. The first was the decision by Deputy President F. W. de Klerk to withdraw the NP from the GNU, leaving the ANC in sole control of the country. The second was Thabo Mbeki's landmark 'I am an African' speech on 8 May 1996, which began the process of re-orientating South African foreign policy, including a renewed focused on the African continent. These factors would systematically influence foreign policy in subsequent years.

The decision by de Klerk to withdraw the NP from the GNU in May 1996 was in one sense a shock (particularly as the party had fought so hard for a power-sharing agreement during the transition), but ultimately it was not entirely unexpected.[1] Since 1994, despite being deputy president, de Klerk had been increasingly marginalized by the ANC and he had become ever more frustrated at his lack of influence and power.[2] There were two significant consequences of this decision: first, the NP's withdrawal placed the ANC in full power of the state; and, second, it provided Thabo Mbeki with the opportunity to increase his own influence on decision making as the sole deputy president. The NP's abandonment of the GNU prompted Mandela to declare that 'the country had reached full political maturity'.[3] The NP had not had that much influence over the GNU, but it had still acted as a counterbalance to the ANC. In a practical sense, the foreign policy of South Africa from 1996 onwards was truly that of the ANC. The issue was, however, that the ANC's foreign policy ideals had not been fully articulated and in practice its principles had been implemented haphazardly and inconsistently. Yet, the mistakes of the previous years had been acknowledged, which prompted a series of foreign policy discussion reviews, in an attempt to clarify what the ANC hoped South Africa would achieve internationally under its leadership.

At the same time as the NP was withdrawing from the GNU, Mbeki delivered his seminal 'I am an African' speech in Cape Town. This was an important statement of intent and a precursor for what South Africa would strive to achieve in the future, particularly under Mbeki's leadership.[4] Mbeki insisted that 'African' was not something that could be simply defined by race, in a rousing speech that reasserted parts of the Freedom Charter. He argued that no matter what the historical actions of white South Africans may have been, they had played an influential part in creating the country and the identity of its entire people. However, the message was a clarion call for Africa. Mbeki declared: 'the time had come that we make a superhuman effort to be other than human, to respond to the call to create ourselves a glorious future'. He emphasized that as a South African, he was 'born of the peoples of the continent of Africa'.[5] Mbeki claimed that South Africans identified with the pain of violent conflicts across the continent, arguing that 'the dismal shame of poverty, suffering and human degradation of my continent is a blight that we share'.[6] Mbeki concluded that it was time for Africa to lift itself out of its predicament. Once this process had been achieved, the continent would begin an unstoppable rise to peace and prosperity. Mbeki's message served several purposes. First, it was an effort to dispel Afro-pessimism and cynicism about the continent being a poor, aid-dependent, and war-ravaged region of the world. Secondly, Mbeki sought to emphasize that Africans could resolve these issues through greater unity, clearly referencing back to ideas of pan-Africanism. Thirdly, it was an attempt to tie South Africa closer to the continent, after several chastening experiences. It is perhaps telling that the ANC felt the need to reaffirm its vows to the continent, indicating a failure in the implementation and explanation of post-apartheid South African foreign policy. Importantly, the speech set in motion the 'African Renaissance', embodied by the New Partnership for Africa's Development (NEPAD), which would become the centrepiece of Mbeki's foreign policy after his accession to the presidency in 1999. Mbeki's speech was the moment when the ANC finally took control of its destiny and began in earnest a strategic review of South African diplomacy.

The DFA's Review of South African Foreign Policy

The first review of South African foreign policy was conducted by the DFA, which published the 'South African Foreign Policy Discussion Document' in 1996.[7] It must be stressed that this review was not undertaken by the ANC, but rather by the civil servants of the DFA; it was intended to provide an overview of foreign policy and make recommendations to the government. In fact, the document emphasized its purpose was 'not to formulate fine-tuned foreign policy for the democratic government' but rather to give 'an overview of the many components of international relations, objectives and priorities which warrant the attention of policy makers and the policy dimensions which government and all its extensions need to consider'.[8] The document was to provide a springboard for further discussion, and was intended to lead to the formulation of a white paper on foreign policy.

The discussion document synthesized the first two years of the post-apartheid foreign policy experience, examining key policies in the context of the international changes of the period, predominantly as evidenced by the speeches of Alfred Nzo and Mbeki. The review examined the principles and cornerstones of the country's foreign policy, and the multilateral activities of the state. The discussion document concluded by condensing the central tenets of South African foreign policy into eight overarching policy recommendations:

1. South Africa must consistently endeavour to pursue a coherent foreign policy, which includes economic, security and political components.
2. Preventive diplomacy and pro-active initiatives should be the approach, rather than reaction, to events. A monitoring network with African partners is essential.
3. South Africa should assume a leadership role in Africa in all those areas where a constructive contribution could be made without politically antagonizing the country's African partners.
4. The Government should continue to pursue a non-aligned approach, with due regard for South Africa's SADC, OAU, NAM and other membership commitments.
5. A diplomacy of bridge-building between the 'North' and the 'South' should be pursued.
6. In multilateral forums, South Africa should strive to promote its interests in regard to the major global issues such as respect for human rights, democracy, global peace, security and the protection of the environment.
7. South Africa should constantly endeavour to positively influence and change the direction of events and developments internationally, to the extent that they affect South Africa.
8. Diplomatic relations and all related aspects should be a means to an end, namely to promote the well-being of the country and its citizens.[9]

In doing so, the document reiterated what had been previously announced by the government and its ministers. In fact, this DFA document barely deviated from the ANC's principles that had been set out in the 'Foreign Policy Perspective in a Democratic South Africa' document.[10] Even though the DFA publication was seen as only one 'further step in the process of policy review', the specific recommendations it offers are few and far between.[11] Its initial proposals were that 'South Africa's policy initiatives should be modest and not overtly ambitious', and 'that economic imperatives and political realities need to be balanced'.[12] However, its main conclusion was that 'South Africa needs to adopt a more pro-active foreign policy approach, within its means, to achieve strategic objectives'.[13] The key recommendations offered by the DFA were that South Africa should scale back its international ambitions, take advantage of the opportunities open to it in order to fulfil its core principles, and to do so on a more realistic basis. Since 1990, the DFA had championed a largely 'realist' approach to foreign policy, and the findings of this review were perfectly attuned to this school of thinking. Although, the review mirrored many of the ANC's principles, the conclusions implied that South Africa had not achieved many of these under the GNU.

What is most interesting about the DFA review is what it does not say. The document did not provide any in-depth case studies of South African foreign policy in action, and certainly did not offer any critical analysis of its successes and failures. For example, it highlighted that democracy and human rights were important pillars of the nation's foreign policy, but there was no comment about how these had been implemented in practice, especially considering what had occurred in Nigeria or whether the country's approach had actually worked. The only mild criticism (which was not expressed explicitly) was made with regard to the seven broad principles that had been set out in early 1994. The document states: 'it may be questioned whether these principles are sufficient ... whether they are achievable, or how far the government should and can go in imposing them on others'.[14] Indeed, for a policy review, there appeared to be a lack of analysis of where the government should change its approach. On the whole, the DFA reverted to reiterating broad aspirational statements that reaffirmed previous ANC positions. A cynical reading would suggest that for reasons of political expediency, the discussion document, sought not to antagonize the government by criticizing its approach.[15] However, it must be noted that the predominantly white civil service, under a new multiracial administration, would be highly unlikely to openly criticize government practice. Although the document includes the caveat that it does not seek to propose policy changes, it could be expected that a major policy review, in a significant government department would do exactly that. Indeed, the core role of the DFA was to advise the minister for foreign affairs (Nzo) and other relevant parties, including the president, on all aspects of foreign policy and to coordinate South Africa's responses to international developments. It therefore begs the question, if the DFA was not in the process of formulating and advising policy for ministers, who was?

Foreign Policy Formulation within the ANC and South Africa: a Democratic Process?

Although the ANC had once openly expressed that foreign policy belonged to South Africa's people, what had in fact occurred was a highly personalized form of policy making. Anthony Butler's study of the ANC's internal democracy illustrated that there had been an increasing centralization of decision making around a small elite, in an apparent throwback to exile-style politics, but also replicating foreign policy decision making under apartheid.[16] The Leninist principles of the ANC in exile had ensured that the lives of its cadres were almost completely controlled by the movement's elite, and such tendencies were increasingly applicable to foreign policy formulation under Mandela. Foreign policy decisions during exile and the transition were made by a small number of ANC officials, and this continued through into democratic government. Moreover, given the legacy of foreign policy creation within the ANC, the process continued to favour external cadres, other those activists that had not gone into exile. The process of foreign policy making was centralized to a handful of people within the government, with Mandela, Mbeki, Nzo and Pahad the key protagonists. This continuity in practice ensured that Mbeki was deeply involved in influencing foreign policy from the latter stages of exile, right through until his presidency. Yet, given the president's overwhelming stature and moral authority, Mandela had the final say on South Africa's foreign policy proceedings.[17] Mandela was a 'foreign policy' president, who busied himself in various aspects of South Africa's international affairs, ranging from trade delegations to peace missions. Consequently, most of South Africa's major foreign policy initiatives were carried out by him. Analyst Greg Mills argued, 'it has thus become a highly personalized affair, with President Mandela's international superstar status overshadowing all else'.[18] In a report written for the South African presidency during Mbeki's administration, it asserted that 'his [Mandela's] command and seeming domination of every major foreign policy decision and issue was so complete as to almost overshadow the role of the DFA, cabinet and parliament'.[19] Additional concerns were raised, especially regarding the government's and the DFA's diminishing role in the process; 'the Department of Foreign Affairs and the Parliamentary Portfolio Committee on Foreign Affairs [PCFA] neither set the agenda nor dominate the discussion; it is mainly the presidency that drives the discourse'.[20] Furthermore, Raymond Suttner, chair of the Portfolio Committee from 1994 to 1997, and later the ambassador to Sweden, was well placed to make observations about South African foreign policy:

> It is not clear that the Presidency relates on a regular and co-ordinated basis with other foreign policy structures when it makes interventions on foreign policy questions. Nor is it clear that there is a structure that relates to the President on an advisory basis, as one finds with other presidencies in other parts of the world.[21]

The *Financial Times* reported that the DFA's ineffectiveness was compounded by the fact that 'Mandela often creat[ed] policy on the spot in his discussions with other world leaders, leaving the foreign ministry stumbling behind, with no idea what is happening.'[22] This was perhaps most notable in his dealings with autocratic leaders such as Suharto or his approach to the Nigerian Crisis. Yet, while Mandela was the figurehead, behind the scenes Mbeki, in the role of deputy president, had an extremely strong influence over South Africa's foreign policy. For example, Mbeki had pushed for Nzo's appointment as foreign minister, because despite his 'incompetence and tendency to sleep on the job', this enabled Mbeki to direct 'foreign policy himself via his trusted client, Aziz Pahad, now deputy minister for foreign affairs'.[23] The control of the levers of power by Mandela, and a small clique of ANC leaders, ensured that the input of other important contributors was largely ignored. Both the DFA and the Portfolio Committee had increasingly become irrelevant to policy formulation in South Africa, and that there was little, if any, democratization of foreign policy in the democratic South Africa.

A pertinent example of the centralization of South Africa's foreign policy was the exclusion of the PCFA from policy formulation. Suttner, in his role as chair of the committee, published several studies during the mid-1990s criticizing South Africa's increasingly centralized foreign policy. Suttner claimed the 'DFA was pretty useless in its policy drafting and they were bypassed almost entirely. Their briefing documents for visits to countries seem to have been ignored by Mbeki, and I think Mandela used his own perceptions.'[24] He added that the PCFA, which circulated documents to MPs and acted as a discussion forum, also 'had no influence on government'.[25] A reason for this was 'the fact that ... decision[s] may well have been taken before the Committee has had the opportunity to meet with the authorities (a clear example of this was around Nigeria in the course of 1995)'.[26] This was neatly encapsulated during media enquiries into Taiwanese donations to the ANC party, about which Suttner was quoted as saying that 'he had no personal knowledge of any donations to the ANC'.[27] Furthermore, the PCFA had lost some of its relevance and independence because the large ANC majority in parliament, led the party to dominate the committee. A key factor that contributed to the marginalization of the PCFA was because the South African parliament is elected via a system of proportional representation, where the party lists are closed. In a system where the party lists are closed, there is almost no attachment between MPs and their constituencies, and accountability to the electorate is diminished. Furthermore, ministers are entirely reliant upon the party leadership for their nomination to office. This system ensured a lack of criticism from the ANC-dominated parliament, as dissidents who did not toe the party line could be easily removed from the electoral rolls. The outcome is that many South African MPs unquestioningly follow the policy positions of the leadership, even on controversial foreign policy issues.[28] Consequently, 'the PCFA receives policy as a fait accompli with very little indication of how its comments may or have impacted on policy adjustment'.[29] This had much to do with the way the presidency, the ANC, the DFA and the South African parliament interacted with each other over foreign policy, which prompted one observer to describe the formulation of foreign policy in South Africa as one of 'vertical integration from conceptualization within the presidency, endorsement from the party, implementation by the DFA and largely unquestioning and compliant support from parliament'.[30]

The ANC leadership's domination of parliament meant that the ruling party could, on the whole, push controversial policies through parliament with little debate or dissent. Andrew Feinstein depicts, for example, the way in which the ANC's National Executive Council (NEC) and the presidency put pressure on him and on the Parliamentary Standing Committee on Public Accounts (SCOPA) to shelve investigations into high-level corruption surrounding South Africa's controversial arms deals.[31] Feinstein revealed how the ANC leadership and party whips stifled debate within parliamentary committees, so that outcomes conformed to their wishes. Yet, many ordinary ANC cadres were all too aware of the undemocratic practices prevalent within the party. Delegates to the ANC's 50th National Conference in December 1997 resolved:

> that the policy process within the ANC ha[s] been fundamentally affected by the ANC's ascension to office in 1994; that since 1994, the point of gravity as regards policy development appears to have shifted to government and away from ANC constitutional structures.[32]

Veteran activist and critic Matthews Phosa weighed into the debate, publicly deriding the movement for its increasing lack of 'regard for the principles of collective leadership, democratic practices, criticism and self-criticism'; he argued that there was a very real danger that the government's policies would now be simply imposed upon a compliant ANC.[33] The conference resolutions and Phosa's criticisms indicate that foreign policy was not a democratic process nor was it, as the ANC claimed, 'owned by the people'. In exile the ANC had consistently spoken on behalf of its supporters without consulting them, and a similar tendency continued through into political power. Although foreign policy is commonly an elite-dominated activity in even the most democratic nations, the situation in South Africa was exceptional and the ANC leadership 'actually [had a] free hand, to a very large extent in foreign policy'.[34]

The fact is that the ANC largely ignored the DFA and the PCFA. However, it does offer an explanation as to why South African foreign policy was regarded as being so inconsistent after 1994. A small group within the ANC controlled the levers of power, an approach grounded in the movement's experiences of exile, its own centralized policy making and the activities of the SCFA during the transition. This group took decisions based upon its members' personal perspectives, without always being appropriately informed by experts. The ANC leadership could do largely as it wished, pursuing policies that served its own narrow perceptions; these policies were unquestioningly supported and adopted by MPs, in part aided by a lack of stringent government oversight. Feinstein's comments that South Africa had witnessed the blurring of national and party interests were to be increasingly significant as events unfolded.[35] The increasing centralization of foreign policy became even more pronounced during Mbeki's presidency, with decision making almost solely the preserve of the President's Office. The origins of this process, however, lay in exile, and was accentuated under Mandela as the ANC evolved from liberation movement into an emerging political party. With little domestic constraint, and ignoring the advice on offer, the ANC approached foreign policy very much in accordance with its leaders' own perceptions of their party's needs.

The ANC's Changing Perspectives on Foreign Policy

The 1997 ANC document, 'Developing a Strategic Perspective on South African Foreign Policy', offered the most effective barometer of the organization's evolving thinking on international relations.[36] While parts of the document presented a pragmatic, realist view on foreign policy, there were sections that had an overtly left-wing/socialist slant, displaying some strikingly undemocratic tendencies in the ANC as a broader movement.[37] This explicit left-wing perspective stemmed from the role that Blade Nzimande, senior SACP and NEC member, had in drafting it, in his position as head of the NEC Committee on International Affairs. The document illustrated the growing tensions that were being played out within the party over the direction of its foreign policy, some of which will be explored later. The document also provided an opportunity for the ANC to assess its experiences of the previous three years; in doing so, it is far more critical and analytical than the DFA's earlier contribution. The ANC was actually quite candid in articulating what it had, and had not, achieved in government, and where it could learn from its mistakes.

Given the many problems the ANC-led government had in implementing human rights, the document recognized directly that 'human rights are often disputed in their interpretation and relevance', and in relation to the Nigerian Crisis admitted that 'it highlighted the potential limits of our influence'.[38] Although it did renew the party's commitment to its 'seven pillars', the ANC did not actually propose solutions to put human rights into effect as the cornerstone of its foreign policy, in any meaningful way. The review simply asserted that 'the difficult challenge is to translate these principles into effective governmental policies'.[39] It might have been expected that the ANC would have developed strategies to implement the central tenet of its foreign policy, but after three years the party was left still pondering how best to do so. In an attempt to reconcile its principled policy with its more pragmatic practices, the ANC insisted that, although South Africa still sought to place human rights at the forefront of its foreign policy, this 'should not mean that we refuse to conduct any diplomatic and trade relations with countries whose record in human rights or democracy we regard as unsatisfactory'.[40] There is a clear link between this statement and the fallout from the crisis in Nigeria; ANC leaders had taken the lessons on board. This was a considerable reversal of the ANC's 1994 vision when it had declared that it would not be selective in highlighting human rights abuses and that this principle would not be 'sacrificed to economic and political expediency'.[41] The ANC was openly admitting that human rights concerns would now be applied on a less idealistic, pragmatic, case-by-case basis, and that it would still maintain links with countries that violated these principles. Gareth van Onselen commented that:

> The romantic period under Mandela was constantly juxtaposed by his personality and the decisions he made personally as an individual, while the party itself, and its particular beliefs always lurked just below the surface and when Mandela went, and Mbeki replaced him, those undercurrents that underpinned his administration came to the fore which were epitomised by him, and you started having hard practical decisions taken that went against human rights.[42]

Given that senior ANC members around Mbeki had major reservations about the inclusion of human rights into foreign policy, this was the first moment in which the party began to publicly disentangle itself from such visions. What appears obvious is that the ANC had started to rationalize its failure to implement its human rights policy consistently. Although the human rights aspects of South Africa's foreign policy were never formally abandoned, from this moment onwards, the ANC government would repeatedly relegate such concerns in the hierarchy of importance.

Africa retained a central place in ANC policy, which the party was eager to reinforce. The review attempted to address African grievances concerning the ANC government by conceding that 'it is not always possible to act in a way that satisfies the expectations of other countries, particularly those on the African continent'.[43] It was acknowledged that in some instances, especially concerning human rights issues in multilateral forums, '[we] have had to vote differently from some of our closest allies', and furthermore it had become clear that 'international relations are not merely based on solidarity ... an important lesson for us'.[44] It was a signal that some ANC leaders recognized that solidarity-based alliances were an insufficient basis for its foreign relations. However, the conclusion to the document contradicted this position, insisting that 'our priority ... should be towards our former allies in the liberation struggle in Southern Africa'.[45] Furthermore, for the first time in political power, some of the more left-wing and communist-inspired views within the ANC began to emerge more prominently. In one section, it was argued that the movement should strengthen its relations between international political parties, because 'the ANC as a political movement, has a critical role to play in cementing solidarity amongst the progressive forces in the world based on the principles of anti-colonialism, anti-imperialism and a democratic world'.[46]

This focus on anti-colonialism and anti-imperialism later became enshrined in the concept of an African Renaissance, and it marked the moment when South Africa first prioritized a developing-world agenda. This would become a central feature of Mbeki's presidency, which will be examined further in the following chapter. Despite the ANC's expressed wish to champion global democracy, the document took a surprisingly undemocratic stance, arguing that: 'while the right to form political parties and participate in democratic elections is undoubtedly a fundamental democratic right, multiparty systems have been introduced in Africa in circumstances where other conditions have had the effect of weakening the capacity of governments'.[47] It was clear that, despite the best efforts at influencing the ANC during the transition process, the true views of certain sections of the party were gaining traction and publicity.

Later in the same year, at the ANC's 50th National Conference at Mafikeng, the importance of liberation solidarity was once again highlighted. At the conference, delegates bemoaned the fact that the world had changed, because 'another problem which arises here is that some of our former allies (political parties) are no longer in government'.[48] This would indicate that some ANC cadres struggled to relate to the new democratic Southern African governments that had replaced some of the movement's former revolutionary allies. The conference recommendations offered an illustration of the diversity of opinions within the ANC. The final resolutions portray a far more radical outlook than the publicly pro-Western outlook of the ANC on taking power; this was exemplified by the stance taken on issues such as Israel, and that of foreign-owned media being too critical of the new government.[49] Such views were actually quite prevalent within the party, but the leadership had the dilemma of appeasing South Africa's Western supporters. Following his 'I am an African' speech, and the increasingly rapid move away from its earlier principles, this was the moment when Mbeki began to assert control over ANC (and subsequently South African) foreign policy, re-orientating its overall direction.

Although both the DFA and the ANC had previously raised concerns about the difficulty of meeting the enormous expectations it faced in Africa, 'Developing a Strategic Perspective on South African Foreign Policy' articulated the grand concept of the 'African Renaissance'. The brainchild of Mbeki, the African Renaissance was 'advanced as the main pillar of our international policy not only relating to Africa, but in all our international relations'.[50] This was a significant re-alignment for South African foreign policy. Despite warnings that South Africa should pursue a more realistic and achievable foreign policy, the African Renaissance was in fact a highly ambitious concept. In principle, it was conceived as a counterbalance to rampant Western globalization, and to act as the focal point for rapid economic development, democracy and stability across the continent. The document claimed that 'an African Renaissance poses a threat to the strategy of globalizing capitalism. In fact, globalization contradicts the very agenda of the African Renaissance. Therefore, the success of the Renaissance depends on the depth of and extent to which it challenges globalization.'[51] Tinged with liberation rhetoric, the African Renaissance is couched in terms of combating Western neo-colonialism. The sentiments appealed strongly to the ANC's radical factions, including its leaders. However, not only was it a highly ambitious ideal, it contradicted many of South Africa's day-to-day policies, not least its ever strengthening ties with Western capital and the acceptance of a neo-liberal approach to economics. South Africa had strenuously sought Western economic investment to alleviate its domestic problems, bringing it ever closer to the Washington Consensus; the implementation of GEAR was a case in point. Yet, the underlying principles of the African Renaissance identified Western capitalism as a threat. The ANC had begun to implement a number of domestic policies such as affirmative action, which, although understandable given the need to redress the imbalances in the country, were hardly in line with neo-liberal principles.[52] In light of the ANC government's acceptance of the SCFA recommendations, the international community were often left surprised when initiatives such as these were implemented. Once again, it raised difficult questions about what South Africa stood for. It must be reiterated that the NP's departure from the GNU had given the ANC leadership greater freedom to assert its own real views; a clear expression of which was the African Renaissance.

Despite repeated assurances that South Africa would not seek to become the leader of Africa, the ANC document presented an overarching and ambitious plan for the reorganization and revitalization of the entire continent. Not entirely surprisingly there was no widespread consultation with its African partners. As part of this envisaged change, the ANC argued that South Africa should take the lead in a campaign to empower the OAU. The ANC government had been under pressure from some quarters to provide clear and strong leadership for the African continent. Since 1994, there had been many such demands; for example in a speech to the South African parliament in 1997, Julius Nyerere had demanded that the country fulfil its responsibilities to southern Africa.[53] This still related to the very real wishes that the ANC should 'repay' its debts to the region. Yet, in a very different vein, the United States wanted South Africa to act as a 'pivotal state', because it believed that it was the only country that could provide effective political and economic leadership in the region.[54] These demands put further pressure on the ANC and created further contradictions within South Africa's foreign policy. However, the party's demand for leadership in Africa was a mantle that the ANC government adopted; Mbeki's ambition and vision, meant that he played a decisive role in enacting continental change. The rapid and significant changes to continental structures would be one of his most impressive foreign policy achievements.

The ANC's 'Developing a Strategic Perspective on South African Foreign Policy' also set out the challenges and tasks that confronted South African foreign policy, particularly relating to its activities in international forums. To achieve long-lasting change, Africa had to be placed more prominently on the global agenda. The purpose was to forge a common 'developing world' through organizations such as the UN, and that South Africa should adopt a leading role in the OAU, to co-ordinate continental economic relations and stability. However, the ANC did warn of overreaching itself, presciently observing that 'we should not overestimate ourselves as a small middle-income country'.[55] All of these changes developed in the latter stages of Mandela's presidency would become extremely important aspects of South African foreign policy during Mbeki's administration.

Just as with the earlier document, 'Foreign Policy Perspective in a Democratic South Africa', this new strategic review by the ANC was predominantly a wish-list of proposals for the future. Once again, the ANC failed to take the opportunity to define exactly what it believed South Africa's national interests were; an important theme as these were increasingly being subsumed by those of the party. The ANC continued to claim that the identification of its seven foreign policy pillars 'should be seen as an essential part of defining the national interest'.[56] However, without a clearer definition of what the national interests were, the ANC's foreign policies lacked an overarching and co-ordinated strategy. Likewise, the African Renaissance, which contained many noble ideas, was largely rhetorical in nature, lacking a definitive vision for how it could realistically be achieved. Peter Vale and Sipho Maseko described the African Renaissance vision as 'an empty vessel', which was 'high on sentiment, low on substance', existing only as 'an undetermined policy goal propounded by a political leadership which faces a particular set of challenges, both domestically and internationally'.[57] The gulf between what the ANC claimed it would achieve and the unfolding reality was very wide.

The White Paper on South African Participation in International Peace Missions

In 1998, the 'White Paper on South African Participation in International Peace Missions' arguably became one of the most crucial policy documents written by the ANC government during Mandela's presidency.[58] On the face of it, the document is unremarkable, acting primarily as the framework for South Africa's entry into international peacekeeping missions. This was a role South Africa had been encouraged to adopt by the Western powers, and one that the ANC government wanted to embrace because of its hope of being chosen as a permanent member of the UN Security Council. It was envisaged that, if proposed UN reforms went ahead, Africa would be granted one permanent seat on the Security Council. The result was that South Africa, Egypt, Libya and Nigeria were all vying for position in order to stake their claim. One way for South Africa to publicize its suitability was through active participation in African peacekeeping missions. Yet the White Paper's impact was far greater than this. One observer argued that, 'from a foreign policy point of view, the White Paper is certainly a groundbreaking document. It is possibly the most important foreign policy document yet to pass Cabinet, since it forced the South African government to outline its national interests and to define ... its general approach towards Africa.'[59] Indeed, after four years, it was the only example of a foreign policy related document during the Mandela period that actually attempted to define South Africa's national interests.

The greater part of the white paper assessed South Africa's future contributions to peacekeeping, emphasizing preventative diplomacy and declaring that only in the last resort would Pretoria send its armed forces overseas, not least because it recognized the legacies of past actions on the psyche of the African continent: 'the South African approach to conflict resolution is thus strongly informed by its own recent history'.[60] The White Paper argued that South Africa's national interests were underpinned by values enshrined in the constitution such as security, promotion of peace and stability, and regional development. It also recognized the primacy of the ANC's 'seven pillars' as a guide to South Africa's foreign policy. However, it ultimately stated that it is 'in the South African *national interest* [original emphasis] to assist peoples who suffer from famine, political repression, natural disasters and the scourge of violent conflict'.[61] The publication of the white paper was also important in terms of South Africa's commitment to conflict resolution on the continent, which had been steadily increasing since 1994. By the end of Mandela's presidency, South Africa was involved in attempts to resolve conflicts across the African continent, most notably in Burundi, Côte d'Ivoire, Lesotho and Zaire (now the Democratic Republic of Congo or DRC).

The various reviews of South African foreign policy did not produce a clearer strategy, but they were nonetheless important steps forward. The ANC's first two years in power had seen the party attempt to pursue an ambitious, non-aligned foreign policy that appealed to many idealistic observers, but was proving problematic in practice. Despite South Africa being regarded as the golden child of the international community, justifiable accusations of inconsistency had been raised. The subsequent policy reviews demonstrated that the DFA and the ANC were fully aware of the criticisms concerning South Africa's failure to practise what it preached. More pertinently, it was recognized that some of the more ambitious principles were not fully compatible with the practical realities of international relations. These various reviews sought to resolve these issues and to extend the foreign policy debate within the country. Crucially, the reviews marked the beginning of a realignment in South African foreign policy. What the reviews did reveal was that the ANC was becoming more cautious about its highly publicized human rights policies, placing qualifications on their use and implementation. There were also mounting concerns about the intentions (largely neo-colonial) of Western powers in Africa, and efforts to combat these perceived threats were developed during Mbeki's presidency; in fact the ANC's explicit alignment with the developing world would inform much of what would unfold over the following decade. The ANC insisted that, from this point forward, fulfilling the African Renaissance would form the basis of all of the country's foreign policy. While this was in a sense an extension of its 'seven pillars', it also marked the shift towards a new approach to foreign policy under Thabo Mbeki, one characterized by an overarching developing-world agenda. Nevertheless, after three review documents, the ANC remained in a position very similar to that when it had gained power, but now harnessed to an even more elaborate and ambitious vision for the future.

South Africa's Foreign Policy Successes under Mandela

Despite the many criticisms of international affairs during Mandela's administration, it would be wrong to depict South African foreign policy as an outright failure. Under Mandela's stewardship, South Africa made rapid progress in reintegrating itself into the international community, and strove to make a telling contribution through its activities. Having been previously isolated internationally, South Africa had, within the space of a few years, made itself central to the developing global agenda. This full reintegration into the international system should be regarded as a major success. The ascension to a position of prominence was in part aided by the profound international changes, with the global community far more sympathetic to the ANC government's development needs. Furthermore, South Africa's successful democratic transition was a shining example for the world, one many nations wished to emulate. South Africa became a key part of the 'new world order' discourse. Based upon the democratic changes and the ANC's self-perceptions, it adopted the mantle of the world's leading moral voice, and in turn became a highly respected and active member of a number of organizations such as the UN, the G20, and the Commonwealth.[62] R. W. Johnson argues that South Africa became 'very noticeable internationally . . . it did mean that everybody . . . came here and wanted to cultivate links, be it China or America'.[63] An illustration of the depth of goodwill towards South Africa was illustrated by the unprecedented decision by the UN General Assembly to absolve the country of payments of its arrears to the organization.[64] South Africa's visible international role and its extensive multilateral activities earned the country the status of a 'middle power'.[65] In fact, South Africa, under Mbeki, became even more active internationally.[66] By playing such a role, the ANC government was making a clear political statement; it was actively distancing themselves from the historic legacies of previous administrations. In doing so the new government earned worldwide prestige for its activities. The foreign policy principles set out by the SCFA, the DFA and the ANC in the early 1990s, all clearly asserted that working with international forums was imperative for the new democracy. It was something that was successfully achieved. For such a young democracy, its international successes were so impressive that Barber argued that they enabled South Africa '"to punch above its weight" in international affairs'.[67]

South African activities in the multilateral environment produced some significant successes, most notably its role in the Non-Proliferation of Nuclear Weapons Treaty (NPT) Conference in 1995.[68] One of the key purposes of the conference was to discuss whether the proposed NPT deal should last for a fixed period or indefinitely. South Africa played a crucial role in pushing for an indefinite position, which was agreed by the majority of signatories. South Africa's position was enhanced by the fact that it was the only country ever to have unilaterally dismantled its nuclear weapons capability, providing it with moral diplomatic leverage in the proceedings.[69] South Africa was also keen to make Africa a non-nuclear weapon region, and this vision was enshrined in the Treaty of Pelindaba.[70] However, despite the success of the OAU agreeing to the treaty in June 1995, it must be noted that by the end of Mandela's presidency only 11 African countries had actually ratified it.[71] Ironically, although there was an extensive armaments industry in the country, which had brought with it much unwanted publicity, the ANC government was particularly active in pursuing a disarmament strategy around the world. South African efforts were key to establishing resolutions and practical proposals on a range of arms control issues. These included its decisive role at the OAU 'Landmine Conference' in May 1997, and the adoption of the Convention on the Prohibition of the Use, Stockpiling, Production and Transfer of Anti-Personnel Mines and on their Destruction, in the same year.[72] This dedication to global disarmament is regarded by former civil servant Tom Wheeler as the greatest success of Mandela's presidency.[73]

South Africa under the ANC government had also made significant progress when it came to economic expansion. In the post-Cold War 'new world order', the West had increasingly shunned the African continent, in favour of Asian and eastern European markets. Western neglect provided a perfect opportunity for South African businesses to fill the economic void; the country rapidly became the single largest economic investor in Africa. The expansion of South African capital northwards was described by the *New York Times* as being 'one of the most vivid illustrations of South Africa's metamorphosis since apartheid ended in 1994'.[74] With little competition, and with significant amounts of money available, South African capital initiated an explosion of trade with Africa.[75] This aptly reflected the 'realist' approach of DFA officials; Suttner pointed out that the mantra of the DFA was that 'foreign policy is trade, trade, trade' and it was a message that South African business eagerly embraced.[76] South African direct investment into Africa reached R 13 billion in 1997. Within two years of the elections, trade with the SADC region alone was valued at R 20.3 billion, a clear indication of just how swiftly South African capital was maximizing its new-found opportunities.[77] Furthermore, the activities of the state-owned Industrial Development Corporation (IDC) illustrates the immense reach of South Africa's investment capabilities on the continent, stretching from neighbouring Swaziland, to Egypt in the north.[78] These figures were extremely positive for South Africa, helping to assist economic recovery and growth. However, many other African nations, especially South Africa's immediate neighbours, were far less enthusiastic about this rapid expansion of 'white' capital. This is not the place for a full discussion on this topic, but many observers have commented on the widespread fear of South Africa's 'selfish' expansion into Sub-Saharan Africa, damaging its neighbour's economies in the process.[79] What this highlights is the dilemma facing the ANC led-government. On the one hand African nations wanted increased investment and trade, something that South Africa could offer, yet simultaneously suspicious of their intentions when it came about.

The best illustration of South African investment in southern Africa is Mozambique. During Mandela's presidency, this was South Africa's most successful economic partnership in southern Africa, proving the ANC government's commitment to regional stability and prosperity. Very quickly after the elections, South Africa became particularly active in Mozambique, helping to stabilize the country following its civil war and embarking upon several ambitious joint projects with the FRELIMO government to rebuild the nation's war-torn infrastructure. By the time of Mbeki's presidency, Mozambique had become South Africa's largest regional trading partner.[80] Two tangible examples demonstrate the strength of this relationship. The first was an agreement on joint police co-operation (funded by South Africa) for cross-border seizure and destruction of small arms filtering into South Africa.[81] The second more concrete initiative began in May 1996, when the Maputo Corridor Project was announced. The project involved the upgrade of road and rail links, plus the expansion of Maputo harbour's capacity.[82] It was envisaged that the project would act as a stimulus to the economies of both countries. By 1997, these links had expanded further to a bilateral agricultural agreement, and the construction of the Mozal aluminium smelter.[83] Mozal I, which has since been upgraded to Mozal II, was South Africa's largest foreign investment, standing at US$1.3 billion, funded by both state and private enterprise. This was also South Africa's first major economic venture beyond its borders under Mandela.[84] The ANC government also acted swiftly to provide humanitarian aid and disaster relief to Mozambique in 1999 after severe flooding, by sending SANDF soldiers and helicopters to assist in the rescue efforts.[85] These were all important initiatives for South Africa to pursue, and Mozambique stands as a practical example of beneficial South African assistance to the region. The success of this relationship not only stemmed from Mozambique's proximity to South Africa, but also because of the close ties between the ANC and FRELIMO. Although in exile this alliance had been at times fractious, the two parties still had a close and strong bond, which continued after the ANC took office. Furthermore, Graca Machel, the widow of former FRELIMO and Mozambican President Samora Machel, married Nelson Mandela in 1998, which further strengthened the relationship.

War and Peace in Southern Africa

Having made peace and stability a core element of its foreign policy, the ANC immediately engaged in various processes of conflict resolution with varying degrees of success. Beginning in Angola and Mozambique, South Africa also got involved in mediation attempts in Burundi, Liberia and Zaire. To strengthen its position the new government also became an active member of the OAU Mechanism for Conflict Prevention, sending envoys and observers to conflict zones.[86] Working closely with the UN and OAU, South Africa pursued all possible avenues to ensure its principles of peace were upheld on the continent. Despite these successful efforts, there were some contradictions in South Africa's initial forays into peacekeeping; only after the Defence White Paper was published did the country clarify its position on overseas peace missions. The pursuit of peace was nevertheless an essential component of the ANC's foreign policy, and one that encompassed several aspects of its overall vision, including working in international forums and the enforcement of human rights.

After the ANC took office, South Africa quickly joined SADC (formerly the SADCC), the regional organization of the former Frontline States. Originally designed as a means of combating racist settler regimes, SADC brought together many of the liberated countries of the region in a loose political alliance. After apartheid had ended, its original remit was defunct, and SADC was redefined as a mechanism for stimulating economic development, promoting closer co-operation on areas of mutual interest, and co-ordinating efforts at regional peace and stability. Some SADC members envisaged that post-apartheid South Africa would be a powerful driving force behind these goals; in 1996, the organization elected Mandela as the chair of SADC.[87] Much has already been written about SADC, its merits and deficiencies, but this section, will confine itself to an examination of the controversies surrounding the SADC Organ on Politics, Defence and Security, and the political in-fighting this caused within the region, exacerbating the ANC's and South Africa's already poor relations with many of its neighbours.[88]

Joining SADC was the natural decision for the new South African government. First, its members were generally the ANC's longstanding former allies from exile, including the ruling parties in Mozambique and Namibia, and others with which it could at least empathize with, such as Zimbabwe. Secondly, SADC provided a means through which the ANC could begin to repay its perceived debts to the region. Thirdly, the recommendations of the SCFA had placed a strong emphasis on SADC, because in its view, a stable and prosperous region was vital to the fortunes of South Africa, an objective the ANC was keen to promote. Finally, it offered South Africa a forum in which it could pursue its declared aim of dedicating itself to Africa's renewal. From 1994 onwards, southern and central Africa had witnessed a number of conflicts including those in Angola, Burundi, Lesotho, Mozambique and Zaire.[89] It was therefore of immense importance for these crises to be solved; not only for regional stability, but also for South Africa's own self interest. Pretoria was increasingly concerned that continuing instability in its own region would scare off foreign investors, jeopardizing South African development, and also damaging its chances of gaining a seat in a reformed UN Security Council. As a means of addressing these problems, working closely within SADC to find peaceful solutions became a key priority for South Africa.

In the early 1990s, SADC leaders had started to discuss the idea of a regional security system, with peacekeeping capabilities. This peace-keeping force was envisaged to be an African-led initiative, in keeping with the principles of the African Renaissance. The proposal to establish an Organ on Politics, Defence and Security was formulated and accepted in principle at the SADC heads of state meeting in June 1996, in Gaborone.[90] However, while the concept had been accepted in principle by the assembled heads of state, the practicalities had been ignored. The negotiation process was seriously compromised by a long-standing feud between Presidents Mugabe and Mandela that subsequently spilled over into SADC; one so severe that it threatened to split the organization. The mutual dislike between the two presidents had been brewing for some time, with South African–Zimbabwean relations coming close to breaking point. This was in part the legacy of divisions between the movements during the exile period, but it was magnified by the abrasive personalities of the two leaders.[91] After Zimbabwean independence in 1980, Mugabe had been fêted as an international liberation hero, and the country stood out as southern Africa's most prominent independent nation. However, after 1994, Zimbabwe's international position changed drastically. Mandela's charismatic personality, moral authority, and South Africa's successful democratic transition knocked Mugabe from his pedestal, which infuriated him.[92] Mandela also personally disliked Mugabe, regarding him as a relic of poor African leadership, who was desperately holding onto power.[93] These tensions came to the fore in the SADC negotiations, with each leader offering their own alternative vision for the future. It resulted in an impasse in the discussions and a failure to reach a definitive agreement for the proposed structure.

The conflict between South Africa and Zimbabwe was reflective of a wider division in the SADC region between opposed democratic and authoritarian systems of government. Although there are some similarities between the region's political parties, most notably in how their independence was achieved (which ensures the pretence of public unity), they do not share common values. The reality is that southern Africa is a highly divided region. The SADC region was split into two camps; authoritarian governments such as Angola, Namibia and Zimbabwe, which preferred a militaristic foreign policy, and more democratically inclined governments such as Botswana, Mauritius, Mozambique and South Africa, which favoured peaceful, negotiated approaches. Given the centralized nature of most SADC states, the majority of regional leaders were unwilling to sacrifice their sovereignty to a multilateral organization specifically concerning security matters. Similar problems concerning the loss of sovereignty and control repeatedly undermined initiatives by the OAU throughout its history. Furthermore, southern African countries are collectively poor, and do not possess the capacity practically to support ventures like the SADC Organ.[94] By the end of Mandela's presidency the issue of regional security had still not been resolved, partly because, 'SADC was polarized around incompatible pacific and militaristic visions of the Organ'.[95] Matters were not helped by Mandela's uncompromising attitude towards the need for political reforms in other African nations; he was personally inclined to pursue his own perceived 'right path' with little concern for the political fallout that might occur. The Goedgedacht Forum noted that 'at a SADC heads of country meeting in 1997, Mandela called Mugabe and Chiluba [the Zambian President] dictators ... the consequences of this were that South Africa became isolated and its neighbours became hostile, forming anti-South African alliances'.[96] Furthermore, Deputy President Mbeki personally disliked the MPLA leader Dos Santos, whom he regarded as a kleptocratic thug.[97] Once again, this put South Africa on the 'wrong side' of continental opinion. The consequence of these attitudes was that it did little to endear the ANC government to its neighbours, which simply generated regional hostility towards South Africa.

The poor state of affairs regarding regional relations was, in part, due to South Africa's grandiose self-defined image, combined with a complete ignorance of the extent of its own power. Former, *Financial Times* Africa editor, Michael Holman depicted the ANC-led South Africa's actions towards southern Africa as being 'like a huge muscular adolescent, who is willing to help old ladies across the street, even if they didn't want to'.[98] The ANC government knew what it wanted, but rarely pursued its objectives in consultation with those whom they would most affect. Ultimately the ANC government failed to unite the region behind its vision for the future. The ANC government quickly discovered that its previously poor relations with political parties across southern Africa had continued through from exile and were affecting its room for manoeuvre. Many SADC leaders still had underlying suspicions of South African intentions, with some accusing it of devoting its attentions elsewhere and neglecting the countries it had pledged to assist the most.[99] South Africa was also seen as interfering with the internal affairs of these nations, rather than simply providing economic assistance. This seething animosity seriously affected South Africa's regional interests during Mandela's presidency, resulting in a switch to consensus building and quiet diplomacy under Mbeki.

These unresolved problems, combined with South Africa's increasing regional isolation, profoundly affected the ANC government's responses to two different conflicts in southern Africa. The summer of 1998 witnessed two major challenges for diplomacy, involving two SADC members: the DRC and Lesotho. The reactions of the ANC government to these incidents starkly revealed the fissures between its foreign policy ideals and those of its closest neighbours. It also brought into sharp relief the deep divisions within SADC, bringing with it a number of problems for South Africa.

In July 1998, the DRC president, Laurent Kabila, faced a significant invasion from the rebel movement the Congolese Rally for Democracy (RCD), backed by Rwanda and Uganda (ironically the very same countries that had only a year previously helped him overthrow the Zairian dictator President Mobutu).[100] Confronted by a well-equipped invading force advancing rapidly on the capital Kinshasa, Kabila urgently requested military assistance to repel the invasion. On 8 August 1998, Mugabe convened a special meeting of the SADC heads of state to discuss the request, but excluded the chair, South Africa, from the deliberations.[101] South Africa's embarrassment about being excluded from a meeting of SADC, an organization that it chaired, was heightened by the ANC government's failure to condemn the invasion of the DRC publicly. The failure to do so went against its own principle of censuring military aggression.[102] It was viewed as a setback to South Africa's authority and political leverage in southern Africa, because 'its neutrality and sincerity as peacemaker [were] questioned'.[103] The dilemma only worsened when Zimbabwe, Angola and Namibia jointly announced that they would send troops to the DRC on behalf of SADC.[104] Mugabe claimed SADC had come to a unanimous decision to assist Kabila, which prompted an indignant Mandela to publicly reproach the Zimbabwean leader for his pre-emptive measures.[105] The fact that the SADC Organ on Politics, Defence and Security was not even yet in place, meant that these three governments had justified and legalized their decision in the name of the region, despite not having the mandate nor the full support of its member states, including South Africa. It brought into question the very survival of SADC.[106] South Africa continued to pursue a peaceful, diplomatic path in the DRC, but its efforts were undermined by the belligerent actions of its neighbours. In the course of the DRC conflict, the ANC government managed to further alienate southern Africa, and failed to avert the continuing conflict.

What made South Africa's non-intervention in the DRC inexplicable was its policy stance concerning Lesotho. In September 1998, elections in Lesotho were once again in dispute, and there were fears of an impending military coup. With tensions mounting, the Lesotho government appealed to South Africa for assistance on 21 September. The next day South African troops, accompanied by a small contingent of soldiers from Botswana, crossed into Lesotho to prevent a coup.[107] The mission was a complete disaster. Expecting no resistance, the South African military was shocked by the reaction from Lesotho's civilians and military forces to its intervention. The capital Maseru was looted, South African businesses were destroyed, and the Lesotho Defence Force killed eight SANDF soldiers during the mission. To make matters worse, the ANC government was accused of acting illegally under international law, and was criticized for undermining its own expressed commitment to non-intervention.[108] South Africa's insistence on a political settlement in the DRC had isolated its position within SADC, yet within weeks its apparently principled stance had been contradicted by invading Lesotho. South Africa's contrasting actions in these two conflicts confused its neighbours and the wider international community.

Although the invasion of Lesotho was an apparent anomaly in South African foreign policy, it once again saw its approach to external relations brought into question. The intervention in Lesotho, at the request of the government, had prevented a coup and maintained a semblance of democracy in the country, but it had done little to dampen criticism of South African inconsistency. Both incidents were striking examples of South Africa's inability to influence its own neighbours and the bad blood this had generated, raising questions about the country's 'middle power' status. Although South Africa was the economic powerhouse on the continent, and one that promoted multilateralism as the preferred means of interaction, it had failed to unite leaders around a solution to the crises afflicting the region.[109] It had attracted renewed domestic and international criticism over its foreign policy and, most importantly, damaged interstate relations. With many similarities to the earlier Nigerian Crisis, the South African government found itself accused by the southern African leaders Kabila, Mugabe, Dos Santos and Nujoma of double standards and of 'promoting regional apartheid policies'.[110] Due to the perceived Western outlook of the ANC, President Kabila went as far as to describe South Africa as the 'puppets of the aggressors'.[111] Given that the ANC had been so keen to accentuate their differences with the previous apartheid regime, this was a major blow. The ANC, and more pertinently Thabo Mbeki, learnt important lessons that had undoubted implications for the country's future policies. Under Mbeki there was a clear re-alignment by the ANC government with regard to the way they interacted with developing world nations. However, by the end of Mandela's presidency, South Africa's attitude to southern Africa was characterized as being one of 'neglect – we have the objectives, but there is no strategy, therefore the objectives are not met'.[112] This was a damning indictment of how one of the centrepieces of the ANC's foreign policy failed.

Conclusion

A key problem for the ANC-led government had been identifying what South African foreign policy entailed during Mandela's presidency. There is no simple answer to this, as South Africa outwardly projected many different diplomatic approaches. For example, South African foreign policy had embraced tenets of Western, neo-liberal ideology, yet simultaneously pursued a pro-developing-world agenda. The contradictions in these polar opposite approaches are stark. However, the ANC-led government ambitiously set out to engage with the international community, and in its self-appointed position as global bridge-builder, had believed it could overcome these contradictions. These chapters on Mandela's presidency have illustrated that there were a number of striking successes for the ANC government's emerging diplomacy. However, the problem of having to appeal to multiple international and domestic constituencies, and the intransigence of the global powers to support a reformist agenda, ultimately resulted in a widely divergent foreign policy.

Following a troubled introduction to foreign affairs, 1996 marked the moment in which the ANC-led government attempted to rectify the challenges that confronted it. Although the ANC had explicitly expressed exactly what it wished to achieve internationally, set out in its seven guiding principles, the government had struggled to fulfil its highly ambitious plans. This inability to implement the ANC's agenda was due in part to the constraints that had been imposed by the SCFA; by the nature of the international community; a lack of operational capacity; the divergent ideals of the movement's leaders and supporters; and the long shadow of history, exemplified by a significant degree of mistrust from African states concerning South African intentions – a direct legacy of the actions of the apartheid state and the ANC in exile. Despite the increasing inability to fulfil its principles, the ANC's foreign policy reviews failed to properly address the problems, and in turn had harnessed South Africa to an even more ambitious, yet unqualified vision for the future.

Some of these problems of inconsistency and contradiction arose because the ANC began to reassert its control over South Africa's foreign policy, once distanced from some of the dictates of the transition. This process was eased considerably by de Klerk's decision to withdraw the NP from the GNU, which granted far more power to Deputy President Thabo Mbeki. One of the first indications of the new emerging reorientation for South Africa was Mbeki's 'I am an African' speech, which was subsequently fleshed out in the transformative ideals of the African Renaissance. The human rights aspects of South Africa's foreign policy, although still included in its policy statements after 1996, were quietly dropped by the ANC government; a development not wholly surprising given the hostility towards its adoption during the transition and the failed pursuit of these principled ideals in practice. The changes in government allowed Mbeki, and the ANC leadership, greater control over foreign policy, which was enhanced by the increasing centralization of power. The development handed a small elite, dominated by Mbeki, the opportunity to control foreign policy, with the advice and recommendations of government committees and the DFA largely ignored, resulting in government decisions being rubber-stamped by a largely subservient parliament. It meant that foreign policy objectives increasingly represented those of the party and not South Africa. Yet the ANC government faced a dilemma. It fully appreciated the need for

Western economic support for South African development, paying lip-service to its demands and protocols; however, the ideals of the party were far more attuned to those of a revolutionary movement and to the developing world. A product of its exile struggle, entwined with its wish to reform the international status quo, the ANC government increasingly championed the developing world, and strengthened its ties with some dubious regimes. Moreover, based upon South Africa's experiences during the first five years of democracy, the explicit reorientation towards the developing world served two purposes. First, the ANC could fulfil some of its revolutionary credentials and, second, it aligned South Africa more closely to continental opinion, especially in Southern Africa. These two dimensions noticeably came to the fore once Mbeki gained office.

The shift in the ANC government's outlook increasingly agitated the West, which had thought that it had 'captured' South Africa's foreign policy during the transition. On the other hand, some of the ANC's initiatives aimed at developing countries and its allies were criticized by the intended recipients of such policies. The result was that South African foreign policy under Mandela was censured for lacking coherence; it failed to conform to either camp, confusing many entrenched interests in the process. Under the leadership of President Mbeki the ANC government was to make its international positions much clearer, but to divide opinion once again.

CHAPTER 8

A NEW PRESIDENT,
A NEW DIRECTION?
THABO MBEKI'S RENAISSANCE

After the first five years of democratic government, South Africa's international relations were at a crossroads. Despite the new ANC government achieving numerous successes in its fledgling foreign policy, it had been dogged throughout its first term in office by accusations of incoherence and contradiction. Unable to apply its foreign policy ideals consistently, the ANC had found itself caught between diverse, yet competing constituencies. The question was whether the incoming President Thabo Mbeki, would implement a new international direction for South Africa to rectify these issues.

Mbeki did initiate a new ideologically coherent foreign policy, but it certainly did not solve South Africa's international relations. South African foreign policy did quite clearly change in outlook post-1999, but Mbeki's inauguration by no means instigated a sudden or 'new' shift in vision or approach. In fact as deputy president, Mbeki had been working behind the scenes to transform South African foreign policy, with almost every aspect of what was to come clearly articulated before he became president. When speeches and documents on foreign policy are examined, the extent of continuity between administrations is remarkable. The important caveat is that the reviews of South African foreign policy after 1996, which had offered the alternative blueprint for the future, had coincided with Mbeki's dramatic increase in influence and authority over the government and the ANC. Mandela had, by his own admission, increasingly stepped aside from the day-to-day business of government and, in doing so, he transferred many of his responsibilities to his deputy president.[1] Mbeki took the opportunities afforded to him to secure a greater degree of control and influence over proceedings. Well before his inauguration Mbeki had started coalescing power around the office of the deputy president, staffed by his allies and confidants.[2] It has been suggested in some quarters that, by 1997, Mbeki was the 'de facto prime minister' of South Africa.[3] As Mandela increasingly devolved his power, the general direction of South African foreign policy was being realigned by Mbeki. The ANC government's initial focus on human rights shifted instead towards a proactive, rather than rhetorical, developing world and anti-imperial position. The purpose of this chapter will not be to repeat the already familiar details of Mbeki's presidency, but will examine how Mbeki corralled power within the ANC and the South African government, the substance of his foreign policy vision, and offer a few pertinent examples of foreign policy in practice. The chapter will also illustrate how Mbeki disentangled the ANC government from the constraints imposed by the transition and examine the consequences of his doing so.

Before assessing South African foreign policy under President Mbeki, two themes raised in the previous chapter must be developed further. The first, which had a significant impact on foreign policy and its formulation, was the increasing centralization of power within the government and the ANC. The second is to unravel what Mbeki's foreign policy vision actually entailed. By doing so, a more coherent and nuanced examination of South Africa's foreign policy can be developed.

Centralization and the Power of the Presidency

It would be a gross generalization about the process of foreign policy formulation to characterize it as the sole preserve of one person; it simply is not feasible and would ignore the work and inputs of multiple people and agencies. However, the centralization and domination of policy making by a select few, under the close watch of the president, had become a feature of Mandela's administration. After 1999, this trend accelerated as power and decision making became concentrated around Mbeki. This section will outline how, as president, Mbeki came to dominate almost every aspect of South African foreign policy. Although clearly he instigated a systematic attempt to centralize executive power, this process had its roots in the years before 1999. Indeed, such centralization was far from a new phenomenon within the ANC; it was simply an enduring legacy of the ANC's exile tradition re-emerging in government. The complete top-down control of all levers of the state and party, typical of many Marxist-Leninist governments, combined with a silencing of internal debate, had been a salient feature of the ANC in exile, and this style of governance was very much a part of Mbeki's political DNA. There was a short period after the ANC was unbanned, when a greater focus on internal party democracy emerged out of the traditions of the United Democratic Front (UDF) and the ANC prisoners on Robben Island. However, it was to be short-lived, and the exile legacies of centralism and top-down control came to the fore once more. The development also highlighted the separation between the internal and external dimensions of the liberation struggle, with priority given to exiled activists in government. This enabled Mbeki to maintain his position of influence over decision making within the ANC. It is important to highlight that this process accelerated during Mandela's term in office and Mandela had done nothing to prevent it from happening. With the centralization of power gathering apace within the ANC, Mbeki had moved to crystallize power around himself and his trusted confidants. In December 1997, decisions made at the ANC's 50th National Conference held in Mafikeng secured Mbeki's dominance over the ANC. This enabled him to expand the scope and depth of his grasp on power. The conference delegates made two key decisions: the first was to elect Mbeki unopposed as the party president, effectively anointing him as Mandela's successor and the second saw the election of a large number of Mbeki's closest allies to the National Executive Council (NEC).[4] This development changed the composition of the ANC's leadership and allowed Mbeki to enforce his almost total domination over the movement's structures.

With his grasp over the ANC almost complete, and safe in the knowledge that he was destined to become South Africa's next president, Mbeki began a similar process within government. Mbeki implemented two vital measures as deputy president that ensured that, once he did become president, he would have an almost unassailable control over the mechanisms and structures of government.

The first measure was to expand the remit and authority of the Office of the Deputy President. This was ostensibly because Mbeki was taking on more government responsibility as Mandela slowly 'retired' from office. In reality it provided the ideal opportunity for Mbeki to exercise a greater degree of control over all aspects of government business. In September 1999, immediately after Mbeki's inauguration, the Offices of the President and Deputy President were integrated to establish the 'Presidency', a change intended to ensure greater coordination across government.[5] The newly established Presidency consisted of the president, the deputy president (Jacob Zuma), a minister in the Presidency (Essop Pahad) and a host of special advisers, with the new office employing 341 staff.[6] Furthermore, key Mbeki loyalists such as Joel Netshitenzhe, Smuts Ngonyama and Trevor Manuel were all recruited to work in the Presidency.[7] A special report 'Democratic Governance: a Restructured Presidency at Work' insisted that the redesign at the top of governmental structures was justified by the need for more effective and efficient policy making. However, it had worrying undertones for the future of free debate and democracy in South Africa. The clique of loyal ministers within the Presidency was seen as a particular concern, as they insulated Mbeki from criticisms and alternative policy ideas; US diplomatic cables believed that the set-up meant that he relied too heavily 'on a core of advisors that lack[s] ... experience and diplomatic seasoning'.[8] The restructuring did however ensure that as president, Mbeki, with a supporting cast of allies, had coalesced government power within the Presidency.

The second important factor, which mutually reinforced the restructuring process, was the establishment of a strategic co-ordinating unit known as the Co-ordination and Implementation Unit, which later evolved into the Policy Co-ordination and Advisory Service (PCAS).[9] Given the green light by the cabinet, the strategic unit – attached exclusively first to the Deputy President's Office, and then the newly established Presidency – was developed to further co-ordinate policies across government departments as a means of streamlining bureaucracy. One of the core purposes of the unit was that it acted as a conduit for all government business, ensuring that decision making was synchronized and mutually reinforced across departments. However, what transpired was that government ministries were required to refer all new policy ideas, documents and draft legislation to the PCAS for approval first. The result was that the Presidency acquired an enormous amount of control over all aspects of government.[10] Nothing could be approved by any part of the government without the consent of Mbeki or the Presidency. Importantly, the strategic unit was answerable to Mbeki only, which made it unaccountable to government oversight. Therefore, in tandem with the newly restructured Presidency, the PCAS acted as an effective mechanism to control ANC ministers, the flow of information and government policies.

As distinctions between the state and the ANC became increasingly unclear in the 'new' South Africa, these two developments served only to further blur the boundaries. Mbeki and his allies in the ANC leadership had engineered a situation in which they had 'gained unprecedented control of both the party and the government, concentrating enormous powers of patronage in the hands of the party bosses'.[11] Given the nature of the South African constitution and electoral system, MPs depended upon patronage from above for their positions within government. Consequently, Mbeki was able to deploy loyalists into key posts, and subsequently to use the threat of removal from future electoral lists to silence any potential criticism. The upshot was that ANC MPs were too frightened to speak their minds for fear of reprisals.[12] This top-down centralism meant that parliament and the ANC were effectively disempowered and, as a consequence, policies could be simply imposed from the Presidency on a compliant government and party. The drift away from democracy was duly noted and even Archbishop Desmond Tutu commented that 'unthinking, uncritical, kowtowing party line toeing is fatal to a vibrant democracy'.[13] Unfortunately, there was very little that could be done to reverse the changes.

In terms of South African foreign policy, Mbeki's control over the government and the party was to have enormous significance. The new structures in place suited Mbeki perfectly. He had a longstanding interest in foreign policy (he was head of the ANC's international department in exile) and was keen to be deeply involved in the process, particularly to promote the African Renaissance.[14] An indication of the underlying importance of foreign affairs to the Presidency (read Mbeki) was highlighted in the 'Democratic Governance' report. The Department of Foreign Affairs (DFA) was the only government department to have an entire section devoted to how the Presidency would enhance its work and results.[15] The DFA's marginalization during Mandela's administration has been outlined previously, and this continued apace under Mbeki. This process was accentuated by the

PCAS, because the Presidency could now dictate and impose the terms of South Africa's foreign engagements or simply do as it wanted. This in turn was aided by the appointment of another ally, Nkosazana Dlamini-Zuma, to the post of foreign minister. Dlamini-Zuma, described by a US ambassador as a 'truculent and petulant foreign minister', was regarded as a political novice for such a post, which consequently allowed Mbeki to 'manipulate foreign policy'.[16] The consequence for South African foreign policy was that there was little room for debate or for outside agency to influence the decision making of the top echelons of the ANC. Without the approval of the Presidency nothing in the realm of international affairs could be formulated or implemented. Mbeki could pursue almost any policy he wished without risk of parliamentary or party recourse.

Mbeki's Vision

When Mandela stepped down as president after one term in office it was seen to mark the end of an overtly idealistic phase in South African foreign policy. Formulated during the transition and then championed by Mandela, the idea 'that human rights will be the light that guides our foreign affairs' had, by 1999, largely been consigned to the sidelines.[17] The ANC government still claims to advocate a human rights based approach, having never removed it from official documents, but it is clear that its importance to foreign policy had diminished significantly.[18] Given Mbeki's strong resistance to the inclusion of human rights in the ANC's policy documents during the transition, it is of little surprise that such idealistic notions were discarded as soon as he had exerted his control over foreign policy. However, Mbeki's inauguration did not necessarily herald the new age of realism that was expected by some.[19] In fact, his foreign policy, which certainly contained pragmatic elements, was in many respects even more idealistic than his predecessors. Mbeki, like Mandela, had entered office set on transforming the world around him primarily by fulfilling the loosely defined concept of the African Renaissance. With the African Renaissance as the overarching principle, South Africa's foreign policy aspirations were: to help rejuvenate Africa and its multilateral institutions; to reform global institutions such as the UN Security Council and the IMF and to achieve Pretoria's desire to play a leading role in international governance, particularly as a representative of the global South.[20] These were and continue to be noble ideals, which would have allowed for some of the injustices of the world to be corrected. This sentiment was summed up in a speech when Mbeki argued that 'the further reproduction of wealth by the countries of the North has led to the creation of poverty in the countries of the South'.[21] Mbeki should be rightly praised for his efforts in attempting to redress the balance of power, while assisting Africa's development. Yet, like Mandela's foreign policy before it, it was an extremely optimistic and highly ambitious blueprint for South Africa.

A hint of Mbeki's alternative, idealistic vision was first expressed in his 'I am an African' speech and was given a degree of substance and formality during the ANC's review of its foreign policy. Perhaps unsurprisingly, the articulation of this new direction in the 1997 document, 'Developing a Strategic Perspective on South African Foreign Policy', coincided with his growing power and influence within the party. The new vision, examined in depth in the previous chapter, set about realigning South Africa towards a greater identification with a developing world agenda. The document, laced with anti-imperial rhetoric, proposed four main things: to advance the African Renaissance 'as the main pillar of our international policy not only relating to Africa, but in all our international relations globally'; to forge alliances with like-minded, progressive nations in order 'to place [the] concerns of Africa and the whole of the developing world more centrally on the international agenda and contest established power relations'; to develop a common agenda of reform to challenge the international status quo; and that South Africa should lead a campaign to transform and empower the OAU (Organization of African Unity).[22] These objectives did not completely alter the course of South African foreign policy, but rather reinforced certain aspects of what had already been started under Mandela. Over the course of Mbeki's presidency it was remarkable how successful the ANC government actually was in achieving these clearly stated aims.

An important theme raised in previous chapters was the legacies and influences of the transition on South Africa's foreign policy, most notably those of the Sub Council on Foreign Affairs (SCFA) and Mbeki's grudging acceptance of them. A core recommendation of the SCFA adopted by Mandela's government had been a strong commitment to multilateral work, especially with Western-orientated organizations such as the UN. After 1994, South Africa's active and prominent multilateral role undoubtedly had an important part in the country 'punching above its weight' on the international stage. Although Mbeki appreciated the importance of the West to South Africa, he wanted to refocus the balance in favour of the developing world. Therefore, instead of keeping the West at the heart of South Africa's multilateral activity, the focus was shifted towards forums outside the direct influence of the G8. Part of the new Mbeki vision was to position South Africa firmly as a beacon of the developing world. Mbeki successfully achieved this stated objective by assuming leadership of important non-Western organizations such as the Non-Aligned Movement (NAM) and the Group of 77; this position was enhanced further when South Africa secured a non-permanent seat at the UN Security Council. South Africa's increasing realignment towards the developing world was advanced by Mbeki's focus on Africa, epitomized by the transformation of the OAU and the pursuit of the African Renaissance. Furthermore, the shift in South Africa's foreign policy orientation was emphasized by an increasing identification with what it deemed 'progressive', anti-imperial governments such as Cuba and Venezuela. Each of these steps clearly demonstrated Mbeki's strong commitment to a developing-world agenda. However, the tightrope that Mbeki walked was that this realignment was not to be at the expense of meaningful work with Western-dominated international organizations. Mbeki was savvy enough to realize the vital importance of organizations such as the EU, not only in terms of trade and international prestige, but also because the African Renaissance was premised on co-operation and partnership. Mbeki's attempt at pursuing a foreign policy that appeased both the developing world and the West was fraught with inherent difficulties and was not always successful.

Yet, it must be emphasized that the ANC government's emphasis towards the developing world was not new. For most of its existence, the ANC's natural bedfellows had been non-Western countries and movements. During its exile, the West (with the notable exception of the Scandinavian nations) had pilloried the ANC and supported the apartheid government instead. The West had therefore been a major impediment in the ANC's liberation struggle. Once in office, Mandela's assertion that 'we never forget our friends' had seen the ANC led-government maintain its exile links, frequently identifying with various authoritarian leaders such as Suharto and Gaddafi, much to the puzzlement of the West.[23] However, Mandela had always been cautious to ensure that such a stance was not official government policy. Guided by the recommendations of the SCFA and the stark diplomatic warnings it had received during the transition, the ANC elite had appreciated the need to adopt an outwardly Western-friendly position. However, Mbeki had never favoured such a position for South Africa's foreign policy and it is clear that at the first opportunity he began to reverse the policy. The outcome was a clear commitment to the developing world, including what might be regarded as 'rogue nations'.

During Mandela's presidency, the ANC government had struggled to fully articulate its commitment to Africa, which had often drawn criticisms of South African indifference to the continent. Therefore Mbeki's concept of the African Renaissance served two purposes. The first was that it allowed the ANC to demonstrate the centrality of the continent to its foreign policy and secondly to clearly set the democratic government apart from apartheid rule. Mbeki thus pledged that South Africa would 'place ourselves among the forces in Africa and together with these forces, for peace, democracy and the reconstruction and development of our continent'.[24] The African Renaissance was a reflection of Mbeki's own outlook. Frustrated by negative perceptions of Africa in the West, he sought to redress the balance. His presidency coincided with efforts to make good this demand, advocating African solutions to African problems, free from external interference and self-serving Western agendas. Deeply suspicious of Western intentions in Africa he wanted to free the continent of its neo-colonial overtures and hypocritical interventions. The anti-Western tone and increasingly exclusivist, pan-African revivalism became an important feature in South African foreign affairs.[25] It may come as no surprise that this shift in direction was not universally welcomed by entrenched interests, either domestically or internationally. It would also lead to a widening gap between rhetoric and action.

The Developing World Champion

Once in office Mbeki rapidly implemented the new developing-world-focused foreign policy that characterized his presidency. In order to meet its objectives, the ANC government calculatedly used South Africa's prominent global position to enhance and expand its international interests by tying its fortunes to those of the developing world. In the 1990s and early 2000s, there had been a widely held belief that reform of international institutions was on the horizon, which would be driven by the non-Western world. For some time, South Africa had coveted a permanent seat on the UN Security Council, but recognized that, for this to become a reality, support from the developing would be crucial. It has previously been mentioned that Mbeki had carefully and skilfully positioned South Africa as one of the developing world's leading countries. South Africa was a prominent and vocal nation, actively participating in or leading many multilateral agencies, such as the NAM, and (although many on the continent might dispute that) regularly 'representing' Africa internationally. To bolster its 'claims' for a Security Council Seat, South Africa also became actively involved in peacekeeping and conflict resolution missions across Africa. Mbeki was frequently abroad, trying to resolve conflicts in countries as varied as the DRC, Burundi, Cote d'Ivoire and Sudan.[26] There is not the space to examine South Africa's interventions fully, but they were well intentioned and had some notable successes. A number of factors lay behind South Africa's new-found dedication to peacekeeping, including a commitment to Africa's development; its own position of strength compared to the rest of the continent and international expectations for the country to act as a mediator.[27] These examples of conflict resolution in Africa acted as a means of situating South Africa at the forefront of the developing world.

The ANC government's foreign policy proposals were heavily centred on Africa and its improving fortunes. According to the South African government, the most important issue for Africa was the need to restructure its existing institutions, primarily the OAU, into effective, operational forums. Not only would this assist Africa's development, it would also act as a vehicle for promoting and implementing many of South Africa's other foreign policy goals. Driven by Mbeki's ideals, South Africa took the lead in formulating and establishing new African institutions. The first priority was OAU reform and Mbeki was the chief architect behind its new-look structures. Modelled on the European Union (EU), the establishment of an African Union (AU) was proposed at an Extraordinary Summit of African heads of state in 1999. The proposals for the new organization were outlined in the Constitutive Act in late 2000, and adopted by delegates in May 2001.[28] The AU was thus formally established in July 2002 in Durban and Mbeki was rewarded with the chairmanship of the organization for his efforts. Given Mbeki's involvement, it is not surprising that many of the objectives of the AU closely mirrored those of the African Renaissance. The AU sought to: forge greater unity on the continent; accelerate political and socio-economic integration; promote and defend common African positions internationally; uphold peace, security, and stability and endorse democracy and good governance.[29] Furthermore, the AU member states agreed to: respect borders; forge a common defence policy; encourage peaceful conflict resolution and to adopt a stance of non-interference on internal matters.[30] In order for these objectives to be achieved, the work of the AU was to be supported by a raft of new structures and organs; it was envisaged that these would include a Pan-African Parliament (PAP), an African Court of Justice, an African Investment Bank and a Peace and Security Council with control over an African Standby Force.[31] South Africa's crucial interventions ensured that Africa's key multilateral forum had been transformed. The AU had been equipped with progressive proposals and backed by a multitude of structures to assist in its empowerment. A new era for Africa appeared to be on the horizon. However, it was fully appreciated that change would not happen without planning, assistance and co-operation on a pan-continental scale. Mbeki's proposed solution was the ambitious New Partnership for Africa's Development (NEPAD).

In 1999, Mbeki, along with his counterparts Obasanjo (Nigeria), Mkapa (Tanzania) and Bouteflika (Algeria), had been mandated by the OAU to prepare a new, comprehensive development programme for the continent. The resulting proposal, designed primarily by Mbeki, known as the Millennium Partnership for the African Recovery Programme (MAP) was envisaged as a means of improving the continent's economic progress and as a way of forging new partnerships with the West. Rather than simply being the recipients of aid, these mutual partnerships were aimed at bridging the development gap between the G8 and the developing world.[32] The leaders travelled extensively to lobby Western governments and organizations in a bid to secure backing for the plan; for example, Mbeki promoted MAP in early 2001, during a speech at the World Economic Forum in Davos.[33] After going through several draft stages, including the incorporation of Senegal President Wade's rival

OMEGA Plan, NEPAD was adopted in October 2001.[34] NEPAD was later described as Mbeki's greatest foreign policy success.[35]

NEPAD as a concept was simple: to generate economic and political confidence in Africa. The initiative was unique because it was not simply premised on economic growth, but also on a continent-wide commitment to democracy, good governance, human rights, peace and stability.[36] Through sustainable growth and development and a clear commitment to political reform, Mbeki hoped that NEPAD would be an important way not only of altering attitudes towards the continent, but attracting foreign investment too. Therefore, as African governments worked to get their houses in order, NEPAD would help facilitate economic partnerships with the developed world.[37] The founding NEPAD document set out a series of envisaged responsibilities, which it hoped would encourage greater debt relief, official assistance and infrastructure development to the continent. Perhaps the most notable and innovative aspect of NEPAD was the proposal for an African Peer Review Mechanism (APRM).[38] The idea was that African nations should 'consider seriously the impact of domestic policies, not only on internal political stability and economic growth, but also on neighbouring countries'.[39] The APRM was a way of demonstrating mutual responsibility for economic and political progress. The NEPAD initiative was also welcomed by the West in 2002, at the G8 Summit in Kananaskis, with delegates endorsing the Africa Action Plan.[40] Importantly, NEPAD was very much a part of the Washington Consensus. The West was encouraged because NEPAD was premised on market liberalization, free trade and liberal democracy, and thus very much in tune with the international status quo. Mbeki's role as NEPAD cheerleader and the West's African 'representative', was demonstrated vividly in July 2003, when George Bush claimed that 'President Mbeki is the point man' in Africa.[41] Mbeki's prominent position meant that, during his presidency, Africa was never far from the international agenda. For example, in 2005, the G8 met at Gleneagles specifically to discuss its contributions to Africa and the prospect of debt relief. Although these pledges have since been broken by the G8 members, the continent would not have received the attention it did without the efforts of Mbeki.[42] R. W. Johnson argues that the acceptance of NEPAD was for Mbeki 'a moment of triumph, for it acknowledged his success in positioning himself as *the* leader of Africa'.[43]

Aside from African concerns, the ANC government utilized its new foreign policy position pragmatically to strengthen its economic and political ties with powerful developing nations. President Mandela had already jettisoned support of Taiwan in favour of closer economic relations with China, and by the turn of the millennium, links with Beijing had been strengthened further. Likewise, similar deals were struck with Brazil and India. These powerful nations, with burgeoning domestic markets and rapid economic growth were regarded as vehicles of opportunity. For example, a forum known as IBSA (India–Brazil–South Africa), which was based on mutual co-operation, was established in 2003.[44] Bilateral links flourished and the participants seemed to genuinely co-operate on economic, diplomatic and technical issues. Mbeki described IBSA's importance to South Africa as being 'a coincidence of interests in so far as we have common hopes, aspirations and challenges and through IBSA have created a platform from which we can attend to these many and varied challenges'.[45]

However, an enduring problem for South Africa is that although compared to the rest of Africa it is an economic powerhouse, in global terms it can hardly be described as a major player. The South African economy paled into insignificance compared to Brazil, China and India and was also in direct competition for markets. South Africa soon found that its role was largely consigned to raw materials exporter and a destination for cheap Chinese products, which seriously damaged several domestic industries.[46] A case in point was the difficulties faced by the South African textiles industry, which saw 63,000 jobs lost between 2002 and 2006 and textile imports rise by 480 per cent in the same period.[47] Yet, for Mbeki it was ideologically important that South Africa was open for business with the world. In terms of international prestige, it was important that powerful nations such as China and India wanted to forge links with South Africa. The depth of its ties with these powers was demonstrated when South Africa was invited into the informal bloc of rapidly growing economic nations known as BRICS (Brazil, Russia, India, China and South Africa) in 2010, and formally initiated in April 2011.[48] This was a major achievement for South Africa. What it demonstrates is that Mbeki's presidency had placed South Africa in a position from which it could repeatedly 'punch above its weight' internationally. As the most prominent (or visible) African nation, South Africa is often chosen by the West and much of the developing world to be the voice of the continent.[49] In his 2002 State of the Nation Address, Mbeki argued that,

> The nations of the world elected to come to our country because they understand and appreciate what we have done in the last seven-and-a-half years to address within our own borders precisely the same questions that constitute the global agenda. They chose to convene in South Africa because they are convinced that we have something of value to contribute to the building of a new and more equitable world order that must surely emerge.[50]

Mbeki has to be commended for successfully ensuring that South Africa continued to occupy such a prestigious position. The vision was clear and the ANC government had made enormous progress in matching its foreign policy objectives to its principles.

South Africa's renewed focus and vigour towards developing world matters earned it many plaudits. However, many of these successes were undermined by the contradictions implicit within this international approach. A particularly contentious point was the ANC government's enduring loyalty to its exile allies and the support of 'progressive nations'. The ANC argued that it was committed to repaying its exile allies and that only through active diplomatic dialogue could reform be encouraged in less democratic countries. This stance had its genesis in the previous administration and President Mbeki had simply formalized it as part of South Africa's foreign policy vision. What transpired in his eight years as president was a deeper and more clearly articulated adherence to the notion of anti-imperialism. There are an ever-diminishing number of authoritarian and anti-imperial regimes around the world, but South Africa's association with nations such as North Korea, Palestine and Iran steadily increased after 1999. South Africa's identification with this anti-Western bloc also moved the country steadily further away from its much-vaulted ideals of human rights and democracy. Mbeki was subsequently accused of placing 'South Africa very firmly on the wrong side of the international street – on the side of would-be dictators and human-rights abusers'.[51]

The underlying tensions within South African foreign policy soon began to emerge. The founding principles of the AU and NEPAD, which Mbeki had played a seminal role in drafting, enshrine the primacy of good governance, democracy, human rights and importantly, neo-liberal economic partnership with the West. However, some of South Africa's allies did not adhere to such principles. Fundamentally the anti-imperial message was at odds with the notion of partnership with the West. It was all well and good preaching democracy and good governance for Africa, but the ANC government did not lead by example. The confusion was compounded by South Africa's continued association with governments with less than palatable records on democracy and human rights. For example, in 2005, Deputy President Jacob Zuma met with the North Korean Vice President Yang Hyong Sop to discuss bilateral issues with the internationally isolated and impoverished country.[52] There was clearly very little the North Korean regime of Kim Jong-il could offer South Africa, other than bolstering the ANC government's anti-imperial credentials. Furthermore, in 2003, on the cusp of the US-led invasion of Iraq, Aziz Pahad visited the country. During his visit Pahad personally 'delivered a letter from President Mbeki to President Hussein pertaining to our bilateral ties'.[53] Irrespective of the war's legality or justification, Saddam Hussein was a brutal dictator, so for South Africa to associate so closely before the Western invasion of Iraq was extraordinary.

Wherever there were anti-imperialist or 'progressive' regimes, President Mbeki was quick to identify with them. Perhaps the most bizarre example of his misguided loyalty and adherence to anti-imperialism was his close affiliation to Haitian President Jean-Bertrand Aristide, leader of one of the world's poorest and worst-governed nations. In 2004, Mbeki elected to not only visit Haiti to mark the bicentennial celebration of its founding; but he also provided R 10 million to fund the event.[54] Mbeki's donation and subsequent visit put him at odds with mainstream international opinion. He was the only president in attendance at the event and, in doing so, the visit was regarded as South Africa offering unconditional support and a 'form of acceptance and tolerance of the fascist regime' of Aristide.[55] Analyst Greg Mills believed that the trip 'could undermine Mbeki's international standing as a progressive democrat'.[56] Aristide was subsequently ousted from power in a coup d'état, but South Africa's largesse did not stop there. Aristide was invited to live in exile in South Africa, at the taxpayers' expense, estimated to be £30,000 per month. Furthermore, Aristide arrived in South Africa to a red-carpet welcome and was met personally by Mbeki at the airport, a courtesy that had not even been extended to US President Bush's visit.[57]

The anti-imperial stance was a clear policy decision by the ANC government, but it fundamentally contradicted other tenets of its foreign policy, especially its stated economic interests. Relations with emerging non-Western nations such as China and Brazil were pragmatic policy decisions, but diplomatic and economic loyalty to nations such as Cuba and North Korea wasted enormous amounts of scarce resources for almost no return. This was starkly illustrated when South Africa was forced to write off Cuba's debt of R 926 million – incidentally not the first time the democratic government had done this for a former exile ally.[58] Despite the ANC government's posturing towards the developing world, South Africa's economic trade partners remained resolutely Western throughout Mbeki's presidency.[59] Although the government's stance could be interpreted as an important way of counteracting Western power, the close identification with regimes that were on the margins of the international mainstream risked alienating many of South Africa's most important trade partners. But what were the benefits of such an approach to South Africa? In reality, very few. The ANC's commitment to forging relationships with anti-imperial nations is another example of how the aims and interests of the party had blurred with those of the government, and not always for the better.

In 2007, South Africa's elevation to the UN Security Council as a non-permanent member should rightly be viewed as an enormous success. Mbeki and the ANC government had, through enormous amounts of effort and politicking, achieved a longstanding foreign policy objective. Having positioned itself strongly in other international forums, South Africa was elected by a groundswell of support from the developing bloc of nations, receiving a record 186 votes.[60] This was a demonstrable example of the support that South Africa could harness. With popular backing for its membership on the Security Council, South Africa used the opportunity to represent the developing world more vociferously and to pursue UN reforms actively at the highest level. However, any successes that were achieved have been obscured by the controversial nature of South Africa's tenure, characterized by strong support for rogue regimes and violators of human rights. South Africa swiftly made a name for itself by refusing to support UN resolutions condemning human rights violations in Belarus, Burma (Myanmar), Iran and North Korea, as well as attempting to delay the onset of

Kosovan independence.[61] Furthermore, South Africa also vetoed UN resolutions on Cuba, Darfur, Uzbekistan and, importantly, Zimbabwe.[62] The shielding of a 'Who's Who' of authoritarian regimes might have allowed the ANC government to fulfil notions of a third world, anti-imperial, internationalist ideology and demonstrate its strong commitment to this constituency, but it had serious repercussions for South Africa's reputation.

South Africa was resoundingly condemned internationally and domestically for its stance in the UN Security Council. After the vote rejecting a resolution condemning the Burmese Junta for its human rights abuses, the opposition DA sarcastically asked the ANC: 'will South Africa ever meet a dictator it does not like?'[63] However, all the UN Security Council membership did was bring into sharp relief the content of South African foreign policy of the previous eight years. Part of the confusion about South Africa's stance in the UN Security Council was due to erroneous perceptions (especially in the West) of what the country actually stood for. The ANC had not forgotten that during the excesses of apartheid, the movement had repeatedly demanded the UN to take concerted and tangible action against South Africa. The ANC government had a unique opportunity to make a difference during its membership of the Security Council, but instead tacitly supported the type of repression that it had spent 30 years in exile so stridently fighting against. There was a widely-held belief that the ideals underpinning the struggle against apartheid and Mandela's commitment to human rights were still applicable. Yet, these had already been sidelined during the latter stages of Mandela's presidency and were no longer applied consistently by the ANC government. Perhaps the world still believed that the warnings epitomized by the Russian Federation during the deliberations of the SCFA, that South Africa's foreign policy could change in style, but not in substance, still rang true.[64] However, contrary to evidence and actions, international perceptions of South Africa were still grounded on an idealized vision of the ANC and its beliefs. In fact, since 1994, the ANC had been gradually moving away from these; Mbeki's presidency marked a decisive shift in South Africa's foreign policy. For the ANC government, solidarity and anti-imperialism took precedence over concerns for human rights and democracy. This stance was epitomized by Mbeki's stance concerning Zimbabwe.

Zimbabwe

When discussing South African foreign policy, nothing else comes closer to clouding the legacy than the Zimbabwe crisis and the diplomatic failures associated with Mbeki. South Africa's stance of quiet diplomacy and Mbeki's continued international protection of Zimbabwe rapidly forfeited the ANC's moral high ground and eroded international goodwill. Moreover, Mbeki's position on Zimbabwe crucially undermined the new principles of good governance and democracy enshrined by the African Renaissance and NEPAD. Mbeki's intransigency over Zimbabwe's crisis damaged his own reputation and weakened many of the founding principles of Africa's newly created institutions. It need not have been this way. However, the ANC government became publicly complicit in the continuing survival of President Robert Mugabe and the deterioration of the Zimbabwean economy. Although a central component of Mbeki's foreign policy efforts, much has already been written on South Africa and Zimbabwe, so to avoid covering well-worn ground this section will be kept relatively brief.

After nearly 20 years as Zimbabwean president, Robert Mugabe, facing deteriorating economic conditions and diminishing voter popularity, held a constitutional referendum in 2000 in a bid to secure more political powers. Failing to recognize the extent of popular discontent or simply complacent about the outcome, Mugabe was caught off-guard when the newly formed opposition, the Movement for Democratic Change (MDC), led by Morgan Tsvangirai, won the referendum vote.[65] In the same year the MDC contested the parliamentary elections in June, winning 57 out of the 120 elected seats, giving ZANU PF only the narrowest of victories.[66] Mugabe's power was under serious threat with challenges not only from the new political opposition, but also from within his traditional support base. Survival and retention of power became key for Mugabe and ZANU PF. Invoking aspects of the guerrilla war, the threat of British imperialism and the need for land redistribution, Mugabe unleashed the so-called 'War Veterans', under the leadership of Chenjerai 'Hitler' Hunzvi, and the Border Gezi youth militia, both authorized and funded by ZANU PF.[67] The upheaval resulted in Zimbabwe becoming engulfed in a tortuous cycle of farmland invasions, violence, repression, political intimidation and rigged elections. Following the land invasions, the urban poor, many of whom had voted for the MDC, were targeted in Operation Murambatsvina. Around 700,000 people were directly affected and the government bulldozed homes and businesses.[68] The two-pronged attack by Mugabe against his opponents contributed to Zimbabwe suffering from severe unemployment, chronic shortages, a sharp decrease in life expectancy and ultimately economic hyperinflation. Amidst the turmoil, Zimbabwe still managed to hold elections in 2002, 2005 and 2008 that ZANU PF manipulated, through a variety of methods, to avoid political defeat.

The 2002 presidential election was the first that really attracted widespread international attention; something that has since become a feature of Zimbabwean elections. One reason behind the increased awareness was because Mbeki had been vociferously championing Africa and the vision for the continent's renaissance; Zimbabwe was the first test case for ideals of democracy, good governance and human rights. Despite indications to the contrary, Mugabe solidly clung to power with 56 per cent of the vote, triggering international condemnation of the rigged outcome. Criticism of the result came from a host of observer missions including Norwegian representatives, the SADC Parliamentary Forum Election Observation Mission and the Report of the Commonwealth Observer Group.[69] The election was clearly not 'free and fair' and had certainly been carried out within a highly volatile atmosphere of intimidation and violence. The international community responded by isolating Zimbabwe, and the Commonwealth elected to suspend it from the organization for a year.[70]

However, in complete contrast to other international assessments of the election result, South Africa, in line with other SADC heads of state, began its sustained defence of the ZANU PF government in earnest. The South African Observer Mission (SAOM), declared the election as legitimate, especially because of the presence of an opposition to Mugabe: 'the SAOM is heartened by the fact that the opposition ... actively participated in the campaign and the elections themselves, thus legitimizing the outcome of the said elections'.[71] Given the extent of the violence and intimidation against the MDC and its supporters, the interpretation of the election results by SAOM was particularly flawed. The ANC reiterated its endorsement of Mugabe and the results in *ANC Today*, which declared that 'the will of the people of Zimbabwe has prevailed ... the ANC believes that the people of Zimbabwe have spoken'.[72] A year later, in 2003, South Africa vocally and publicly committed its support to Zimbabwe at the Commonwealth Summit in Abuja. The collective heads of state took the decision to maintain Zimbabwe's suspension from the organization; Mbeki refused to accept this and simply withdrew. His position was backed by SADC members (with the exception of Botswana), who had argued against the Commonwealth making the expulsion permanent.[73] During the summit Mbeki had frantically attempted to defuse the international criticism of Zimbabwe and lobbied to have its membership restored; it was to no avail. It has been argued that the rejection of his proposals by the heads of state represented 'above all a defeat for the ambitious foreign policy that has emerged under Thabo Mbeki'.[74] Furthermore, Moses Mzila of the MDC believed that:

> it was most humiliating for [Mbeki] and for his country to attempt to prevent the decision the Commonwealth took in the first place, to be seen to defending a dictator who has brought ruin to his country ... it was diplomatic bungling at such a high level that Mbeki will feel hurt ... that his stand was tossed out the window.[75]

Mbeki was absolutely furious with the outcome and he penned his views of the Commonwealth in a vitriolic polemic for *ANC Today*, in which he lashed out at the West, blamed Britain for the farm invasions and argued that Africa should be left to deal with its own issues.[76] This was a clear indication of Mbeki's anti-imperial perspectives. Despite mounting international criticism of his lack of progress, Mbeki steadfastly maintained a stance of 'quiet diplomacy', attempting to coax a remarkably resilient Mugabe into reform. Nothing substantive changed through a further two flawed electoral processes and South Africa's stance was widely interpreted as providing support for Mugabe and ZANU PF.

Mbeki's defence of Mugabe came at a significant cost, inflicting enormous damage to his reputation and ambitious international visions. The first obvious impact was that in defending Zimbabwe he effectively sacrificed NEPAD and the ideals of the African Renaissance. There was a vast discrepancy between Mbeki's much vaunted commitment to continental renewal and Zimbabwe's collapse. NEPAD had widely publicized the onset of an era of good governance, democracy and human rights in Africa. Zimbabwe was the perfect test case for this new approach. However, instead of enforcing these principles and demonstrating the beginning of a new era, South Africa simply watched (and tacitly supported) the economic, social and political collapse of Zimbabwe. It was argued that 'President Mbeki [had] no credibility as a leader because he is not prepared to stand by the principles he is espousing in terms of NEPAD and a vision of an African renaissance ... the danger is that the ... G8 (industrialized nations) and other forums, could very well withdraw that support'.[77] Mbeki could seek Western assistance and partnership for NEPAD all he liked, but it was easy for institutions such as the EU or the Commonwealth to point out that despite the rhetoric, things were not changing, and indeed were rapidly deteriorating on South Africa's doorstep. The West simply withheld their investment and NEPAD had effectively withered by the end of Mbeki's presidency. This had a serious effect on the practical implementation of NEPAD, with Senegalese President Wade finally abandoning any hope of success: 'Expenses adding up to hundreds of millions of dollars have been spent on trips, on hotels. But not a single classroom has been built, not a single health centre completed. NEPAD has not done what it was set up for.'[78] In the *Mail and Guardian* an unnamed European diplomat argued that the crisis in Zimbabwe affected NEPAD because serious investment and development aid would not be forthcoming until they had got 'their house in order', stating that NEPAD 'is a wonderful idea but it all falls down at the Zimbabwe hurdle'.[79] South Africa did not help get 'the house in order' and the 'wonderful idea' declined in importance. Accentuating the problem was Zimbabwe's proximity to South Africa. It seemed inexplicable to the international community that for all the positive rhetoric, Mbeki, who arguably held the economic and political aces, had done nothing to prevent or even ease the ongoing crisis.

The second issue was the damage to South Africa economically, socially, and ultimately politically. Throughout the eight years of Mbeki's 'quiet diplomacy' there appeared to be a lack of recognition of the domestic cost of the Zimbabwe crisis in South Africa. From as early as 2000, South Africa found itself underwriting huge economic losses in Zimbabwe. For example in February 2000, South Africa offered an economic 'rescue package' of $133 million and it transpired that the South African electricity company ESKOM, which supplied energy to

Zimbabwe, was owed \$3.3 million.[80] These sums have since escalated further, with little prospect of repayment. For all his intellectualizing of grand ideas and concepts, the establishment of new continental organizations and the travelling of the world on official business, Mbeki was detached from matters affecting ordinary South Africans. The vast majority could not care less about an African Renaissance, NEPAD or the plight of other 'progressive' regimes when their daily reality was one of unemployment, poverty and poor service delivery at home. The ongoing crisis in Zimbabwe exacerbated domestic tensions, as millions of refugees flooded across the border, adding further pressure on limited jobs and housing in South Africa. An illustration of this discontent occurred in 2008, when waves of xenophobic attacks against foreigners, particularly Zimbabweans, broke out.[81] It served to highlight the enormous disconnect between the ANC elite and the population at large. Foreign policy is supposed to serve the best interests of the country, but this case tragically demonstrated how it was neither serving the majority of South Africans nor the Zimbabweans fleeing Mugabe's autocratic rule.

Why did the ANC government resolutely defend Zimbabwe? It was due in part to the overt anti-imperial foreign policy pursued by Mbeki, the desire not to deviate from the wider African consensus and the strong historical notion of liberation solidarity. The ANC government had moored South Africa to developing world opinion and was thus keen to remain in step. The Nigerian Crisis in 1995 and the disagreement about military intervention in Zaire in 1998 had been chastening experiences for the ANC leaders. Mbeki's stance of quiet diplomacy was a direct consequence; he was adamant that South Africa would not violate the principle of African solidarity during his presidency. Given the ANC's long history of fractious relations with Southern African governments in particular, staying attuned to regional opinion was especially important. Accordingly Mbeki became increasingly 'sensitive to being a part of the African family'.[82] Therefore, by consciously eschewing intervention in Zimbabwe's internal affairs, the ANC government was acting with continental opinion in mind. There had been frequent demands from domestic and foreign observers for South Africa to be more assertive against Mugabe, mirroring the actions of apartheid President John Vorster towards the then Rhodesian Prime Minister Ian Smith.[83] However, the thought of taking coercive action against Zimbabwe was inconceivable because, since 1994, the ANC government had been desperately trying to avoid acting like the apartheid regime. Some of the contradictions within South Africa's foreign policy towards southern Africa stemmed from the ANC's attempts to differentiate the government clearly from apartheid rule. Moreover, Mugabe was regarded by many on the continent and elsewhere as a progressive, revolutionary leader and a liberation hero.[84] Mugabe's land invasions were also popular across the continent, where issues surrounding farming and land redistribution still fester. Influential South African politicians continue to express their admiration for Mugabe and his policies; this sentiment was typified by firebrand Julius Malema who 'praised Mr Mugabe as an "exemplary" African leader because of his willingness to "say no to imperialists"'.[85] Mbeki was also extremely wary of Western intervention in African affairs and his suspicions were hardened by hypocritical Western interferences, especially when white interests were threatened. If South Africa had bowed to Western pressures to intervene it would have undermined Mbeki's anti-imperial credentials.

The history of the ANC's liberation struggle also had an extremely important bearing on the course of action taken by Mbeki. It must be stressed that the notion of liberation solidarity continues to have an enormous cachet in southern Africa amongst political elites. For the ANC in particular, the romanticized idea of the Frontline States, and the role they had in its struggle against apartheid, has a special place in its psyche. In spite of the obvious tensions within the region, and the clear absence of common values amongst states, there is a shared historic bond. The ANC, ZANU PF, FRELIMO, SWAPO and the MPLA all waged successful liberation struggles against white minority rule (some clearly more successful than others), culminating in their achieving and retaining political power ever since. The shared experiences in the battle against white minority rule and the solidarity this engendered has been a strong unifying force for the collective movements. ANC spokesman Keith Khoza argued that 'our shared history means that we have a responsibility to assist each other whenever and wherever possible ... Our interaction has never been defined within state relations – it's purely a party-to-party thing'.[86] Consequently both as a liberation movement and a governing political party, the ANC had been quick to recognize and celebrate the support it received. However, as the book has identified, there were many longstanding problems in the ANC's relationship with southern African governments originating from exile. Take Zimbabwe for instance: ZANU had been excluded from the Soviet backed 'authentic' group of movements, the newly elected Mugabe in 1980 was extremely reticent to support the ANC and, after the demise of apartheid, presidents Mugabe and Mandela personally despised each other.[87] Therefore, given a 'shared history' characterized by tension, and the enormous damage the Zimbabwe policy had upon his and South Africa's reputation, how can Mbeki's actions be explained?[88]

What has emerged in southern Africa is a collective amnesia concerning the past and a reinvention of history. Although the fractious inter-state relations continued, they were glossed over through the official rewriting of the historical narrative to suit specific political agendas. In its place, a narrow, self-selective reading of the past, embellishing the closeness of these relationships and emphasizing the heroic, revolutionary struggle has been established. Although the various liberation movements did clearly share close fraternal links, they certainly were never as smooth or as harmonious as has been subsequently depicted. Thus in the rewriting of its past the ANC systematically distorted the historical reality and created a highly filtered and idealistic interpretation, propagating certain 'myths'. Through the creation of this 'myth' of regional solidarity and the outward projection of unity, the ANC hoped to underscore its revolutionary credentials; align South Africa more closely with African opinion after its 'failures' under Mandela; and importantly legitimize its perpetual retention of power. The invention of tradition is not an isolated phenomenon in the region. Henning Melber argues that the position of the ruling political elites in each southern African nation is 'strengthened by selective narratives and memories related to the war(s) of liberation. These create new (to some extent invented) traditions to establish an exclusive post-colonial legitimacy under the sole authority of one particular agency of social forces'.[89]

In the case of Zimbabwe, the reinterpretation and rewriting of the historical record by the ANC to defend its policies, based upon the notion of liberation solidarity, has been startling. Mavivi Myakayaka-Manzini extolled the legacy of liberation alliances by arguing that the ANC would not criticize ZANU PF because 'these are our comrades we fought with in the struggle. Our relations have been sealed by blood.'[90] This is a wilful reinterpretation of the past, as it is historical fallacy to argue that the ANC and ZANU-PF were 'sealed by blood'; however, the concept and myths of liberation solidarity are far more important than the reality.

A reason behind the rise of pan-regional solidarity and the creation of a 'patriotic' history was the mounting political challenges that these former liberation parties were beginning to face. Although the SADC region outwardly projects a commitment to democracy, the vast majority of composite member states are noticeably authoritarian; 'it is clear that most Southern African leaders have absolutely no interest in entrenching democracy in their countries and the region'.[91] However, the electoral rise of the MDC, a party of the trade unions and civil society, complicated the dominant liberation narrative. The MDC had not fought a liberation war against white minority rule and its leaders had not been in exile. Accordingly, southern Africa's former national liberation movements, and now parties of government, deemed the MDC unfit to lead Zimbabwe due to its lack of past experience. The party was branded as 'illegitimate'. Moreover, the ANC were wary of the MDC because it lacked the necessary liberation credentials, and seemed to be in the thrall of Western interests. Not only did the MDC threaten regional solidarity, it was a threat to the anti-imperial positions of the ANC. For Mbeki it was inconceivable that Tsvangirai could become president of Zimbabwe. At the time Mbeki had been facing problems at home over his frankly ruinous HIV/AIDs stance, corruption within the ANC, and debates about the suitability of his neo-liberal economic policies.[92] South Africa's domestic opposition also originated from civil society and the trade unions. Therefore there was a fear within the ANC, that a successful democratic election victory for the MDC would trigger similar domestic challenges and threaten its own political hegemony in South Africa.

The emergence of a distinct form of regional solidarity between the ANC and these movements under Mbeki was a remarkable occurrence, especially because it masked a long history of inter-party disputes, a litany of broken promises and soured relations. The creation of the self-serving 'myth' of solidarity became a convenient unifying tool and a means of legitimizing the perpetual retention of power. Given this mindset, it is hardly a surprise that Mbeki acted in this fashion and helps to explain SADC's toothless response to Mugabe. Consequently, it was the ANC's perceived interests that were being served in shielding Mugabe, rather than the national interest. Despite the unfolding crisis, this band of brothers stood firmly behind ZANU PF. The outcome was concerted support of Mugabe and ZANU PF throughout Mbeki's presidency.

Conclusion

In September 2008, Thabo Mbeki's presidency came to an acrimonious end, when the ANC's National Executive Committee chose to recall him, prompting his immediate resignation.[93] Mbeki's resignation as South African president was the culmination of months of bitter infighting within the ANC.[94] Previously in December 2007, during the 52nd National Conference at Polokwane, Mbeki's attempt to secure a third successive term as ANC president was foiled by the challenge of his rival Jacob Zuma. The rise of what was dubbed the 'Zuma Tsunami' by the South African press was caused by the growing dissatisfaction not only within the ANC but also its alliance partners, COSATU and the SACP, concerning the course of Mbeki's presidency.[95] There was evident discontent from a number of quarters over a range of issues including: the centralized nature of power; favouritism within the upper echelons of government and the ANC; corruption; growing inequality exemplified by high crime, poverty and poor service delivery and Mbeki's apparent disinterest in the plight of ordinary South Africans. By September 2008, there was a lengthy charge sheet against Mbeki. The result has been widespread vilification of Mbeki and his record as president.

Yet as this chapter has demonstrated, the reality was far more nuanced. The furore surrounding some of Mbeki's more bizarre decisions and the manner of his demise from power has meant that his foreign policy achievements have been obscured or wilfully ignored. From the moment he gained office, Mbeki had explicitly articulated the content and objectives for South Africa's foreign policy, pledging to work towards the rejuvenation of Africa through the concept of the African Renaissance and the transformation of its multilateral institutions, to reform global institutions such as the UN Security Council and to play a leading role in international governance, particularly as a representative of the developing world. For nine years, the foreign policy of South Africa was fully geared towards fulfilling the clearly stated aims of the ANC government. Close confidant Frank Chikane, Director-General of the Presidency, argued that for Mbeki 'the renewal of the African continent and the freedom of Africans to determine their own destiny defined everything he was about'.[96] When the objectives are compared to the actual outcomes, there was a remarkable degree of success. Mbeki certainly helped transform Africa through the creation of the AU and the creation of NEPAD; South Africa worked closely with a number of multilateral organizations, including a stint on the UN Security Council; and Pretoria forged links with and represented the developing world wherever possible. The prominent role adopted by the ANC government ensured international prestige and recognition, which can only be regarded as a major achievement for South Africa. Mbeki deserves some recognition for his efforts at trying to transform the world.

However, the vast majority of these foreign policy achievements were a veneer. Replicating Mandela's government, there was an overriding emphasis on rhetoric over substance combined with inherent contradictions in the strategic approach. For example, the AU, and in particular the associated NEPAD and PAP, are now merely symbols of an era of optimism and idealism. The problem is that they are the product of grandiose yet largely unsubstantiated ideas. The intentions behind them for genuine change and progress for Africa cannot be doubted, but they were grounded largely in the convictions of Mbeki. Once he resigned from the presidency, there was no longer a prominent international cheerleader for these initiatives. An observer commented that 'his removal from office felt like the removal of the African Renaissance vision from the agenda of the African continent and a dampening of the spirit of enthusiasm'.[97] This was a characteristic of Mbeki's presidency: grand ideas, linked to instant international acclaim, with little thought about the practicalities or realities. Furthermore, the ANC government fundamentally undermined its own positions and efforts through not leading by example. The ideals of democracy and good governance enshrined by institutions such as the AU and NEPAD were flagrantly disregarded in the ANC government's foreign policy. Zimbabwe serves as a striking example of this practice. The reinterpretation of the ANC's history, and the influence this had on the implementation of South Africa's foreign policy, particularly in southern Africa, further dented the ideals and visions set out by the ANC. The consequence was that Mbeki's anti-imperialism and notions of historic regional solidarity trumped principled foreign policy action every time. Here was the heart of the contradiction. Mirroring the end of

Mandela's presidency, Mbeki was trying to perfect a seemingly impossible balancing act between diametrically opposed constituents. The success of many of Mbeki's grand projects rested upon forging partnerships and good relations with the West, yet the priority was an ideology that ran contrary to this very notion. The resultant outcome was entirely predictable.

CHAPTER 9

CONCLUSIONS

Throughout the ANC's existence, international activity in a variety of forms has played an important role in the movement's historical trajectory. The development and application of its foreign policy has neither been simple nor necessarily coherent, encompassing a myriad of twists and turns, yet its interactions with foreign actors have left an indelible mark upon the political psyche of the ANC. In examining the evolution in thought and implementation of the movement's foreign policy vision, this book has demonstrated how a range of historical factors, often neglected by political analysts, have shaped and constrained the ANC in government. By approaching the history of the ANC through an analysis of its foreign policy activities from exile through to its accession of political power, a central purpose has been to provide fresh insights into this array of international interactions. Breaking from the tendency of periodizing the history of the ANC into neat compartmentalized time frames (exile, South Africa's transition, and political power) important themes of continuity and discontinuity have now been revealed. A key consequence has been that decisions made during the previously neglected transition, with demonstrable significance to post-apartheid South Africa have been brought into sharp relief. By adopting a long view of the ANC's foreign policy, this book has provided the framework to link together previously separately analysed periods of the movement's history. Moreover, this has allowed for a deeper understanding of the continuities and discontinuities throughout these periods, offering new insights into the historic evolution of the ANC's foreign policy.

The pivotal era in this narrative is South Africa's negotiated transition from apartheid to democracy, 1990–4. Not only does the transition bridge the divide between exile and political power, it sheds light on the very nature of the country's negotiated revolution. In all areas of government, decisions were made and elites co-opted that would be of immense significance to a democratic South Africa. Yet, despite the importance of foreign policy formulation in this period, the significance of the transition has never been fully acknowledged. Due to the nature of South Africa's 'miracle' transition, the focus has tended to have been primarily on the dramatic domestic political and economic changes that occurred. The consequence has been that foreign policy in the Mandela era is often misleadingly represented as beginning 'anew' in May 1994, with the ANC-led government starting its international work with a clean slate. This, however, is historical fallacy and ignores the direct relevance of events that preceded the ANC's election to power. The demise of global communism, the unbanning of the ANC and the movement's readjustment to its new-found conditions contributed to a period of profound changes not only internationally, but also within the ANC itself. These past experiences acted as an important point of reference for the post-apartheid governments of Mandela and Mbeki. This book has argued that such an oversight has resulted in the ANC's, and consequently democratic South Africa's, foreign policies being misunderstood. It therefore directly questions the prevailing over-simplification in the current analysis and illustrates the significant impact both exile and the transition had upon South Africa's post-apartheid foreign policy.

An important aspect of this book has been to reveal the extent to which the ANC as a movement and political party has had a foreign policy and how increasingly its vision and perspectives have replaced those of the state. Since its inception the ANC has had an historic and deeply significant relationship with the international community. The ANC's extensive international dimension, especially during its exile was crucial for its own survival and acted as a key weapon in the demise of the apartheid regime. However, an important, yet rarely acknowledged point is that the ANC's foreign policy did not cease once it entered political office. In fact, there is a remarkable amount of continuity between the periods of exile and political power. It must of course be recognized that theoretically there are distinctions between South African foreign policy as a sovereign country, the foreign policy perspectives of civil servants and those of the ANC as a movement/political party. Nonetheless such distinctions have become increasingly impossible to differentiate in the democratic South Africa. The creeping centralization of political power during Mandela's and Mbeki's presidencies has made it ever more apparent that South Africa's 'national interests' have come to replicate those of the ANC as a party. This blurring of interests has resulted in several problems for South Africa internationally. There are a number of instances in which the ANC government has pursued policies that clearly benefited itself and not the country as a whole. For example, Mandela, on official state visits to Indonesia and Taiwan procured financial donations for the ANC coffers, while Mbeki saw fit to cancel Cuban debts to South Africa. These two instances typify the way in which the distinctions between party and state started to blur.

Despite the ANC's extensive links with the wider international community it has not always been a happy union; in fact the relationship was highly complicated and often fractious. Throughout the ANC's exile and current period of political power it has relied enormously upon the international community in order to achieve its goals.[1] However, its relations with international partners led to conflicting pressures on the ANC once it was in power. A range of global and domestic constituents had preconceptions about what the ANC and South Africa stood for internationally and consequently what an ANC-led South Africa would offer to their disparate interests. Simultaneously, drawing on the experiences of its liberation struggle, the ANC developed its own self-perception of what it could offer the international community, including acting as a global bridge-builder between different international cultures, a champion of human rights and the leader of the developing world.

However, seeking to meet competing, even opposed, interests has been a path fraught with complexity for the ANC in government. Each influential bloc held widely divergent expectations and desires for the direction of post-apartheid South African foreign policy. The ANC found that in power it was unable to fulfil its own anointed self-image, let alone the expectations placed upon it domestically and internationally. The ANC's foreign policy has thus fluctuated between these divergent audiences, trying to please them all at different times and in different ways. For example, the ANC adopted and pursued a Western-friendly, neo-liberal economic policy, but simultaneously made contradictory political statements through initiatives such as the African Renaissance and Mbeki's declared wish to lead and represent progressive forces and oppose Western power. While in exile the ANC had been remarkably successful in interacting with protagonists on either side of the Cold War divide. This was a major success for its foreign policy and an impetus for its later attempts to become an international bridge-builder. However, once in power such an approach proved largely impractical. The ANC government's ambitious foreign policy initiatives for South Africa failed to please the majority of the intended recipients and were subsequently criticized extensively.

The Legacies of Exile

By demonstrating the continuity in the ANC's thinking, incidents from its exile provide insights into the formulation of the movement's foreign policy both in the transition and once in government. The ANC's broad-based international support network spanned the Cold War divide, yet it had a predominantly socialist orientation, influenced by the close relations with the Eastern Bloc.[2] Not only did this have implications for the ANC's future foreign policy, but also on the ideological perspectives of the movement's supporters. A vital aspect of the ANC's foreign policy in exile was establishing relationships with independent southern African states and various Marxist-inspired liberation movements. Without these links the very survival of the ANC as a viable liberation movement would have been in serious doubt. Materially and rhetorically, the ANC was supported by various southern African nations, which allowed the movement to function organizationally, and to establish bases for its guerrilla fighters from which to launch armed attacks against South Africa. Although these relations with Southern African nations and movements were rhetorically strong, in reality they were fragile, and the ANC's position in the region was extremely tenuous at times. For example, by the end of the 1960s, the ANC had fallen out with its hosts in Tanzania and Zambia, with the former expelling the movement from its bases, and the latter threatening to do likewise. Later, during the 1980s, the ANC was expelled from Mozambique after the Liberation Front of Mozambique (FRELIMO) government had signed the Nkomati Accords with apartheid South Africa. Swaziland had earlier signed a similar deal in 1982, and, following the New York Accords in 1988, the ANC was also banished from Angola.

The legacy of these notoriously poor relations survived the immediate transition, and continued once the ANC took power in South Africa. This was typified by Mandela's conflict with President Mugabe over the Southern African Development Community (SADC) and the People's Movement for the Liberation of Angola's (MPLA) enduring hostility towards the ANC for not recognizing and rewarding the enormous sacrifices of the region in supporting the movement's struggle. It was only under Mbeki, who made a conscious decision to alter the orientation of the ANC's foreign policy, that relations began to gradually improve with its immediate region. Armed with a foreign policy vision, which emphasized the desire to work in tandem with the continent and identify more closely with developing nations, the ANC revived the notion of exile liberation solidarity, exemplified by South Africa's stance towards Zimbabwe. The conscious reinterpretation of history by the ANC to suit its current political goals was telling. The revitalization of an outward projection of regional unity and solidarity enabled Mbeki to utilize the past in such a way as to fulfil the ANC's anti-imperial aspirations, while also attempting to negate some of the enduring tensions amongst southern African governments. Yet, in spite of these efforts, South Africa's relations with its neighbours have not thawed to any great extent. The ANC government has found it can do little to please regional governments. Paradoxically, it has been criticized for not being active enough, but also for being too assertive. This no-win situation demonstrated both the continuity of regional fears of South African hegemony, and also the inability of the ANC to overcome the legacy of its apartheid-era foreign relationships.

Most pertinent to South African foreign policy was the ANC's overwhelming lack of strategic vision for the future. After 30 years in exile, the ANC was remarkably unprepared for the impending transition and its subsequent negotiations. In exile the ANC had been forced to be pragmatic in accepting assistance from any group or nation that could help the struggle, although much of this aid was sourced from the socialist bloc. However, this was not conducted in a co-ordinated fashion; the focus was on the immediate need for material assistance and the aim of overthrowing the apartheid regime. This was not just symptomatic of foreign policy issues, but all aspects of the future day-to-day running of government. The ANC had endlessly theorized about taking power, but never fully articulated its plans for South Africa once it had been achieved. The only two documents from the exile period with any immediate relevance to foreign policy were the Freedom Charter created in 1955, and the more detailed 'Final Report of the Commission on Foreign Policy' from the Kabwe Conference of 1985. These two documents could in no way be described as an adequate basis for foreign policy. The ANC's lack of readiness for the transition and the negotiations was further magnified by the collapse of international communism, removing the ideological lodestar of the movement, which seriously affected its cadres' thinking. After the ANC was unbanned by de Klerk in 1990, these eventualities combined to put the movement at a marked disadvantage during the initial stages of the transition. However, the legacy of the exile liberation struggle did not end in 1994. Although South Africa courted the West during Mandela's administration, the ANC-led government frequently interacted with some of the world's more dubious regimes, many of which had contributed to its liberation struggle. Moreover, after 1999, the ANC government explicitly reverted to a developing world programme. Couched in anti-imperialist language and reminiscent of the Cold War, this stance was exemplified by South Africa's ties to nations that stood on the edge of the global mainstream, such as North Korea and Haiti. What it demonstrated was the enduring and powerful legacy of the ANC's past, which continued to inform the party's actions and perspectives in government.

The Effect of the Transition

This book has emphasized the importance of events and decisions made during South Africa's transition, which are pivotal to understanding the evolution of the ANC's thinking and the initial stages of its post-apartheid foreign policy. The first was the ANC's own process of policy formulation during the transition. The movement faced numerous difficulties after being unbanned: it entered the 1990s with no definitive foreign policy vision; initially it struggled to adapt to the immense global changes; it was forced to establish new international alliances and it encountered unexpected competition from the NP government, which sought to re-establish its own international influence and legitimacy. The movement gradually adapted to these problems, but faced with more pressing domestic concerns the ANC subsequently delegated parts of the process of formulating foreign policy to academics. Through these processes, which certainly involved ANC leaders, these academics aligned the movement to the prevailing international norms of human rights, democracy and multilateralism. In the early 1990s, the ANC publicized the human rights aspects of its future foreign policy widely, most notably in the ghost written *Foreign Affairs* journal article.[3] Although the ANC leadership accepted the bold and assertive proposals created for them, there were some misgivings about this general direction; notable dissent concerning the human rights aspects came from a number of ANC leaders, particularly those allied to Mbeki. It was not only some of the leadership that was displeased with the ANC's direction. The movement's more militant supporters desired a more socialist-revolutionary approach to foreign policy, reflecting the ANC's own recent past. Not surprisingly, it was only after Mbeki took office that the ANC government moved away from these ideals, choosing to focus on the developing world and prominent anti-imperialist states. This dramatic change saw South Africa relegate its highly vaunted focus on human rights in favour of courting authoritarian regimes; a considerable policy U-turn from the ANC's earlier idealism. The revelations about the transition process raise important questions about the ANC's ownership of its stated foreign policy in 1994 and thus have implications for understanding democratic South Africa's international relations in the immediate post-apartheid era.

The question of foreign policy direction and ownership during and after the transition becomes even more complex when the concurrent activities and recommendations of the Sub Council on Foreign Affairs (SCFA) are factored into the equation. The under-studied Transitional Executive Council (TEC) and the SCFA, were tasked, as part of the final stage of South Africa's transition from apartheid to democracy, with establishing a comprehensive set of recommendations on foreign policy for the new government. The significance of the SCFA was that its work had the ability to shape and influence the direction of post-apartheid foreign policy. The power of the SCFA to shape foreign policy was not lost on the DFA, and its civil servants manipulated the process so that the final recommendations closely mirrored both its own, and the Western international community's prevailing perspectives on the world. Therefore entrenched elite interests partially 'captured' the 'new' South Africa's initial foreign policy by ensuring that the recommendations of the SCFA were attuned to the international status quo of the early 1990s.

This was part of a wider process of 'domestication' of the ANC underway by external forces in South Africa at this time. The SCFA process was a means of encouraging the SCFA, and the ANC, into conforming to international norms, as well as demonstrating the advantages that doing so would bring to South Africa. Essentially, the new ANC-led government was forced to accept these proposals in order to be accepted back into the fold of international respectability, which helps to explain why certain policies such as GEAR were subsequently introduced under Mandela's stewardship.

ANC Foreign Policy in Office

When the ANC-led Government of National Unity (GNU) came to power in May 1994, it faced a number of cumulative pressures and constraints that arose both from exile and the transition period. However, these neglected aspects of the ANC's history are vital in explaining and understanding some of its foreign policy initiatives, and thus its policy successes and failures. Throughout Mandela's and Mbeki's terms in office, the ANC government recorded a number of successes in its foreign policy. The bold and clear assertions made in the ANC's various foreign policy documents demonstrated that the movement was clear in what it wished to achieve internationally, albeit with rather conflicted objectives. Mandela's administration pro-actively sought to promote democracy, peace, development and human rights across the world, as set out in its seven guiding principles. These principles were publicly outlined from the earliest moments of the ANC-led government. South African attempts to fulfil these principles were evident in the country's dynamic work within multilateral organizations; the key role it played in several international treaties, most notably in the field of disarmament; efforts at bridging global divisions by adopting an all-encompassing 'universalistic' policy towards all nations; active involvement in conflict resolution, especially in promoting peaceful, democratic solutions and standing up to international abuses of power. Within five years, South Africa became a highly active and respected member of the international community. This in itself was a significant achievement. Moreover, the ANC was not afraid to speak out on issues that it thought should be placed on the global agenda, and refused to be deflected from its guiding philosophies, even if it meant upsetting its Western or African allies.

This commitment, in the face of hostility from entrenched interests, was admirable. The ANC did not wish to sit back, but to actively engage the international community with ambitious and challenging policies. All of these had been clearly elucidated by the ANC before and after taking power. Tom Lodge believes that these achievements offer a 'strong case for representing the foreign policy of Mandela's presidency as ... more success than failure'.[4]

Although Mbeki altered the underlying ideological focus of South Africa's foreign policy, the ANC had clearly articulated this alternative vision for the future in a number of prior policy documents. The core tenet of Mbeki's administration was to address global inequalities, positively transform Africa and support the developing world. During his presidency Mbeki helped oversee the creation of the AU and the ambitious development plan known as NEPAD; South Africa worked closely with a number of multilateral organizations such as the NAM; served a high-profile term on the UN Security Council; and Pretoria actively forged relations with and represented the developing world wherever possible. That South Africa achieved these successes was in part due its unrivalled economic and political position in Africa, which allowed it to act in ways other similar sized or even larger nations could not. Furthermore, in its self-perceived role as a bridge-builder, the ANC government has been able to engage with a range of global constituents in pursuit of different outcomes. The prominent role adopted by Mbeki ensured international prestige and recognition, which can only be regarded as a major achievement for South Africa. Mbeki was not wrong in 2000 when he announced that 'South Africa's voice is indeed listened to with a certain degree of attention by many on our Continent and the rest of the world.'[5] This success illustrates that because of South Africa's unique status on the continent, and the country's own self-perceived 'exceptionalism', the ANC has been able to take advantage of its international position and the patronage of the global community to carve out unique opportunities for its foreign policy. When the ANC's objectives are compared to the outcomes in South African foreign policy during Mbeki's presidency, there was a remarkable degree of success, although it was not always popular. James Barber's view that the ANC's activities in government ensured that South Africa could 'punch above its weight' in international affairs' certainly holds true.[6] Mbeki's successor, President Jacob Zuma, maintained this tradition of

South Africa's global prominence by gaining a second term on the UN Security Council and securing admission to the prestigious bloc of developing nations known as BRICS.

Yet, for all the high-profile successes, the ANC government has been dogged by accusations of failure and ideological incoherence in its approach to foreign policy from the first moments it gained office. Importantly, many of the problems and constraints that have been encountered stem from the ANC's exile, the transition period, the nature and realities of the international environment, as well as the distinctive character of the ANC as a party and a movement. The difficulty of having to reconcile the conflicting international expectations on the ANC-led administration has already been discussed. This was however only one of a multitude of factors that have conspired to constrain the 'new' South Africa since 1994.

Constraints and Contradictions

The GNU adopted many of the recommendations of the SCFA, which enabled South Africa to 'hit the ground running' in foreign policy matters and allowed for swift and easy reintegration into the international community. However, it also brought about a number of problems for the ANC-led government in its first term in office. By accepting the recommendations of the SCFA, the ANC-led administration committed South Africa to an orthodox 'realist' path for its international interactions. In doing so, it had agreed to interact within the constraints of the then prevailing normative practices of the international community. This meant that the ANC's 'own' principles of universal recognition and moral interactions in foreign policy clashed with the neo-liberal, Western-friendly recommendations of the SCFA. In the initial years of the GNU, these widely divergent and ultimately contradictory perspectives contributed to a foreign policy riddled with inconsistency and apparent incoherencies.

Another factor that has contributed to this 'clash' is the very nature of the ANC as a movement. Although the ANC has and continues to speak as a monolithic organization, stressing the overriding need for unity, this is far from the reality. The ANC has always been a broad nationalist umbrella organization, containing a vast spectrum of views within its structure, ranging from socialism to neo-liberalism.[7] The result is that behind the external image of unity, the ANC is internally a divided movement. For example, during its exile, the ANC leadership found it difficult to meet the demands of some of its more militant cadres, and in some instances worked closely with allied African governments, such as the MPLA in Angola, to quell internal dissent. Furthermore, the foreign policy that the ANC had officially promoted at the end of the transition was not universally popular within the movement, most strikingly amongst a section of the leadership. What has become clear in this book is that through the SCFA, parts of the old regime and the Western international community had succeeded in influencing a section of the ANC elite, which had duly indicated that South Africa would adhere to the international status quo. However, due to the characteristics of the ANC and its umbrella structure, this small (divided) elite was unable to contain all of the contradictory elements that resided within the party and its leadership, especially those who during exile had been influenced by socialist and anti-imperialist interpretations of the world. Although the influence of the SCFA diminished in importance as Mbeki exerted power and control over the ANC, the movement continued to remain ideologically divided throughout his presidency. A consistent feature between the administrations is that the ANC leadership has been unable to placate all the demands of either the international community or its domestic supporters. The result has been an oscillating and incoherent foreign policy.

Some of the fluctuations in South African foreign policy stemmed from the ever-increasing centralization of decision making in the structures of the ANC and government. During the ANC's first term in office, presidential personality became a dominant feature under Mandela's stewardship and consequently South Africa witnessed a creeping centralization in decision making amongst a small number of the ANC's leaders.[8] This was not an alien development for the movement as its exile structures had been organized in a top-down manner, not only for issues of security, but also representing its Leninist ideological tendencies. The preponderance of democratic centralism after the transition ensured the continued domination of decision making by a small elite, most of whom were perfectly attuned to this style of governance having served the ANC in exile. As previously discussed, once in government the ANC ignored the recommendations of parliamentary committees and the DFA was increasingly marginalized.

The developments enabled the ANC to conceptualize and pursue a foreign policy that suited its own needs rather than those of the country. This was taken a stage further once Mbeki became president. Aided by the power of the President's Office and the invasive nature of the Policy Co-ordination and Advisory Service (PCAS), Mbeki had an unrivalled control of all aspects of government, including foreign policy. Not only did this circumvent party and government oversight or input, Mbeki had the final say on decisions and took an active role in directing and shaping South African foreign policy towards his developing world agenda. Without either the guidance of experts or an effective process of accountability to the wider party, foreign policy increasingly became based upon Mbeki's personal view of the world.

Furthermore, the ANC's bold but inherently contradictory foreign policy principles led to numerous constraints, which became increasingly apparent in South Africa's interactions with countries like Indonesia, where economic matters took precedent over human rights concerns. The concept of a human rights based foreign policy had been largely imposed upon the ANC leadership during the transition, which did little to help matters of coherence or even practicality. Although the new South Africa did initially strive to implement this publicly declared policy in the case of Nigeria in 1995, championed specifically by Mandela, these efforts were short-lived and the ANC government increasingly began to ignore it. In policy initiatives such as the AU, NEPAD and the APRM, the ideals of democracy and human rights were enshrined as core components; however, the ANC government has repeatedly paid them only lip-service, as typified by its dealings with Zimbabwe and its acrimonious term on the UN Security Council. Moreover, the ANC-led government repeatedly undermined its own stated democratic and human rights principles by the party's willingness to accept donations from any willing nation or organization; by permitting continued arms sales to foreign regimes with dubious human rights records; and by acting internationally as if it was still a liberation movement, through its links with nations such as Cuba and North Korea. As a result, analysts such as Greg Mills accuse the ANC government of lacking 'the necessary broad orientation and strategic purpose'.[9] This may be true, but many Western actors have fundamentally misunderstood the foreign policy of South Africa.

There is still a belief that the ANC remains the champion of democracy and human rights ideals, a position that the party had once so vociferously promoted. In reality, nothing could be further from the truth, because when issues of democracy and human rights are pitted against the anti-imperial agenda, the ANC's anti-imperialism triumphs every time. This only serves to fuel perceptions of incoherence and contradiction.

The dichotomy within South African foreign policy needs to be understood historically to provide an explanation for some of the outcomes for its foreign relations. Part of the problem in understanding the foreign policy of the ANC government is premised on Western-perceptions of South Africa, and the notion that during the transition the nation's economic/trade policies were 'captured' by dominant neo-liberal interests. A clear demonstration of this is the ANC-led government's adoption of neo-liberal principles, epitomized by Growth, Employment and Redistribution (GEAR). It is typified by its international trade balances: eight of South Africa's top ten trading partners in 1999 were Western states and this pattern was replicated throughout Mbeki's administration.[10] This occurrence reflects the extent to which South Africa's continued integration with Western partners during the 1990s made anything other than a free market, neo-liberal approach unlikely. Adherence to these economic principles led Western leaders to believe that the ANC-led government also subscribed to the other basic tenets of Western international thinking. However, post-apartheid South Africa surprised the West. The ANC's links with regimes in Libya, Cuba and Iran were the antithesis of Western opinion. The West had believed that through the capture of trade relations, South Africa's foreign policy would simply follow suit. There was thus a failure by the West to recognize or fully understand the principles and political culture of the ANC. The ANC's publicly stated desire to pursue such a foreign policy seems to have been disregarded, or treated as largely rhetorical. The West also failed to take into account the lack of homogeneity within the ANC. Despite having influenced a small number of ANC leaders during the SCFA process, as a broad-based movement the variance in ideals amongst its supporters was striking. In fact, after the withdrawal of the NP from the GNU in 1996, Mbeki was able to assert personal control over South African foreign policy, directing it away from the recommendations of the SCFA and towards the earlier tenets of the ANC's principles. This trend continued throughout his presidency. In fact, the developing world focus, tinged with anti-imperialism, became the driving force in South African foreign policy after 1999. The Western-dominated international community, regardless of its own perceptions, had therefore not fully 'captured' or understood all elements of South Africa's foreign policy. This was starkly demonstrated by Western surprise and anger towards South Africa during the rebel uprising against Colonel Gaddafi's rule in Libya, in August 2011. As the rebel movement took control of the capital Tripoli, its leaders appealed to the UN to immediately release $1.5 billion of frozen assets to provide humanitarian aid.[11] However, South Africa's 'blocking tactics' in the UN Security Council towards its anti-imperial ally prevented the funds from being released, prompting a furious response from the US and British governments.[12] The then British Defence Secretary, Liam Fox, urged South Africa to think again, arguing that 'there will be huge moral pressure on South Africa', adding that, 'they wanted the world at one point to stand with them against apartheid. I think they now need to stand with the Libyan people.'[13] Yet, as this book has explained, although the international community may have regarded such actions as incoherent, the decision by the ANC government to support Gaddafi was a conscious and coherent part of its foreign policy. Historical analysis and interpretation is thus crucial as a means of explaining post-apartheid South African foreign policy.

'Punching Above its Weight'

Many of the ANC's guiding foreign policy principles ultimately failed to be implemented because they were far too ambitious, and were constrained by forces outside of their control. The ANC demonstrated its inexperience in foreign affairs through many of its international activities. Former DFA Director General Jackie Selebi, himself a veteran of the exile struggle, acknowledged this inexperience:

> South Africa went from pariah state to being a significant player on the world stage in the very short space of five years. This meant we were thrust into immediate action on the international stage, a situation not all of our own choice, but one dictated to us by the

international community which forced the country to both plan and execute simultaneously.[14]

A telling point made by Selebi was the recognition that the ANC's foreign policy was not entirely of its own volition. He tacitly acknowledged that the government's room for manoeuvre had been checked not only by the outcomes of the transition period, but also the realities of the 'new world order'. Yet, the ANC continued to persevere with its foreign policy agenda that was at odds with the reality. This was both admirable and naïve. Furthermore, the ANC in government has continued to pile pressure upon its foreign policy, desperately wanting South Africa to match the high international expectations placed upon it and forge its own niche in international affairs. In part, this has meant that the ANC government engaged with the international community with little time for effective planning or reflection. Given the severe limitations on the new South Africa's operational capabilities, the ideals of the government could not always be matched in practice. There has been a tendency by the ANC to think 'big' internationally, epitomized by the notion of the African Renaissance and grand initiatives such as the restructuring of the OAU into the AU, the launch of NEPAD, and the establishment of the African Parliament. Pioneered by the vision and drive of Mbeki, all of these initiatives were central pillars of ANC foreign policy, and provided enormous steps forward in African multilateral structures. Yet for all the success and prestige these initiatives brought to South Africa and Mbeki personally, they have failed to live up to the lofty expectations. This is due to an abundance of rhetoric, unmatched by reality; the desire for an instant fix rather than gradual, evolutionary development; a lack of organizational capacity to make the newly created structures function and, like so many things, a serious shortfall in funding. The reality has been that the ANC government has been unable to fulfil its own expectations, let alone those of other nations.

Many of the ANC's foreign policy principles did not fit neatly with the realities of power, and were poorly or incoherently executed. The 'new' South Africa came into being with an idealistic vision for the future, but also faced many constraints. The picture that emerges is that the initial, seemingly unconstrained possibilities for South African foreign policy were in fact highly constrained, by: leading individuals in the ANC; the movement's historic experiences from exile and the enduring influence these continued to have once in government; the nature of the international community; and by South Africa's democratic transition. Thus the bright new dawn for South African foreign policy, epitomized by two idealistic presidents, was shaped, restricted and influenced by a range of factors that can only be fully understood through an historical assessment of the ANC.

NOTES

Chapter 1   Introduction

1. Mandela, Nelson, 'South Africa's future foreign policy', *Foreign Affairs* 72 (1993), p. 88.
2. For example, see: Speech by O. R. Tambo, 'Statement of the National Executive Committee on the Occasion of the 60th Anniversary of the ANC', 8 January 1972, http://www.anc.org.za/show.php?id=2642 (9/8/11); *The New Age*, 17 June 2011.

Chapter 2   The ANC in Exile, 1960–76

1. Lelyveld, Joseph, *Move Your Shadow: South Africa Black and White* (London, 1985), p. 328.
2. Slovo, Joe, 'SACP; one of the great pillars of our revolution', *The African Communist* 107 (1986), p. 28.
3. Sapire, Hilary, 'Liberation movements, exile, and international solidarity: an introduction', *Journal of Southern African Studies* 35 (2009), p. 273. For more on the internal struggle see, for example: Jeffery, Anthea, *People's War: New Light on the Struggle for South Africa* (Johannesburg, 2009); Marx, Anthony, *Lessons of Struggle: South African Internal Opposition, 1960–1990* (Cape Town, 1992); Seekings, Jeremy, *The UDF: a History of the United Democratic Front in South Africa 1983–1991* (Cape Town, 2000); Suttner, Raymond, *The ANC Underground in South Africa to 1976* (Auckland Park, 2008).
4. Johns, Sheridan, 'Obstacles to guerrilla warfare – a South African case study', *The Journal of Modern African Studies* 11 (1973), p. 271.
5. Callinicos, Luli, *Oliver Tambo: Beyond the Engeli Mountains* (Cape Town, 2004), p. 253.
6. Callinicos, *Tambo,* pp. 258–61.

7. The Anti-Apartheid Movement (hereafter AAM) Archive, Bodleian Library of Commonwealth and African Studies, University of Oxford, MSS AAM 938, Death of Oliver Tambo, ANC Chairperson, April 1993, Memoriam O. R. Tambo Programme.

8. Barber, James, *South Africa in the Twentieth Century, a Political History: in Search of a Nation State* (Oxford, 1999), p. 169.

9. University of Fort Hare (hereafter UFH), Liberation Archives, ANC Lusaka Additions (Mayibuye II), Box 36, File 1, Morogoro Conference Resolutions.

10. The Freedom Charter, adopted at the Congress of the People, Kliptown, 26 June 1955, http://www.anc.org.za/show.php?id=72 (25/11/09); 'Second National Consultative Conference: Report of the Commission on Foreign Policy, 17 June 1985, Kabwe, Zambia', UFH, Liberation Archives, ANC Lusaka Additions (Mayibuye II), Box 37, File 1, Conference documents and reports.

11. Some examples include: Barrell, Howard, *MK: The ANC's Armed Struggle* (Johannesburg, 1990); Ellis, Stephen and Tsepo Sechaba, *Comrades Against Apartheid: The ANC and the South African Communist Party in Exile* (London, 1992); Ellis, Stephen, 'The ANC in exile', *African Affairs* 90 (1991), pp. 439–47; Kasrils, Ronnie, *Armed and Dangerous: From Undercover Struggle to Freedom* (London, 1998); Legassick, Martin, 'Myth and reality in the struggle against apartheid', *Journal of Southern African Studies* 24 (1998), pp. 443–58; Lissoni, Arianna, 'Transformations in the ANC external mission and Umkhonto we Sizwe, c.1960–9', *Journal of Southern African Studies, Special Issue: Liberation Struggles, Exile and International Solidarity* 35 (2009), pp. 287–301; Lodge, Tom, *Black Politics in South Africa Since 1945* (London, 1987); Marx, *Lessons*; Manghezi, Nadja, *The Maputo Connection: ANC Life in the World of FRELIMO* (Auckland Park, 2009); Mckinley, Dale, *The ANC and the Liberation Struggle: A Critical Political Biography* (London, 1997); Meli, Francis, *A History of the ANC: South Africa Belongs to Us* (Harare, 1988); Morrow, Sean, 'Dakawa Development Centre: an African National Congress settlement in Tanzania, 1982–1992', *African Affairs* 97 (1998), pp. 497–521; Ndlovu, Sifiso, 'The ANC's diplomacy and international relations', in SADET, *The Road to Democracy in South Africa*, vol. 2, 1970–1980 (Pretoria, 2006), pp. 615–67; Ndlovu, Sifiso, 'The ANC in exile, 1960–1970', in SADET, *The Road to Democracy in South Africa*, vol. 1, 1960–1970 (Cape Town, 2004), pp. 411–78; Ndlovu, Sifiso, 'The ANC and the world, 1960–1970', in SADET, *The Road to Democracy in South Africa*, vol. 1, 1960–1970 (Cape Town, 2004), pp. 541–71; Pfister, Roger, 'Gateway to international victory: the diplomacy of the African National Congress in Africa, 1960–1994', *Journal of Modern African Studies* 1 (2003), pp. 51–73; Shubin, Vladimir, *The ANC: a View From Moscow* (Cape Town, 1999); Thomas, Scott, *The Diplomacy of Liberation: the Foreign Relations of the ANC since 1960* (London, 1996); Trewhela, Paul, *Inside Quatro: Uncovering the Exile History of the ANC and SWAPO* (Auckland Park, 2009).

12. Ellis, 'The ANC in Exile', p. 442.
13. Fatton, Robert Jr., 'The African National Congress of South Africa: the limitations of a revolutionary strategy', *Canadian Journal of African Studies* 18 (1984), p. 598.
14. University of Western Cape (hereafter UWC), Mayibuye Centre Historical Papers (hereafter MCH) 70, Survey of the External Mission of the African National Congress of South Africa, February 1965.
15. On 16 December 1961, a series of explosions across South Africa marked the formation of the guerrilla fighting force known as Umkhonto we Sizwe (Spear of the Nation). After Sharpeville there had been a division of opinion within the ANC leadership about the turn to armed struggle, particularly in light of the ANC's historical commitment to non-violence. The result was that MK, a semi-autonomous group, remained separate from the ANC, and contained members from both the ANC and SACP under the leadership of Nelson Mandela and Joe Slovo.
16. Ralinala, Rendani Moses, et al., 'The Wankie and Sipolio Campaigns', in SADET, *The Road to Democracy in South Africa*, vol. 1, 1960–1970 (Cape Town, 2004), pp. 479–540.
17. Houston, Gregory, 'International solidarity: introduction', in SADET, *The Road to Democracy in South Africa*, vol. 3, *International Solidarity* (Pretoria, 2008), p. 35.
18. Thomas, *Diplomacy*, p. 2.
19. Filatova, Irina & Davidson, Apollon, *The Hidden Thread. Russia and South Africa in the Soviet Era* (Cape Town, 2013), p. 236.
20. The countries buffering South Africa from 'black Africa' in 1960 included the annexed territory of South West Africa (Namibia), the British Protectorates of Bechuanaland (Botswana), Basutoland (Lesotho), Nyasaland (Malawi), Southern Rhodesia (Rhodesia), Swaziland, and Northern Rhodesia (Zambia), and the Portuguese colonies of Angola and Mozambique. Although Tanganyika was still officially a British Protectorate until its independence in December 1961, the country was granted internal self-government in 1960, after the Tanganyika African National Union (TANU) had won the 1959 election. Its president, Julius Nyerere, became an active supporter of African independence and he allowed numerous liberation movements to settle in the country, predominantly in Dar es Salaam.
21. The southern African states granted independence during the 1960s were: Tanganyika, 1961; Nyasaland, 1964; Northern Rhodesia, 1964; Bechuanaland, 1966; Basutoland, 1966 and Swaziland, 1968. Southern Rhodesia announced a Unilateral Declaration of Independence (UDI) from Britain in 1965, renaming itself Rhodesia, which kept the country under white minority rule, closely allied to South Africa.
22. Nothling, F. J., 'Co-operation with neighbouring states', in Thomas Wheeler (ed.), *History of the South African Department of Foreign Affairs, 1927–1993* (Johannesburg, 2005), p. 279.

23. Shubin, *Moscow*, pp. 29–30.
24. Karis, Thomas and Gail Gerhart, *From Protest to Challenge*, vol. 5, *Nadir and Resurgence*, 1964–1979 (Bloomington, 1997), p. 6.
25. *The Guardian*, 24 September 1961.
26. Lodge, Shubin and Thomas have argued that Ghana pressurized the ANC and PAC to unite, though Ndlovu refutes this, believing it was less clear-cut. See: Lodge, *Black Politics*, p. 297; Ndlovu, 'The ANC in exile', p. 429; Shubin, *Moscow*, p. 49; Thomas, *Diplomacy*, p. 35.
27. For example see: Tambo, Oliver R., 'Statement on behalf of the South Africa United Front', New York, 20 October 1960, http://www.anc.org.za/show. php?id=4257 (6/2/11); AAM Archive, Mss Afr. S 1681, Box 209, File 2, ANC documents, AB 209/2, Item 11, 'Press Statement by the African National Congress, Pan Africanist Congress and the South African Indian Congress'; Historical Papers Archive, William Cullen Library, Witwatersrand University, ANC AD2186, Box 4, Da9.
28. Cited in Shubin, *Moscow*, p. 50.
29. Davenport, Rodney and Chris Saunders, *South Africa: a Modern History*, 5th edn (Basingstoke, 2000), p. 416.
30. Barber, James and John Barratt, *South Africa's Foreign Policy: the Search for Status and Security, 1945–1998* (Cambridge, 1990), p. 81.
31. *The Guardian*, 16 January 1961.
32. Barber and Barratt, *Foreign Policy*, p. 82; Nothling, F. J., 'South Africa, Great Britain and the Commonwealth', in Wheeler (ed.), *South African Department of Foreign Affairs* (Johannesburg, 2005), pp. 248–51.
33. *The Guardian*, 16 March 1961.
34. AAM Archive, Mss Afr. S 1681, Box 209, File 2, ANC documents, 'South Africa United Front, Newsletter. Press Statement, 16.3.61' (AB 209/2, item 10).
35. Spence, Jack, 'South African foreign policy: the "Outward Movement"', in Christian Potholm and Richard Dale (eds), *Southern Africa in Perspective: Essays in Regional Politics* (New York, 1972), p. 47.
36. Ndlovu, 'The ANC in exile', p. 432; Shubin, *Moscow*, p. 50.
37. Thomas, *Diplomacy*, p. 41.
38. Turok, Ben, *Nothing but the Truth: Behind the ANC's Struggle Politics* (Jeppestown, 2003), p. 199.
39. Slovo, Joe, *Slovo: the Unfinished Autobiography* (Melbourne, 1997), p. 178.
40. Feit, Edward, *Urban Revolt in South Africa, 1960–1964: a Case Study* (Evanston, 1971), p. 232.
41. Ndlovu, 'The ANC in exile', p. 454.
42. Benson, Mary, *Nelson Mandela: the Man and the Movement* (Harmondsworth, 1994), p. 89; Mandela, Nelson, *Long Walk to Freedom* (London, 1995), pp. 321–4; Sampson, Anthony, *Mandela: the Authorised Biography* (London, 2000), pp. 150–2.

43. UFH, Liberation Archives, Oliver Tambo Papers, Box 81, File B 2.3.1, 'Political report of the NEC to the Consultative Conference of the ANC', Morogoro, April 1969.

44. The National Archive (hereafter TNA), 'Commonwealth Relations Office Southern Africa Department', African National Congress (ANC) and Pan-African Congress 1961, Document 38, Discussion about Lutuli's prize, AR.4/9/50, DO 180/6.

45. Mandela, *Long Walk*, p. 338.

46. Mandela, Nelson, 'Address by Nelson Mandela to the Conference of the Pan-African Freedom Movement of East and Central Africa', Addis Ababa, 12 January 1962, http://www.anc.org.za/show.php?id=4297 (7/2/11).

47. Mandela, *Long Walk*, p. 342.

48. Feit, *Urban Revolt*, p. 232.

49. Between January and June 1962, Mandela visited 12 African nations including Egypt, Morocco, Ghana, Nigeria and Sudan. For a full list of countries and map of his trips across the continent, see: Mandela, Nelson, *Conversations with Myself* (Basingstoke, 2010), pp. 418–19.

50. Mandela, *Conversations*, pp. 93–103; Mandela, *Long Walk*, pp. 354–64; Sampson, *Mandela*, pp. 166, 169–70.

51. Turok, *Truth*, p. 124.

52. Johns, 'Obstacles', p. 277.

53. Sampson, *Mandela*, p. 167.

54. Mandela, *Long Walk*, p. 352.

55. Ibid., p. 361.

56. Tandon, Yashpal, 'The Organisation of African Unity and the liberation of Southern Africa', in Potholm and Dale (eds), *Southern Africa in Perspective*, p. 245.

57. Shubin, *Moscow*, pp. 10–53.

58. Filatova, *Thread*, p. 243.

59. Kasrils, *Armed and Dangerous*, pp. 83–92; O'Malley, Padraig, *Shades of Difference: Mac Maharaj and the Struggle for South Africa* (New York, 2007), pp. 88–9.

60. Interview with Joe Matthews cited in Ndlovu, 'The ANC and the world', p. 547.

61. Callinicos, *Tambo*, p. 278.

62. Thomas, *Diplomacy*, p. 42.

63. The notion that the ANC was destroyed internally after Rivonia is the accepted view in the historiography, but this has been dismissed by Raymond Suttner as incorrect. Suttner has argued that the ANC's internal underground was, although quiescent in the late 1960s, still active, and 'despite heavy repression by the state, underground work continued'. The lack of publicity about the ANC's activity in South Africa is because its structures were not uniform across the country, it was difficult to communicate between cells, and

those still operational were understandably kept secret due to the security threat. See: Suttner, *Underground*, pp. 59–83.

64. Callinicos, *Tambo*, p. 307.
65. Shubin, *Moscow*, p. 70.
66. Turok, *Truth*, pp. 202–11.
67. Hugh Macmillan, 'The African National Congress of South Africa in Zambia: the culture of exile and the changing relationship with home, 1964–1990', *Journal of Southern African Studies* 35 (2009), p. 308.
68. Tandon, 'Organisation of African Unity', p. 250.
69. 'Review of the State of Organisation of the Liberation Movement', 1966, http://www.disa.ukzn.ac.za/index.php?option=com_displaydc&recordID=mem19660000.032.009.013 (4/5/11).
70. Ralinala et al., 'Wankie', p. 483.
71. The suppression of ANC dissenters was also in the interest of the host governments, as they did not want such actions to act as inspiration to their own populations, and neither did they want bands of armed fighters at loose within their territories.
72. FRELIMO had begun its independence war in September 1964: Cabrita, Joao, *Mozambique: the Tortuous Road to Democracy* (Basingstoke, 2000), p. 29.
73. 'ANC-ZAPU alliance', *Sechaba* 1/10 (October, 1967), p. 3.
74. *Morning Star*, 23 November 1967, cited in Ralinala et al., 'Wankie', p. 488.
75. The 'Ho Chi Minh Trail' was an intricate system of support, weaving through several countries, which acted as a strategic supply route for the North Vietnamese guerrillas during the Vietnam War. The ANC and ZAPU sought to recreate this in Rhodesia.
76. 'Victory or Death', *Dawn Souvenir Issue* (December 1986), pp. 2–3.
77. For an alternative view on the Wankie Campaign, see: Flower, Ken, *Serving Secretly: Rhodesia's CIO Chief on Record* (London, 1987).
78. 'ANC-ZAPU alliance', p. 3.
79. Johns, 'Obstacles', p. 283.
80. 'The Wankie Campaign', *Dawn Souvenir Issue* (December 1986), p. 37.
81. Barber and Barratt, *Foreign Policy*, p. 141.
82. Turok, *Truth*, p. 223.
83. Resha, Robert, 'Statement by Robert Resha, member of the National Executive Committee of the ANC before the Special Committee against Apartheid', 18 March 1969, http://www.anc.org.za/show.php?id=4781 (15/2/11).
84. Permanent Secretariat of the Afro-Asian Peoples' Solidarity Organisation, 'International Conference in Support of the Peoples' of Portuguese Colonies and Southern Africa, Khartoum, 18–20 January 1969', Cairo, 1970.
85. Permanent Secretariat of the Afro-Asian Peoples' Solidarity Organisation, 'International Conference', pp. 52–76.
86. Ibid., pp. 37–45; 'The Khartoum Conference', *Sechaba* 3/3 (March 1969), p. 3.

87. Thomas, *Diplomacy*, pp. 21–2.
88. TNA/FCO 45/69, Commonwealth Office and Foreign and Commonwealth Office, Liberation Movements 1968 Document 8 – Khartoum Conference, January 1969.
89. Hugh Macmillan, 'The "Hani Memorandum" – introduced and annotated', *Transformation: Critical Perspectives on Southern Africa* 69 (2009), pp. 107–9.
90. Ibid., pp. 107–9.
91. Full Hani Memorandum cited in ibid., pp. 114–21.
92. Shubin, *Moscow*, p. 87.
93. *Mayibuye* 10 (May 1969), p. 2.
94. 'Close Ranks!' *Sechaba* 7 (July 1969), p. 2.
95. Document 13, 'What is Wrong?' Memorandum by Ben Turok before the ANC's Morogoro Conference, April 1969, in Karis and Gerhart, *Nadir*, pp. 383–7.
96. 'Close Ranks!', p. 2.
97. 'Strategy and Tactics of the ANC', adopted by the Morogoro Conference of the ANC, Tanzania, 25 April – 1 May 1969, http://www.ancyl.org.za/docs/political/1969/Morogoro%20Strategy%20and%20Tacticsg.pdf (16/2/11).
98. Ibid.
99. Ibid.
100. An agreement amongst the former Congress alliance in 1960 had ensured that the ANC would be the only one represented abroad. The decision left the allied Indians, Coloureds and whites in exile without official organizational representation.
101. 'Strategy and Tactics of the ANC'.
102. Thomas, *Diplomacy*, p. 53.
103. Johns, 'Obstacles', p. 287.
104. Shubin, *Moscow*, pp. 91–2.
105. 'Close Ranks!', p. 2.
106. Ibid., p. 3; 'Extracts from the Political Report of the National Executive Committee of the African National Congress', April 1969, http://www.anc.org.za/show.php?id=143 (16/2/11).
107. *The Lusaka Manifesto*, http://www.anc.org.za/show.php?id=4836&t=Organisation+of + African + Unity (16/2/11).
108. Ibid.
109. Ibid.
110. 'A disturbing Manifesto', *African Communist* 40 (1970), p. 9. The remark about the 14 states denotes independent African countries that had signed the Lusaka Manifesto.
111. Ibid., p. 10.
112. Ibid., p. 8.
113. Karis and Gerhart, *Nadir*, p. 35.
114. The processes of Dialogue and Détente should not be confused as these were two separate attempts by South Africa to break its isolation on the continent.

Pretoria's initial efforts, primarily focused on economic links, were labelled as Dialogue, and were relatively well received by conservative governments such as the Ivory Coast and Malawi. After Dialogue publicly broke down at the OAU meeting in June 1971, overt efforts at wooing Africa ceased. However, Vorster was not deterred, and his efforts to initiate an 'outward policy' was renewed in 1974, when he offered Africa 'the way of peace'; the ensuing attempts became known as Détente.

115. Records of the Africa Bureau and related organizations, Bodleian Library of Commonwealth and African Studies, University of Oxford, MSS Afr. S 1681, Box 70, File 8, ff. 1–29, AB 70/8 Item 1, The Simonstown Agreements 1970, Christie, M. J., *The Simonstown Agreements: Britain's Defence and the Sale of Arms to South Africa*, published by The Africa Bureau, Sept. 1970 (pamphlet).

116. Quoted in: 'Dialogue – South Africa's Imperialist Mask', *Sechaba* 5/8 (August 1971), p. 3.

117. Ndlovu, 'The ANC and the world', p. 566.

118. Karis and Gerhart, *Nadir*, p. 7.

119. Macmillan, 'The African National Congress of South Africa in Zambia', p. 313.

120. Ellis and Sechaba, *Comrades*, p. 59.

121. Shubin, *Moscow*, p. 99.

122. Ibid., p. 99.

123. 'Dialogue: the viewpoint of the people of South Africa', *Sechaba* 5/10 (October 1971), p. 4.

124. For example, Tambo wrote a letter to the Mauritius government criticizing its foreign policy towards South Africa; the response from the prime minister was terse and concise, arguing that although the government was behind the ANC, it was still going to trade with South Africa. 'Mauritius Collaboration', *Sechaba* 5/1 (January 1971), p. 7; and 'Dialogue is Betrayal', *Sechaba* 5/7 (July, 1971), p. 7.

125. Cited in Turok, *Truth*, p. 230.

126. 'Banda's Treachery', *Sechaba* 1/5 (May, 1967), p. i.

127. 'Banda belly-crawls to Vorster', *Sechaba* 5/10 (October, 1971), p. 2.

128. Cited in Barratt, John, 'South Africa's outward policy: From isolation to Dialogue', in N. J. Rhoodie (ed.), *South African Dialogue: Contrasts in South African Thinking on Basic Race Issues* (Johannesburg, 1972), p. 554.

129. Ibid., p. 554.

130. It must be noted that the vast majority of African governments did not publicize their links to South Africa during this period. Although a number of conservative countries such as Malawi did openly express their ties with Pretoria, most southern African nations, including the closest allies of the ANC, kept their links with the apartheid regime secret.

131. Ndlovu, 'The ANC's diplomacy', p. 619.

132. 'Beware the temptor', *Sechaba* 5/1 (January, 1971), pp. 2–3.

133. Ibid., pp. 2–3; 'Dialogue is betrayal', p. 2; 'The battle for the middle ground', *Sechaba* 5/7 (July 1971), pp. 9–13.
134. Ibid., p. 3.
135. 'OAU declaration on Dialogue', *Sechaba* 5/10 (October 1971), p. 5.
136. Ibid., p. 5.
137. Hirschmann, David, 'Southern Africa: Détente?', *The Journal of Modern African Studies* 14 (1976), p. 107; Spence, Jack, 'Detente in Southern Africa: An Interim Judgment', *International Affairs* 53 (1977), p. 1.
138. Houston, 'International solidarity: introduction', p. 33.
139. Pfister, 'Gateway', p. 63.
140. Karis and Gerhart, *Nadir*, p. 52; Shubin, *Moscow*, pp. 101–2; Suttner, *Underground*, pp. 68–70. For more information on Radio Freedom in the struggle, see Davis, Stephen, 'The African National Congress, its radio, its allies and exile', *Journal of Southern African Studies* 35 (2009), pp. 349–73.
141. Suttner, *Underground*, pp. 65–6.
142. 'The second stage: attempts to get back', *Dawn Souvenir Issue* (December 1986), p. 33.
143. Joe Matthews interview cited in, Karis and Gerhart, *Nadir*, p. 51.
144. Ibid., p. 51.
145. Shubin, *Moscow*, p. 104.
146. 'The second stage', p. 34.
147. Ibid., p. 34; 'The adventurer episode', *Dawn Souvenir Issue* (December 1986), p. 44.
148. Ibid., p. 34.
149. Ellis and Sechaba, *Comrades*, p. 64.
150. 'Conspirators Expelled', *Sechaba*, 10 (April 1976), p. 40.
151. Karis and Gerhart, *Nadir*, p. 55.
152. Bruneau, Thomas. 'The Portuguese coup: causes and probable consequences', *The World Today* 30 (1974), p. 277.
153. For more information about the Angolan Civil War, the different protagonists, and its consequences see: Baines, Gary and Peter Vale (eds), *Beyond the Border War: New Perspectives on Southern Africa's Late-Cold War Conflicts* (Pretoria, 2008); Crocker, Chester, *High Noon in Southern Africa: Making Peace in a Rough Neighbourhood* (New York, 1992); Davis, Nathaniel, 'The Angola Decision of 1975: a personal memoir', *Foreign Affairs* 57 (1978), pp. 109–24; Gleijeses, Piero, *Conflicting Missions* (London, 2002); Graham, Matthew, 'Covert collusion? American and South African relations in the Angolan Civil War, 1974–1976', *African Historical Review* 43 (2011), pp. 28–47; Guimaraes, Fernando, *The Origins of the Angolan Civil War* (Basingstoke, 2001); Marcum, John, *The Angolan Revolution*, vol. 2, *Exile Politics and Guerrilla Warfare (1962–1976)* (Cambridge, 1978); Steenkamp, Willem, *South African Border Wars: 1966–1989* (Gibraltar, 1989); Stockwell, John, *In Search of Enemies* (London, 1979).

154. AAM Archive, MSS. Afr. S 2151 2/2, pp. 683–921, 'Interview with Ivan Pillay, conducted by Howard Barrell, 20 and 23 July 1989, Lusaka', pp. 776–7.

155. Ellis and Sechaba, *Comrades*, pp. 70–4.

156. Barber, *South Africa*, p. 212.

157. Anthony Marx describes claims of ANC involvement in Soweto as being greatly exaggerated and that 'those who see increased ANC involvement are based on a strong dose of retrospective wishful thinking or pro-ANC bias': Marx, *Lessons of Struggle,* pp. 67–8.

158. Barber, *South Africa*, p. 215; Davis, *Rebels*, pp. 28–9; Marx, *Lessons of Struggle,* pp. 67–8.

159. AAM Archive, MSS AFR. S. 2151 1/2, pp. 151–334, 'First Interview with Ronnie Kasrils, Conducted by Howard Barrell, Lusaka, August 19 1989', p. 250.

160. Cited in Ellis and Sechaba, *Comrades*, p. 83.

161. Tambo, O., 'Political Report by Oliver Tambo on the National Executive Committee to the National Consultative Conference of the African National Congress', 17 June 1985, Kabwe, Zambia, http://www.anc.org.za/4464 (3/3/11).

162. 'ANC report to the OAU Liberation Committee', *Sechaba* 11 (July, 1977), p. 3.

163. Interview with Pallo Jordan, cited in Ndlovu, 'The ANC's diplomacy', p. 638.

164. Lodge, *Black Politics*, p. 339.

165. Marx, *Lessons of Struggle*, p. 93.

166. Thomas, *Diplomacy*, p. 234.

Chapter 3   From Exile to Liberation, 1976–90

1. It was not until the elections of Margaret Thatcher in Britain (1979) and Ronald Reagan in the USA (1981) that Western governments became more openly hostile towards the ANC. Previously the Jimmy Carter administration and the British Labour government in the 1970s had been far more sympathetic to African liberation.

2. Cited in Nadja Manghezi, *The Maputo Connection: ANC Life in the World of FRELIMO* (Auckland Park, 2009), p. vi.

3. Kasrils, Ronnie, *Armed and Dangerous: from Undercover Struggle to Freedom* (London, 1998), pp. 181–2.

4. Macmillan, Hugh, 'The African National Congress of South Africa in Zambia: the culture of exile and the changing relationship with home, 1964–1990', *Journal of Southern African Studies* 35 (2009), p. 317.

5. Ibid., pp. 317–19.

6. Shubin, Vladimir, *The ANC: a View from Moscow* (Cape Town, 1999), pp. 165–6.

7. Meli, Francis, *A History of the ANC: South Africa Belongs to Us* (Harare, 1988), p. 189; Shubin, *Moscow*, p. 179; Tambo, O., 'Political Report by Oliver Tambo on the National Executive Committee to the National Consultative

Conference of the African National Congress', 17 June 1985, Kabwe, Zambia, http://www.anc.org.za/4464 (3/3/11).

8. 'Lesotho's struggle to safeguard independence', *African Communist*, 102 (1985), p. 60.

9. Ibid., p. 61.

10. Shubin, *Moscow*, p. 208.

11. Sifiso, Ndlovu, 'The ANC's diplomacy and international relations', in SADET, *The Road to Democracy in South Africa*, vol. 2, 1970–1980 (Pretoria, 2006), p. 658.

12. After temporarily withdrawing from Angola by March 1976 after its involvement in the Civil War, South Africa renewed its offensive against the MPLA. For example, the ANC camp at Novo Catengue was bombed by the South African air force. For a first-hand account see: Document 111, 'Diary of Jack Simons at Novo Catengue camp, Angola, January–March 1979 (abridged)', in Karis, Thomas and Gail Gerhart (eds), *From Protest to Challenge*, vol. 5, *Nadir and Resurgence, 1964–1979* (Bloomington, 1997), pp. 707–15.

13. Ndlovu, 'The ANC's diplomacy', pp. 658–9.

14. Shubin, *Moscow*, pp. 196–8.

15. Email correspondence with Dr Gary Littlejohn, 24 June 2011.

16. Manghezi, *The Maputo Connection*, pp. 78–9.

17. Ibid., p. 81.

18. Ibid., p. 81.

19. Ellis, Stephen and Tsepo Sechaba, *Comrades Against Apartheid: The ANC and the South African Communist Party in Exile* (London, 1992), p. 100.

20. 'The battle for South Africa is on!', *Dawn* 2 (December 1979), pp. 15–20.

21. McKinley, Dale, *The ANC and the Liberation Struggle: A Critical Political Biography* (London, 1997), p. 49.

22. 'The Year of the Spear', *Sechaba* 13 (April, 1979), p. 1.

23. 'The National Executive Council meeting', *Sechaba* 12 (January, 1978), p. 1.

24. Document 108, 'Report on meeting of the ANC National Executive Committee, Morogoro, 15–24 July 1977 (abridged)', in Karis and Gerhart (eds), *Nadir*, pp. 696–701.

25. 'The National Executive Council meeting', p. 1.

26. Barber, James, *South Africa in the Twentieth Century, a Political History: in Search of a Nation State* (Oxford, 1999), p. 217; 'Year against apartheid', *Sechaba* 13 (June, 1979), pp. 21–3; The 1978 UN Declaration against Apartheid, http://domino.un.org/UNISPAL.NSF/db942872b9eae454852560f6005a76fb/d7340f04b82a2cb085256a9d006ba47a (3/3/11).

27. 'Honecker meets Tambo', *Sechaba* 13 (May, 1979), pp. 12–13; 'Statement by Comrade Oliver Tambo', *Sechaba* 13 (December, 1979), pp. 12–19.

28. Oliver Tambo, 'Political report by Oliver Tambo, 17 June 1985; AAM Archive, Bodleian Library of Commonwealth and African Studies, University of Oxford, MSS Afr. S. 2151 2/3, pp. 922–1063, 'First interview with Joe Slovo, Conducted by Howard Barrell, 12–16 August 1989, Lusaka', p. 982.

29. Jeffery, Anthea, *People's War: New Light on the Struggle for South Africa* (Johannesburg, 2009), p. 52.

30. For more on armed propaganda see: Houston, Gregory and Bernard Magubane, 'The ANC political underground in the 1970s', in SADET, *The Road to Democracy in South Africa*, vol. 2, 1970–1980 (Pretoria, 2006), p. 413.

31. Gerhart, Gail and Clive Glaser (eds), *From Protest to Challenge*, vol. 6, *Challenge and Victory, 1980–1990* (Bloomington, 2010), pp. 54–5, 67, 129–30; Jeffery, *People's War*, pp. 64–5.

32. This is questioned by Anthea Jeffery who argues that the formation of the UDF 'was carefully planned and then pushed and prodded into existence' by the ANC. Furthermore, 'the ANC welcomed the UDF's formation and claimed this as its most important achievement since 1961'. See: Jeffery, *People's War*, p. 61.

33. Gerhart and Glaser, *Challenge*, p. 120.

34. 'The fires of freedom', *Sechaba* 14 (August 1980), p. 1.

35. The Report of the Study Commission on US Policy toward Southern Africa, *South Africa: Time Running Out* (Berkley, 1981), p. 140.

36. 'Ball of fire', *Sechaba* 15 (October 1981), p. 12; 'Koeberg – power house for war', *Sechaba* 17 (February 1983), p. 20; *The Guardian*, 22 and 23 May 1983.

37. *The Guardian*, 6 August 1983.

38. Lodge, Tom, 'State of exile: the African National Congress of South Africa, 1976–86', in Frankel, Philip, Noam Pines and Mark Swilling (eds), *State, Resistance and Change in South Africa* (London, 1988), p. 230.

39. AAM Archive, MSS Afr. S. 2151 1/2, pp. 151–334, 'Interview with Pallo Jordan, conducted by Howard Barrell, Lusaka, 4 July 1989', p. 233.

40. Ibid. 2/2, pp. 683–921, 'First interview with Sue Rabkin, conducted by Howard Barrell, 7, 9 July and 16 August 1989, Lusaka', pp. 809–10.

41. For example, the ANC named its school in Morogoro, Tanzania, after the executed MK combatant Solomon Mahlangu.

42. AAM Archive, MSS. Afr. S 2151 2/2, pp. 683–921, 'Interview with Ivan Pillay, conducted by Howard Barrell, 20 and 23 July 1989, Lusaka', p. 773.

43. See: Historical Papers, University of Witwatersrand. Karis-Gerhart Collection, Folder 36, Part I. Howard Barrell interview with Garth Strachan, 28 December 1990, pp. 1, 199–200, 1,204, cited in Thula Simpson, 'Toyi-Toying to freedom: the endgame in the ANC's armed struggle, 1989–1990', *Journal of Southern African Studies* 35 (2009), p. 509.

44. AAM Archive, MSS Afr. S. 2151 1/3, pp. 335–535, 'Third interview with Mac Maharaj, conducted by Howard Barrell, Johannesburg, 30 November 1990', pp. 499–501.

45. Hanlon, Joseph, *Beggar your Neighbours: Apartheid Power in Southern Africa* (London, 1986), p. 7.

46. The Bantustans or Homelands were ten areas within South Africa, set aside for the separate development of Africans. The four territories granted

'independence', were the Transkei, Bophuthatswana, Venda, and Ciskei (sometimes referred to as the TBVC states).

47. AAM Archive, MSS AAM 932, ANC combatants and prisoner of war status, 'Armed Resistance in South Africa', by Reddy, E. S., Director, UN Centre against Apartheid, 6 February 1980, p. 4; Davies, Robert and Dan O'Meara, 'Total strategy in Southern Africa: an analysis of South African regional policy since 1978', *Journal of Southern African Studies* 11 (1985), pp. 189–91; Hanlon, *Beggar,* pp. 14–15.

48. Amin, Samir, Derrick Chitala and Ibbo Mandaza (eds), *SADCC: Prospects for Disengagement and Development in Southern Africa* (London, 1987), pp. 8–9.

49. Ibid., pp. 9–10.

50. AAM Archive, MSS AAM 1027, Gifford, Tony, *Memorandum and Leaflets, South Africa's Record of International Terrorism* (SWAM/AAM Publication, London, 1981), p. 3.

51. 'SA declares war on Africa', *African Communist* 85 (second quarter, 1981), pp. 5–6; 'Apartheid murder in Matola', *Sechaba* 15 (March 1981), p. 1.

52. Ibid., pp. 5–6.

53. 'Racist South Africa invades Lesotho', *Sechaba* 17 (January 1983), pp. 4–7; 'The force of people power' and 'Victims of the Maseru Massacre', *Sechaba* 17 (February 1983), pp. 1–5.

54. Hanlon, *Beggar*, p. 113.

55. Barber and Barratt, *Foreign Policy*, p. 315; *The Guardian*, 15 June 1985.

56. Gerhart and Glaser, *Challenge*, p. 131; 'Obituary: Comrade Ruth First', *Sechaba* 16 (October 1982), pp. 24–8.

57. Stiff, Peter, *Warfare by Other Means: South Africa in the 1980s and 1990s* (Alberton, 2001), p. 117–18.

58. Jaster, Robert, 'Evolution of a regional conflict in "war and diplomacy"', in Robert Jaster (ed.), *Changing Fortunes: War, Diplomacy, and Economics in Southern Africa* (New York, 1992), p. 30; Shubin, *Moscow*, p. 231.

59. For more information on RENAMO and UNITA see: Bridgland, Fred, *Jonas Savimbi: a Key to Africa* (Edinburgh, 1986); Brittain, Victoria, *The Death of Dignity: Angola's Civil War* (London, 1998); Cabrita, Joao, *Mozambique: the Tortuous Road to Democracy* (Basingstoke, 2000); Minter, William, *Apartheid's Contras: an Inquiry into the Roots of War in Angola and Mozambique* (London, 1994).

60. Barber and Barratt, *Foreign Policy*, p. 318; Ellis and Sechaba, *Comrades*, pp. 165–8.

61. 'Third interview with Mac Maharaj, Conducted by Howard Barrell, Johannesburg, 30 November 1990', p. 456.

62. Gevisser, Mark, *Thabo Mbeki: the Dream Deferred* (Johannesburg, 2007), p. 488.

63. Macmillan, 'The African National Congress of South Africa in Zambia', p. 318.

64. For example see: 'Minutes of a meeting between President Kenneth Kaunda and South African Representatives, Lusaka, 25 June 1984', http://www.disa.

ukzn.ac.za/index.php?option=com_displaydc&recordID=min19840625. 035.017.d1.18a; 'Meetings between Dr Kenneth Kaunda, President of Zambia, and Ministers R. F. Botha, General M. A. de M. Malan and the Administrator General Dr W. A. van Niekerk, April 1984', http://www.disa. ukzn.ac.za/index.php?option=com_displaydc&recordID=min19840425. 035.017.d1.18.

65. AAM Archive, MSS AAM 1044, Background, Martin, Roger, 'Southern Africa: the price of apartheid. A political risk analysis', The Economist Intelligence Unit, Special Report No. 1130, July 1988', pp. 45–6; Larmer, Rethinking.

66. Macmillan, 'The African National Congress of South Africa in Zambia', p. 325.

67. Ellis and Sechaba, Comrades, pp. 129–31; Lodge, 'State of exile', p. 235; Amnesty International, 'South Africa: Torture, Ill-treatment and Executions in African National Congress Camps' (December 1992), http://www.amnesty. org/en/library/asset/AFR53/027/1992/en/fba1e35c-ed9a-11dd-9ad7–350 fb2522bdb/afr530271992en.html (2/4/11).

68. Ibid., (December 1992).

69. Ketelo, Bandile, Amos Maxongo, Zamxolo Tshona, Ronnie Masango and Luvo Mbengo, 'A miscarriage of democracy: The ANC Security Department in the 1984 Mutiny in Umkhonto we Sizwe', in Paul Trewhela (ed.), Inside Quatro: Uncovering the Exile History of the ANC and SWAPO (Auckland Park, 2009), p. 8.

70. Amnesty International, 'South Africa: Torture, Ill-treatment and Executions'.

71. Ketelo, Maxongo, Tshona, Masango and Mbengo, 'A miscarriage', pp. 22–3.

72. Ibid., p. 37.

73. Telephone interview with Ann Grant, former Consul and Head of Chancery at the British Embassy in Maputo, Mozambique (1981–4) and British High Commissioner to South Africa (2000–5), 7 December 2009.

74. For example see: 'We are ready to accept the challenge', Sechaba 15 (April, 1981), pp. 21–3; Institute of Commonwealth Studies (ICS), PP.SA.ANC.56, 'Hands off Mozambique'; ICS, PP.SA.ANC.259, 'Statement by comrade Oliver Tambo at a mass rally, Bairro de Liberdade, Maputo, 14 February 1982'.

75. 'First interview with Sue Rabkin, pp. 857–8.

76. Interview with Professor Deon Geldenhuys, Johannesburg, 29 March 2010.

77. Hanlon, Joseph, Mozambique: the Revolution Under Fire (London, 1990), p. 257; Email correspondence with Dr Gary Littlejohn, 24 June 2011; Manghezi, The Maputo Connection, pp. 3–5; Shubin, Moscow, p. 256–7; The Guardian, 6 April 1984.

78. 'First interview with Sue Rabkin, p. 857.

79. Gevisser, Dream Deferred, pp. 431–3.

80. Ellis and Sechaba, Comrades, p. 104.

81. Gevisser, Dream Deferred, p. 437.

82. Ibid., p. 437.

83. The Guardian, 6 April 1984.

84. Davis, Stephen, *Apartheid's Rebels: Inside South Africa's Hidden War* (New Haven, 1987), p. 68; UFH, Liberation Archives, ANC Zimbabwe Mission, Zimbabwe Additions, Box 4, Folder 34, Correspondence and statements on raid of ANC offices Harare, 1986.
85. Interview with Professor Deon Geldenhuys, Johannesburg, 29 March 2010.
86. Davis, *Rebels*, p. 127; Martin, Roger, 'Southern Africa: the price of apartheid, pp. 42–3.
87. UFH, Liberation Archives, ANC Lusaka Mission 1923–96, Box 149, Folder 44, Statements Kwanhgwane, Ingwauuma 1982.
88. Kasrils, *Armed and Dangerous*, p. 201.
89. *The Economist*, 21 January 1982, pp. 6–7.
90. UFH, Liberation Archives, ANC Lusaka Mission 1923–96, Box 136, Folder 303, Swaziland-SA land deal 1982–3.
91. Martin, Roger, 'Southern Africa: the price of apartheid. A political risk analysis', p. 40.
92. UFH, Liberation Archives, ANC Senegal Mission, Box 1, Folder 2 – ANC Campaigns 1986–9.
93. Ellis and Sechaba, *Comrades*, pp. 199–120; Hanlon, *Beggar*, p. 111; Kasrils, *Armed and Dangerous*, p. 200; *The Guardian*, 3 July 1984.
94. Email correspondence with E. S. Reddy, 9 November–1 December 2010.
95. For example, see: UFH, Liberation Archives, ANC Lusaka Mission 1923–96, Box 136, Folder 303, Swaziland-SA land deal 1982–3; AAM Archive, MSS AAM 946, Miscellaneous Papers, 'Memorandum to the Government of Swaziland on the Agreement between Swaziland and the Pretoria regime on Ka-Ngwane and Ngwavuma'.
96. 'Memorandum to the Government of Swaziland', p. 5.
97. 'Third interview with Mac Maharaj', p. 496.
98. Email correspondence with E. S. Reddy, 9 November–1 December 2010.
99. UFH, Liberation Archives, ANC Zimbabwe Mission, Box 9, Folder 64, SA-Mozambican Relationship 1984.
100. *The Guardian*, 6 April 1984.
101. Shubin, *Moscow*, p. 254.
102. AAM Archive, Mss Afr. S. 2151 2/3, pp. 922–1063, 'First interview with Joe Slovo, conducted by Howard Barrell, 12–16 August 1989, Lusaka', pp. 999–1000.
103. Manghezi, *The Maputo Connection*, pp. 2–3
104. Hanlon, *Revolution*, p. 261.
105. 'Obituary: Hamba Kahle Comrade Moses Mabhida', *Sechaba* 20 (May 1986), p. 27.
106. Shubin, *Moscow*, p. 260.
107. Manghezi, *The Maputo Connection*, p. 206.
108. Gerhart and Glaser, *Challenge*, p. 136; For examples of documents see: UFH, Liberation Archives, ANC Lusaka and London, ANC Lusaka Additions (Mayibuye II), Box 32, Folder 1, Contributions ANC units, discussion papers.

109. Shubin, *Moscow*, p. 279.
110. 'We are revolutionaries, internationalists and Africans', *Sechaba* 19 (August 1985), p. 1.
111. Callinicos, *Tambo*, pp. 552–4; 'We are revolutionaries', pp. 1–3.
112. UFH, Liberation Archives, ANC Lusaka and London, ANC Lusaka Additions (Mayibuye II), Box 38, Folder 1, ANC National Consultative Conference 1985, 'NEC (Secretary General's) Report'; 'We are revolutionaries', pp. 1–3.
113. Ibid., p. 2.
114. UFH, Liberation Archives, ANC Lusaka and London, ANC Lusaka Additions (Mayibuye II), Box 38, Folder 3 (b), ANC National Consultative Conference 1985, 'International Situation'.
115. AAM Archive, MSS AAM 948, Miscellaneous ANC, 'African National Congress National Consultative Conference June 1985: Report of the Commission on Foreign Policy'.
116. A noteworthy feature is that the title of the 'Report of the Commission on Foreign Policy' points to the ANC publicly considering itself to have a foreign policy. What is most surprising is that the current literature on the topic neglects to acknowledge this point.
117. 'African National Congress National Consultative Conference June 1985: Report of the Commission on Foreign Policy'.
118. Ibid.
119. Ibid.
120. Barrell, Howard, 'Conscripts to their age: African National Congress operational strategy, 1976–1986', D. Phil. (University of Oxford, 1993), p. 384.
121. ANC NEC 1985, 'Take the struggle to the white areas: make the whole of South Africa ungovernable! Paralyse apartheid!', http://www.anc.org.za/show.php?id=4677 (24/3/11); Gevisser, *Dream Deferred*, p. 505; Jeffery, *People's War*, pp. 97–99; Meli, *South Africa*, pp. 192–3; Suttner, *Underground*, pp. 152–3.
122. de Klerk, F. W., *The Last Trek: a New Beginning. The Autobiography* (London, 1999), p. 105.
123. *The Guardian*, 16 August 1985.
124. Ibid., 17 August 1985; *The Guardian*, 10 September 1985; 'Pik Botha reacts to UK Sanctions decision', *Johannesburg Domestic Service* (accessed via Foreign Broadcast Information Service (FBIS) Daily Reports), 25 September 1985.
125. Sampson, Anthony, *Black and Gold: Tycoons, Revolutionaries and Apartheid* (London, 1987), pp. 25, 29–30.
126. Ibid., pp. 23–5.
127. *The Guardian*, 14 September 1985.
128. UFH, Liberation Archives, ANC Lusaka Mission 1923–96, Box 148, Folder 27, Discussions between ANC and SA big business 1985.
129. Sampson, *Black and Gold*, p. 195.
130. Ibid., pp. 198–200.

131. Shubin, *Moscow*, p. 296; *The Telegraph*, 16 May 2010.

132. ICS, JQ2026 AFR fol., 'The Dakar declaration', 12 July 1987.

133. Ibid.

134. 'Apartheid nervousness over the Dakar meeting', *Sechaba* 21 (September, 1987), p. 1.

135. Document 136, 'A few points on the current state of the struggle in SA', ANC intelligence report, mid-1987, in Gerhart and Glaser, *Challenge*, p. 608.

136. For example see: 'Omelettes cannot be made without breaking eggs', *Sechaba* 23 (June 1989), pp. 11–18.

137. Gerhart and Glaser, *Challenge*, p. 147; Gevisser, *Dream Deferred*, pp. 526–54.

138. Simpson, 'Toyi-Toyi-ing', p. 512.

139. Political report by Oliver Tambo on the National Executive Committee to the National Consultative Conference of the African National Congress, 17 June 1985, Kabwe, Zambia, http://www.anc.org.za/show.php?id=4464 (3/4/11).

140. Gevisser, *Dream Deferred*, p. 531.

141. Mandela, Nelson, *Long Walk to Freedom* (London, 1995), pp. 625–7, 633–65.

142. Crocker, Chester, *High Noon in Southern Africa: Making Peace in a Rough Neighbourhood* (New York, 1992), pp. 67–70; Saunders, Chris, 'The Angola/Namibia crisis of 1988 and its resolution', in Sue Onslow (ed.), *Cold War in Southern Africa: White Power, Black Nationalism* (Abingdon, 2009), p. 227.

143. Crocker, *High Noon*, pp. 392–400.

144. *The Observer*, 19 November 1989; 'Simple Majority Celebrated', *Johannesburg SAPA* (accessed via FBIS Daily Reports), 14 November 1989.

145. Crocker, *High Noon*, pp. 407, 441–2.

146. Shubin, *Moscow*, p. 350; Simpson, 'Toyi-Toyi-ing, p. 508.

147. Ibid., p. 508–9.

148. Ibid., p. 509.

149. *The Independent*, 19 August 1989.

150. Simpson, 'Toyi-Toyi-ing', p. 511.

151. Political report by Oliver Tambo, 17 June 1985.

152. UFH, Liberation Archives, ANC Lusaka Mission 1923–96, Box 9, Folder 33, Negotiations, 1989–91.

153. Ibid., ANC Dar es Salaam Office, Box 20, File: Declarations 1969, 1989.

154. Ibid.

155. *The Guardian*, 11 October 1989.

156. Jeffery, *People's War*, p. 233; *The Guardian*, 17 October 1989.

157. Although finding peaceful, negotiated solutions to regional conflicts was the preferred option of the Soviet Union, Gorbachev's announcement did not start an immediate reappraisal of its relations with the ANC, and it continued to provide the movement with substantial assistance in a variety of fields throughout the 1980s. For example, the Soviet Union airlifted MK cadres from Angola as late as 1989 and, more significantly, had played a part in the planning for 'Operation Vula', the ANC's attempt to strengthen the

underground in South Africa through the infiltration of guerrilla fighters. For more on Operation Vula see: O'Malley, Padraig, *Shades of Difference: Mac Maharaj and the Struggle for South Africa* (New York, 2007), pp. 247–99; Shubin, *Moscow*, pp. 332–9.

158. Shubin, Vladimir, 'The Soviet Union/Russian Federation's relations with South Africa, with special reference to the period since 1980', *African Affairs* 95 (1996), p. 19.

159. Ibid., pp. 20–30.

160. Onslow, Sue, 'The fall of the Berlin Wall and the end of apartheid', *IDEAS Today* 1 (2009), p. 19; Interview with Tom Wheeler, Johannesburg, 31 March 2010.

161. 'Statement of the National Executive Committee on the occasion of the 78th Anniversary of the ANC', http://www.anc.org.za/show.php?id=71 (28/3/11).

Chapter 4   ANC Foreign Policy during South Africa's Transition: the Search for Direction, 1990–4

1. Elements of this chapter were previously published as 'Foreign policy in transition: the ANC's search for a foreign policy direction during South Africa's transition, 1990–1994', *The Round Table Journal* 101 (2012), pp. 1–19. Bush, President G. H. W., Address before the Joint Session of Congress on the End of the Gulf War, 6 March 1991.

2. Barber, James, *Mandela's World* (Oxford, 2004), p. 44.

3. du Pisani, Andre, 'Post-apartheid South Africa and the region in the 1990's', paper prepared for BISA Annual Conference, University of Newcastle-upon-Tyne, 17–19 December 1990, pp. 4–6.

4. Lodge, Tom, *Mandela: A Critical Life* (Oxford, 2006), p. 158; Mandela, Nelson, *Long Walk to Freedom* (London, 1995), pp. 625–65; Sampson, Anthony, *Black and Gold: Tycoons, Revolutionaries and Apartheid* (London, 1987), pp. 195–200; Saunders, Chris, 'The Angolan/Namibian crisis of 1988 and its resolution', in Sue Onslow (ed.), *Cold War in Southern Africa: White Power, Black Liberation* (Abingdon, 2009), pp. 234–5.

5. Mr de Klerk's speech at the opening of the South African Parliament, 2 February 1990, http://www.info.gov.za/speeches/1996/101348690.htm (18/11/09).

6. Ibid. (18/11/09).

7. Mandela, Long Walk, pp. 666–7.

8. 'The Groote Shuur Minute', http://www.sahistory.org.za/pages/governence-projects/constitution/doc17-groote-schuur.htm (2/6/11).

9. 'The Pretoria Minute', http://www.sahistory.org.za/pages/governence-projects/constitution/doc18-pta-minute.htm (2/6/11).

10. Examples include: Bond, Patrick, *Elite Transition: from Apartheid to Neoliberalism in South Africa* (London, 2000); Adam, Heribert and Kogila Moodley, *The Negotiated Revolution: Society and Politics in Post-Apartheid South*

Africa (Johannesburg, 1993); Friedman, Steven and Doreen Atkinson (eds), *South African Review 7: The Small Miracle. South Africa's Negotiated Settlement* (Johannesburg, 1994); Friedman, Steven (ed.), *The Long Journey: South Africa's Quest for a Negotiated Settlement* (Johannesburg, 1993); Marais, Hein, *South Africa: Limits to Change* (London, 2001); Rantete, Johannes and Hermann Giliomee, 'Transition to democracy through transaction? Bilateral negotiations between the ANC and NP in South Africa', *African Affairs* 91 (1992), pp. 515–42; Sparks, Alistair, *Tomorrow is Another Country: the Inside Story of South Africa's Negotiated Revolution* (London, 1996).

11. Vale, Peter, 'The search for Southern Africa's security', *International Affairs* 67 (1991), pp. 699–704.

12. Pisani, 'South Africa and the region', p.10.

13. Vale, 'The search for Southern Africa's security', pp. 704–6.

14. Johnson, R. W., *South Africa: the First Man, the Last Nation* (London, 2004), p. 200.

15. University of Fort Hare (hereafter UFH), Liberation Archives, ANC Botswana Mission, Box 1, File 8, ANC Missions 1990.

16. Barber, James, *South Africa in the Twentieth Century* (Oxford, 1999), p. 278.

17. The ANC Freedom Charter, adopted at the Congress of the People, Kliptown, 26 June 1955, http://www.anc.org.za/show.php?id=72 (25/11/09); UFH, Liberation Archives, ANC Lusaka Additions, Box 37, File 1, Conference Documents and Reports.

18. Ibid. (25/11/09).

19. UFH, Liberation Archives, ANC Dar es Salaam Office, Box 20, File: Declarations 1969, 1989.

20. Pfister, Roger, 'Gateway to international victory: the diplomacy of the African National Congress in Africa, 1960–1994', *Journal of Modern African Studies*, 1 (2003), p. 65.

21. Interview with Professor Peter Vale, University of Rhodes, 31 August 2009.

22. Keynote address of Comrade Nelson R. Mandela, Deputy President of the ANC, to the ANC National Consultative Conference, 14–16 December 1990, http://www.anc.org.za/show.php?id=123 (22/11/09).

23. Ibid. (22/11/09).

24. Conference Resolutions from the ANC National Consultative Conference, 14–16 December 1990, http://www.anc.org.za/show.php?id=120 (22/11/09).

25. Gevisser, Mark, *Thabo Mbeki: the Dream Deferred* (Johannesburg, 2007), p. 599.

26. Tambo, O. R., Opening address to the ANC National Consultative Conference, 14 December 1990, http://www.anc.org.za/show.php?id=104 (22/11/09).

27. Mandela, *Long Walk*, p. 707.

28. *Financial Times (FT)*, 27 June 1990.

29. Quote from John Carlin cited in, Adam and Moodley, *Negotiated Revolution*, p. 51.

30. For example, after 1990, the United Democratic Front (UDF) disbanded, with the majority of its leaders and supporters joining the ANC.
31. Tambo, O. R., Speech to the ANC Rally at Soccer City, Johannesburg, 16 December 1990, http://www.anc.org.za/show.php?id=125 (22/11/09).
32. Landsberg, Chris, 'Directing from the stalls?: the international community and the South African negotiation forum', in Steven Friedman and Doreen Atkinson (eds), *South African Review 7: The Small Miracle*, p. 283.
33. *Washington Post*, 16 December 1990.
34. Landsberg, Chris, *The Quiet Diplomacy of Liberation: International Politics and South Africa's Transition* (Johannesburg, 2004), p. 88.
35. UFH, Liberation Archives, ANC Swedish Mission, Box 88, File: Correspondence: ANC DIA (outgoing faxes, 1990–2).
36. *FT*, 9 February 1991.
37. Ibid., 16 April 1991.
38. *The Guardian*, 11 July 1991.
39. van der Westhuizen, Janis. 'South Africa's emergence as a middle power', *Third World Quarterly* 19 (1998), pp. 449–51.
40. Tambo, O. R., Opening address to the ANC 48th National Conference, Durban, 2 July 1991, http://www.anc.org.za/show.php?id=104 (22/11/09).
41. Mandela, Nelson, Opening address to the 48th National Conference of the ANC, http://www.anc.org.za/show.php?id=106 (22/11/09).
42. Ibid. (22/11/09).
43. Ibid. (22/11/09).
44. Adopted Resolutions on Foreign Policy, ANC 48th National Conference, Durban, July 1991, http://www.anc.org.za/show.php?id=113 (23/11/09).
45. Ibid. (23/11/09).
46. Ibid. (23/11/09.
47. Ibid. (23/11/09).
48. *FT*, 2 November 1991. Such political changes in Africa were themselves part of the unfolding post-Cold War world, allowing pro-democracy movements to make gains across the continent.
49. Ibid., 7 June 1991.
50. Ibid., 10 June 1991.
51. Ibid., 18 December 1991.
52. Pfister, 'Gateway', p. 66.
53. *FT*, 11 April 1992.
54. Ibid., 8 April 1992.
55. Landsberg, *Diplomacy*, p. 127.
56. Waldmeir, Patti, *Anatomy of a Miracle: the End of Apartheid and the Birth of the New South Africa* (New Brunswick, 1998), p. 191.
57. Mandela, *Long Walk*, p. 724.
58. Marais, *Limits to Change*, p. 89.
59. Pfister, 'Gateway', p. 67.
60. Friedman, *Long Journey*, p. 156.

61. *FT*, 18 and 19 August 1992.
62. Mandela, *Long Walk*, p. 726.
63. Email correspondence with Alan Hirsch, 18 June 2011; Telephone interview with Professor Peter Vale, 5 March 2010.
64. Telephone interview with Professor Peter Vale, 5 March 2010.
65. University of Western Cape (hereafter UWC), Mayibuye Centre Historical Papers (hereafter MCH) 236, Draft Foreign Policy by Peter Vale, comments by Rob Davies, and page edits by Renfrew Christie.
66. Ibid. p. 2.
67. Ibid. p. 4.
68. Ibid. p. 4.
69. Ibid. p. 10.
70. Ibid. p. 14.
71. Ibid. p. 17.
72. Telephone interview with Professor Peter Vale, 5 March 2010.
73. 'Foreign Policy in a New Democratic South Africa: A Discussion Paper', October 1993, http://www.africa.upenn.edu/Govern_Political/ANC_Foreign.html (1/12/09).
74. This 'moral' struggle that was elucidated in these discussions documents differed from the more politicized version of the ANC's thinking in the 1970s and 1980s.
75. Mbeki, Thabo, 'South Africa's international relations: today and tomorrow', in Greg Mills (ed.), *From Pariah to Participant: South Africa's Evolving Foreign Relations 1990–1994* (Johannesburg, 1994), p. 201.
76. Mandela, Nelson, 'South Africa's future foreign policy', *Foreign Affairs* 72 (1993), pp. 86–97.
77. Ibid. p. 87.
78. Ibid. pp. 90–1.
79. Ibid. p.88.
80. Ibid. pp. 93–5.
81. Interview with Professor Peter Vale, University of Rhodes, 31 August 2009; email correspondence with Alan Hirsch, 18 June 2011.
82. Telephone interview with Professor Peter Vale, 5 March 2010.
83. Email correspondence with Alan Hirsch, 18 June 2011.
84. Ibid.
85. Gevisser, *Dream*, p. 705.
86. The South African Constitution, adopted in 1996, http://www.info.gov.za/documents/constitution/1996/a108–96.pdf (5/5/11).
87. Email correspondence with Alan Hirsch, 18 June 2011.
88. The Interim South African Constitution, adopted in 1993, http://www.info.gov.za/documents/constitution/93cons.htm (5/5/11).
89. Mandela, *Long Walk*, p. 733.
90. Adam, Heribert, and Kogila Moodley, *The Opening of the Apartheid Mind: Options for the New South Africa* (Berkley, 1993), p. 35.

Chapter 5   The Sub Council on Foreign Affairs of the Transitional Executive Council: The Effects on the ANC's Post-apartheid South African Foreign Policy

Elements of this chapter were previously published as 'Coming in from the cold: the Transitional Executive Council and South Africa's reintegration into the international community', *Commonwealth and Comparative Politics* 49/3 (2011), pp. 359–78

1. Act No. 151 of 1993: Transitional Executive Council Act, 27 October 1993, http://www.info.gov.za/view/DownloadFileAction?id=88467 (17/6/2010).
2. *Financial Times (FT)*, 18 July 1994.
3. Spitz, Richard and Matthew Chaskalson, *The Politics of Transition: a Hidden History of South Africa's Negotiated Settlement* (Oxford, 2000), pp. 27–8.
4. '"Record of Understanding", Meeting between the State President of the Republic of South Africa and the President of the African National Congress Held at the World Trade Centre on the 26 September 1992', http://www.anc.org.za/show.php?id=4206&t=Transition%20to%20Democracy (6/7/2010).
5. Ibid.
6. Spitz and Chaskalson, *Transition*, p. 30.
7. Atkinson, Doreen, 'Brokering a miracle?: the multiparty negotiating forum', in Steven Friedman and Doreen Atkinson (eds), *South African Review 7: The Small Miracle. South Africa's negotiated settlement* (Johannesburg, 1994), pp. 21–3.
8. Spitz and Chaskalson, *Transition*, pp. 34–6.
9. Ibid. p. 48.
10. Atkinson, 'Miracle', p. 24.
11. 'First Report of the Technical Committee on the Transitional Executive Council 13 May 1993', http://www.nelsonmandela.org/omalley/index.php/site/q/03lv02039/04lv02046/05lv02097/06lv02100.htm (2/7/2010).
12. Ibid.
13. Ibid.
14. Ibid.
15. Act No. 151 of 1993: Transitional Executive Council Act, 27 October 1993 (TEC Act 1993), http://www.info.gov.za/view/DownloadFileAction?id=88467 (17/6/2010).
16. South African History Archive (hereafter SAHA), William Cullen Library, University of Witwatersrand, John Barratt Collection, AL3081, A1.7.14.
17. TEC Act 1993.
18. Ibid.
19. Ibid.
20. Ibid.
21. For example, if the DFA wanted to send a delegation to an international conference, they would first have to seek the approval of the SCFA. Some

examples of the DFA's requests to send conference delegations include: the Symposium on Conflict Management in Africa in Cairo; the World Health Organisation Conference and the 30th International Conference of Military Medicine: SAHA, John Barratt Collection, AL3081, A1.6.54, A1.7.23, and A1.7.25.

22. Interview with Tom Wheeler, Johannesburg, 31 March 2010.

23. Ivor Sarakinsky, 'Rehearsing joint rule: the Transitional Executive Council', in Steven Friedman and Doreen Atkinson (eds), *South Africa Review 7: The Small Miracle*, p. 78.

24. *The Star*, 10 September 1993.

25. SAHA, John Barratt Collection, AL3081, A1.7.14.

26. TEC Act 1993.

27. Although it should be noted that the NP had close ties to the civil servants of the DFA.

28. SAHA, John Barratt Collection, AL3081, A2.4.

29. *The Star*, 10 September 1993.

30. SAHA, John Barratt Collection, AL3081, A1.6.5.

31. Ibid.

32. Ibid.

33. Ibid.

34. Ibid., A1.7.14.

35. Interview with Tom Wheeler, Johannesburg, 31 March 2010.

36. 'Junketing on a junk', contribution for the *Meintjieskop Courier* for publication after 27 April, from Tom Wheeler's personal papers.

37. Ibid.

38. Interview with Tom Wheeler, Johannesburg, 31 March 2010.

39. Ibid.

40. SAHA, John Barratt Collection, AL3081, A1.6.5.

41. Interview with Tom Wheeler, Johannesburg, 31 March 2010.

42. Interview with Professor Deon Geldenhuys, Johannesburg, 29 March 2010.

43. SAHA, John Barratt Collection, AL3081, A1.3.11.

44. Ibid., A1.6.5.

45. Ibid., A1.5.5.

46. For example, at an SCFA meeting in Pretoria on the 29 April 1994, 11 days before the GNU's inauguration, three members of the DFA were in attendance. SAHA, John Barratt Collection, AL3081, A1.6.53.

47. Examples include: reports on the implications of NAFTA, the ways US foreign policy could affect South Africa, return to the UN, SAHA John Barratt Collection Al3081, A1.7.9, A1.7.10, A1.7.59.

48. SAHA, John Barratt Collection AL3081, A1.7.35.

49. Ibid.

50. Interview with Tom Wheeler, Johannesburg, 31 March 2010.

51. SAHA, John Barratt Collection, AL3081, A1.3.15.

52. Ibid., A1.6.40.
53. Interview with Tom Wheeler, Johannesburg, 31 March 2010.
54. SAHA, John Barratt Collection, AL3081, A1.3.3 & A1.3.4.
55. Internal DFA Document, Multilateral Conference: New York 4–7 February: proposed visit of sub-council on foreign relations – New York, 6 January 1994, Tom Wheeler's Personal Papers.
56. Ibid.
57. SAHA, John Barratt Collection, AL3081, A1.2.3.
58. Ibid., A2.14.
59. Internal DFA Document, Multilateral Conference: New York 4–7 February.
60. Ibid.
61. SAHA, John Barratt Collection, AL3081, A1.2.3.
62. Ibid., A1.3.15.
63. Ibid., A2.6.
64. Ibid., A1.7.21.
65. Ibid., A1.3.3.
66. Ibid., A2.14.
67. Ibid., A1.6.40.
68. Ibid., A1.2.3.
69. Ibid.
70. Ibid., A1.3.4.
71. Landsberg, 'Directing', p. 289.
72. Ginsburg, David, 'The democratisation of South Africa: transition theory tested', *Transformation* 29 (1996), pp. 96–7.
73. SAHA, John Barratt Collection, AL3081, A1.7.24.
74. Vladimir Shubin, 'The Soviet Union/Russian Federation's relations with South Africa, with special reference to the period since 1980', *African Affairs* 95 (1996), pp. 5–30.
75. SAHA, John Barratt Collection, AL3081, A1.7.60.
76. Ibid.
77. Landsberg, 'Directing', p. 289.
78. Cited in Southall, Roger, 'The new South Africa in the new world order: beyond the double whammy', *Third World Quarterly* 15 (1994), p. 124.
79. Barber, *Mandela's World*, p. 61.
80. SAHA, John Barratt Collection, AL3081, A1.3.15.
81. Ibid., A1.3.11.
82. Evans, Richard, 'South African foreign policy and the new world order', *Institute of Strategic Studies* (ISS) Paper 4 (1993).
83. Thanks to Professor Peter Vale for this point, telephone discussion, 5 March 2010.
84. Interview with Tom Wheeler, Johannesburg, 31 March 2010.
85. Patrick Bond, *Elite Transition: from Apartheid to Neoliberalism in South Africa* (London, 2000), pp. 55–6; Samuel Huntington, 'Democracy's third wave', *Journal of Democracy* 2,/2 (1991), pp. 12–34.

86. South African Foreign Policy: Discussion Document, DFA, http://www.info. gov.za/greenpapers/1996/foraf1.htm#3.2 (1/7/2010).

87. SAHA, John Barratt Collection, AL3081, A1.3.10.

Chapter 6   Idealism versus Realism? The Contested Nature of South African Foreign Policy, 1994–6

1. Examples include: Habib, Adam and Nthakeng Selinyane, 'South Africa's foreign policy and a realistic vision of an African century', in Elizabeth Sidiropoulos (ed.), *Apartheid Past, Renaissance Future: South Africa's Foreign Policy 1994–2004* (Johannesburg, 2004); Greg Mills, 'South Africa's Foreign Policy: from Isolation to Respectability', in David Simon (ed.), *South Africa in Southern Africa* (Oxford, 1998); Spence, Jack, 'South Africa: an African exception or just another country?', *Conflict, Security & Development* 7 (2007), pp. 341–7; Spence, Jack, 'The new South African foreign policy: incentives and constraints', in Francis Toase and Edmund Yorke (eds), *The New South Africa: Prospects for Domestic and International Security* (Basingstoke, 1998).

2. Information about Nzo sleeping in meetings provided during an interview with former ANC MP Andrew Feinstein, London, 1 July 2009.

3. Examples include: Adam, Heribert, Frederik van Zyl Slabbert and Kogila Moodley, *Comrades in Business, Post-liberation Politics in South Africa* (South Africa, 1998); Bond, Patrick, and Meshack Khosa, *An RDP Policy Audit* (Pretoria, 1999); Bond, Patrick, *Talk Left Walk Right: South Africa's Frustrated Global Reforms* (Scottsville, 2004); Saul, John, 'Liberal democracy vs. popular democracy in Southern Africa', *Review of African Political Economy* 24 (1997), pp. 219–36; Saul, John, *The Next Liberation Struggle, Capitalism, Socialism and Democracy in Southern Africa* (Toronto, 2005); Taylor, Ian, *Stuck in Middle Gear: South Africa's Post-apartheid Foreign Relations* (Westport, 2001).

4. RDP was first initiated in 1994 and GEAR was introduced in 1996. The RDP's primary goal was to tackle poverty and invest in the country's shortfall in service. Using a mix of socialist and neo-liberal tendencies, RDP incorporated massive infrastructure spending, trade liberalization, reducing government debt, and lowering taxes to alleviate the problems. GEAR on the other hand, demonstrated the ANC-led South Africa's commitment to free trade and privatization. It was seen by Finance Minister Trevor Manuel as a means of encouraging foreign investment, which, it was hoped, would aid massive job creation and increase GDP by 6 per cent year.

5. A prime example was when South African brewing company SABMiller (the second largest brewer in the world) was forced to cease operations in Kenya due to poor returns and local hostility, *Daily Nation* (Kenya), 28 July 2010. For academic studies on South African business expansion see: Daniel, John, Varusha Naidoo and Sanusha Naidu, 'SA expansion into Africa. Can the leopard change its spots?', *South African Labour Bulletin* 27 (2003), pp. 14–16;

Daniel, John, Varusha Naidoo and Sanusha Naidu, 'The South Africans have arrived: post-apartheid corporate expansion into Africa', in John Daniel, Adam Habib and Roger Southall (eds), *State of the Nation: South Africa 2003–2004* (Cape Town, 2004), pp. 368–90; Daniel, John, Jessica Lutchman and Alex Comninos, 'South Africa in Africa: trends and forecasts in a changing African political economy', in Sakhela Buhlungu (ed.), *State of the Nation: South Africa 2007* (Cape Town, 2007), pp. 508–32.

6. Gevisser, Mark, *Thabo Mbeki: the Dream Deferred* (Johannesburg, 2007), p. 693.

7. Lyman, Princeton, 'South Africa's promise', *Foreign Policy* 102 (1996), pp. 105–19; Warren Christopher, cited in Barber, *Mandela's World*, p. 85.

8. South African History Archive (hereafter SAHA), William Cullen Library, University of Witwatersrand, John Barratt Collection, AL3081, A1.3.11.

9. See: Bond, Patrick, *Elite Transition: from Apartheid to Neoliberalism in South Africa* (London, 2000), pp. 55–6; Samuel Huntington, 'Democracy's third wave', *Journal of Democracy*, 2 (1991), pp. 12–34.

10. Leon, Tony, *On the Contrary: Leading the Opposition in a Democratic South Africa* (Cape Town, 2008), p. 272.

11. SAHA, John Barratt Collection, AL3081, A1.3.11.

12. Ibid., A1.3.15.

13. Ibid., A1.3.11.

14. 'OAU officially informs government of acceptance', *Johannesburg SAPA*, 23 May 1994.

15. 'Building Democracy, Securing Economic Development, Advancing Social Justice and Peace', remarks by Mr Alfred Nzo, Minister of Foreign Affairs, at the Council of the Socialist International, Cape Town, 10 July 1995.

16. Statement by President Nelson Mandela at the OAU Heads of State and Government, Tunis, 13 June 1994.

17. 'Deputy Minister Pahad on Foreign Policy Priorities', *Johannesburg SABC TV 1 Network*, 29 May 1994.

18. Speech by the Minister of Foreign Affairs, Mr Alfred Nzo, Foreign Affairs Budget Vote, Parliament, 8 August, 1994.

19. 'Mandela Addresses Parliament', *Johannesburg SABC CCV Television Network*, 24 May 1994.

20. Ibid.

21. Speech by the Minister of Foreign Affairs, Mr Alfred Nzo, Foreign Affairs Budget Vote, Parliament, 8 August 1994.

22. For Western assistance of apartheid see: Harshe, Rajen, 'Africa: trends in US imperialism', *Social Scientist* 12 (1984), p. 29; Vale, Peter, 'Pivot, Puppet or Periphery: the Cold War and South Africa', The Cold War as Global Conflict International Centre for Advanced Studies, New York University, Unpublished Working Paper #9 (September 2003), p. 11.

23. Telephone interview with Ann Grant, Consul and Head of Chancery at the British Embassy in Maputo, Mozambique (1981–4) and former British High Commissioner to South Africa (2000–5), 7 December 2009.

24. Speech by the Minister of Foreign Affairs, Mr Alfred Nzo, Foreign Affairs Budget Vote, Parliament, 8 August 1994.

25. Ibid.

26. Cited in Southall, Roger, 'Regional security: the 'new' security in Southern Africa', *Southern Africa Report* 10 (1995), p. 3.

27. Speech by Nelson Mandela at a breakfast meeting with Business and Media, Harare, 21 May 1997.

28. SAHA, John Barratt Collection, AL3081, A1.3.11, A1.3.15.

29. Speech by the Minister of Foreign Affairs, Mr Alfred Nzo, Foreign Affairs Budget Vote, Parliament, 8 August 1994.

30. 'Building Democracy, Securing Economic Development, Advancing Social Justice and Peace', remarks by Mr Alfred Nzo, Minister of Foreign Affairs, at the Council of the Socialist International, Cape Town, 10 July 1995.

31. 'Mandela Interviewed on First 100 Days', *Johannesburg SABC TV 1 Network*, 18 August 1994.

32. Statement by President Nelson Mandela at the OAU Heads of State and Government, Tunis, 13 June 1994.

33. Speech made by Minister Alfred Nzo to the Council of Ministers on the occasion of the accession of South Africa to the SADC Treaty, Gaborone, 26 August 1994.

34. *Sunday Times* (SA), 19 June 1994.

35. Ibid.

36. Ibid.

37. 'Lesotho Minister Discusses Recent Military Uprising', *Gaborone Radio Botswana Network*, 21 April 1994.

38. 'Nzo: Commission on Lesotho Army Working Well', *Johannesburg SAPA*, 25 July 1994.

39. 'Praises Agreement Signed in Lesotho', *Johannesburg SAPA*, 14 September 1994.

40. 'Nujoma Leaves with Debt Relief', *Johannesburg SABC TV 1 Network*, 6 December 1994.

41. Ibid.

42. 'Mandela Comments on Cancelling Namibian Debt', *Johannesburg SAPA*, 13 December 1994.

43. 'Foreign Policy Perspective in a Democratic South Africa', http://www.anc.org.za/show.php?id=230 (9/08/10).

44. 'Foreign Policy in a New Democratic South Africa: A Discussion Paper', October 1993, http://www.inform.umd.edu/EdRes/Topic/Diversity/General/Government/International/ANC/Policy_Docs/foreign.txt (1/12/09).

45. 'Foreign Policy Perspective in a Democratic South Africa'.

46. Ibid.

47. Ibid.

48. Ibid.

49. Ibid.

50. For more information on Jimmy Carter's and Tony Blair's attempts see: Carleton, David, and Michael Stohl, 'The foreign policy of human rights: rhetoric and reality from Jimmy Carter to Ronald Reagan', *Human Rights Quarterly* 7 (1985), pp. 205–29; Schmitz, David, and Vanessa Walker, 'Jimmy Carter and the foreign policy of human rights: the development of a post-Cold War foreign policy', *Diplomatic History* 28 (2004), pp. 113–43; Little, Richard, and Mark Wickham-Jones (eds), *New Labour's Foreign Policy: A New Moral Crusade?* (Manchester, 2000).

51. 'Foreign Policy Perspective in a Democratic South Africa'.

52. Ibid.

53. Ibid.

54. 'Human rights group begins anti-execution campaign', *Paris AFP*, 13 July 1995.

55. Barber, *Mandela's World*, p. 110.

56. 'Mandela Prefers "Quiet Persuasion" With Nigeria', *Johannesburg Channel Africa Radio* (accessed via Foreign Broadcast Information Service (FBIS) Daily Reports), 1 November 1995.

57. van Aardt, Maxi, 'A foreign policy to die for: South Africa's response to the Nigerian crisis', *Africa Insight* 26 (1996), p. 111.

58. *The Star*, 24 July 1995.

59. Ibid., 16 November 1995.

60. 'Mugabe rules out isolated response to Nigeria', *Johannesburg SAPA*, 18 November 1995.

61. Barber, James, 'The new South Africa's foreign policy: principles and practice', *International Affairs* 81 (2005), p. 1084.

62. *The Observer*, 26 November 1995. Popularized by Thabo Mbeki, the concept of the 'African Renaissance' was to unite the continent politically and philosophically in a bid to end Afro-pessimism, and to move Africa towards peace, development and democracy.

63. 'Parliamentary Briefing Week: The Minister of Foreign Affairs, Nzo', 13 February 1996.

64. *Mail and Guardian*, 17 November 1995.

65. *The Star*, 13 December 1995.

66. Ibid.

67. 'Abacha: Mandela lacks understanding of diplomacy', *Paris AFP*, 23 November 1995.

68. Ibid.

69. Ibid.

70. 'Evaluating the Effectiveness of South Africa's Foreign Policy Since 1994', Goedgedacht Forum for Social Reflection, 12 April 2003.

71. *The Star*, 13 December 1995.

72. *Mail and Guardian*, 17 November 1995.

73. Ibid.

74. Ibid.

75. *Sunday Independent* (SA), 7 March 2010.
76. Ibid.
77. 'Shell to continue Nigerian gas project', *Johannesburg SAPA*, 29 November 1995.
78. *The Star*, 13 December 1995.
79. van Aardt, 'A foreign policy to die for', p. 115.
80. Interview with Professor Deon Geldenhuys, Johannesburg, 29 March 2010.
81. van Aardt, 'A foreign policy to die for', p. 115.
82. Interview with Professor Deon Geldenhuys, Johannesburg, 29 March 2010.
83. *The Independent*, 28 August 2006.
84. 'US, other delegations described', *Johannesburg SAPA*, 9 May 1994.
85. 'DP also criticises Omar', *Johannesburg SAPA*, 25 July 1994.
86. Interview with Andrew Feinstein, London, 1 July 2009.
87. Telephone interview with R. W. Johnson, 13 November 2009.
88. 'On efforts to resolve Lockerbie', *Johannesburg SAPA*, 3 February 1995.
89. *The Citizen*, 14 February 1996.
90. *Mail and Guardian*, 6 August 2010.
91. Email correspondence with Dr Gary Littlejohn, 24 June 2011.
92. *New Nation*, 30 June 1995.
93. *Mail and Guardian*, 23 June 1995.
94. Leon, *On the Contrary*, p. 273.
95. *Mail and Guardian*, 1 December 1995.
96. Ibid.
97. *Mail and Guardian*, 23 June 1995.
98. Ibid., 1 March 1996.
99. Ibid.
100. 'Mandela: "no intention" of ending ties with Taiwan', *Johannesburg SAPA*, 6 July 1995.
101. *Mail and Guardian*, 8 December 1995.
102. *Sunday Independent* (SA), 7 March 2010.
103. Spence, 'The new South African foreign policy', p. 161.
104. *Mail and Guardian*, 8 December 1995.
105. Ibid.
106. Ibid.
107. Skosana, Xolani, 'Arms Control South Africa Style: the Dynamics of Post-1994 Arms Export Control Policy', ISS Paper 62 (October 2002), p.1.
108. Ibid., p. 4.
109. Findings of the Cameron Commission, cited in ibid., p.4.
110. Interview with Professor Roger Southall, Johannesburg, 14 September 2009.
111. 'South Africa: a question of principle. Arms trade and human rights', *Human Rights Watch* 12/5 (A), (October, 2000), section vii.
112. Ibid.
113. Interview with Andrew Feinstein, London, 1 July 2009.
114. *Mail and Guardian*, 26 May 1995.

Chapter 7   The Changing Nature of South African Foreign Policy

1. *Financial Times (FT)*, 13 May 1996.
2. Barber, James, *Mandela's World: the International Dimension of South Africa's Political Revolution 1990–99* (Oxford, 2004), p. 128.
3. *FT*, 13 May 1996.
4. 'I Am an African', Thabo Mbeki's speech at the adoption of The Republic of South Africa Constitution Bill, 8 May 1996.
5. Ibid.
6. Ibid.
7. 'South African Foreign Policy Discussion Document', DFA, 1996, http://www.info.gov.za/greenpapers/1996/foraf1.htm (11/5/11).
8. Ibid.
9. Ibid.
10. 'Foreign Policy Perspective in a Democratic South Africa', http://www.anc.org.za/show.php?id=230 (9/08/10).
11. 'South African Foreign Policy Discussion Document', DFA, 1996.
12. Ibid.
13. Ibid.
14. Ibid.
15. Civil servants don't generally attack the approach of the government in power, so the lack of criticism in the 'South African Foreign Policy Discussion Document' is not especially unusual.
16. Butler, Anthony, 'How democratic is the African National Congress', *Journal of Southern African Studies* 31 (2005), pp. 719–36.
17. Barber, *Mandela*, p. 88.
18. Mills, Greg, 'Leaning all over the place? The not-so-new South Africa's foreign policy', in Hussein Solomon (ed.), *Fairy Godmother, Hegemon or Partner? In Search of a South African Foreign Policy* (ISS, 1997), p. 21.
19. I.e. Pere, Garth, 'South Africa's foreign policy in a globalising world an overview: 1994–2002', *The Policy Co-ordination and Advisory Services in the Presidency as part of a 10 year review*, http://www.thepresidency.gov.za/docs/pcsa/irps/pere1.pdf (2/9/10), p. 15.
20. Ostheimer, Andrea, 'Foreword', in Tim Hughes, *Composers, Conductors and Players: Harmony and Discord in South African Foreign Policy Making* (Johannesburg, 2004), p. iii.
21. Suttner, Raymond, 'Foreign policy of the new South Africa: a brief review', in Samuel Guimaraes (ed.), *South Africa and Brazil: Risks and Opportunities in the Turmoil of Globalization (Brasilia, 1996), p. 193*.
22. *FT*, 27 August 1998.
23. Johnson, R. W., *South Africa's Brave New World: The Beloved Country Since the End of Apartheid* (London, 2009), p. 55.
24. Email correspondence with Raymond Suttner, 26 January 2010.

25. Ibid.
26. Suttner, Raymond, 'South African foreign policy since April 1994', *African Communist* 145 (1996), p. 69.
27. *Mail and Guardian*, 8 December 1995.
28. Hughes, *Composers, Conductors and Players*, p. 30.
29. Ibid., p. 188.
30. Ibid., p. 145.
31. Feinstein, Andrew, *After the Party: A Personal and Political Journey Inside the ANC* (Johannesburg, 2007), pp. 156–207.
32. 'Resolutions - Role of State and Governance', ANC 50th National Conference, Mafikeng, December 1997, http://www.anc.org.za/show.php?id=2425 (10/11/10).
33. *New Nation* (SA), 1 November 1996.
34. Interview with Professor Deon Geldenhuys, Johannesburg, 29 March 2010.
35. Interview with Andrew Feinstein, London, 1 July 2009.
36. 'Developing a Strategic Perspective on South African Foreign Policy', July 1997, http://www.anc.org.za/show.php?id=2348 (2/9/10).
37. 50th National Conference: Report of the Secretary General, 17 December 1997, Mafikeng, Section 4: Activities of the National Executive Committee, http://www.anc.org.za/show.php?id=2484 (6/6/11).
38. 'Developing a Strategic Perspective'.
39. Ibid.
40. Ibid.
41. 'Foreign Policy Perspective in a Democratic South Africa', http://www.anc.org.za/show.php?id=230 (11/5/11).
42. Interview with Gareth van Onselen, the DA's Executive Director of Research and Communications, Cape Town, 7 September 2009.
43. 'Developing a Strategic Perspective'.
44. Ibid.
45. Ibid.
46. Ibid.
47. Ibid.
48. 'Discussion Document for Commission on International Relations', ANC 50th National Conference, Mafikeng, December 1997, http://www.anc.org.za/show.php?doc=ancdocs/history/conf/conference50/discomms3.html#Discuss per cent20Inter per cent20Relations (2/8/10).
49. Ibid.
50. 'Developing a Strategic Perspective'.
51. Ibid.
52. Johnson, *Brave New World*, pp. 110–16.
53. Former Tanzanian President Dr Julius Nyerere speaking to the South African Parliament, Cape Town, 16 October 1997.
54. Chase, Robert, Emily Hill and Paul Kennedy, 'Pivotal states and US strategy', *Foreign Affairs* 75 (1996), pp. 33–51.

55. 'Developing a Strategic Perspective'.

56. Ibid.

57. Vale, Peter, and Sipho Maseko, 'South Africa and the African Renaissance', *International Affairs* 74 (1998), pp. 276–7.

58. 'White Paper on South African Participation in International Peace Missions', 21 October 1998, http://www.info.gov.za/view/DownloadFileAction? id=70438 (2/8/10).

59. Neethling, Theo, 'The emerging South African profile in Africa: reflections on the significance of South Africa's entrance into peacekeeping', *African Journal of Conflict Resolution* 2 (2002), p. 101.

60. 'White Paper', 1998, p. 20.

61. Ibid.

62. Telephone interview with Ann Grant.

63. Telephone interview with R. W. Johnson, 13 November 2009.

64. 'Parliamentary Briefing Week: The Minister of Foreign Affairs, Mr A. B. Nzo', 13 February 1996.

65. The term 'middle power' is multifaceted, but when applied to South Africa, it often refers to its status as a semi-peripheral world power, yet because of its political, economic and military dominance in Southern Africa, this power makes it the pre-eminent nation in the region. For more details see: Schoeman, Maxi, 'South Africa as an emerging middle power: 1994–2003', in John Daniel, Adam Habib and Roger Southall (eds), *State of the Nation: South Africa 2003–2004* (Cape Town, 2004), pp. 349–67; and van der Westhuizen, Janis, 'South Africa's emergence as a middle power', *Third World Quarterly* 19 (1998), pp. 435–55.

66. Pertinent examples of this visibility internationally are South Africa's role in the formation of the African Union (AU) – the successor of the OAU – and in 2006 it became a non-permanent member of the UN Security Council.

67. Barber, *Mandela*, p. 200.

68. Statement by Mr Alfred Nzo, Minister of Foreign Affairs, at the General Debate of the 50th Session of the General Assembly of the UN, 6 October 1995.

69. Ironically, this process of decommissioning South Africa's nuclear arsenal was carried out by the NP in the years 1989–93.

70. Statement by Mr Alfred Nzo, Minister of Foreign Affairs, at the General Debate of the 50th Session of the General Assembly of the UN, 6 October 1995.

71. The 11 countries were – Algeria, Botswana, Burkina Faso, Gambia, Ivory Coast, Mali, Mauritania, Mauritius, South Africa, Tanzania and Zimbabwe – although 39 had signed it: 'African Nuclear Weapons Free Zone Treaty (ANWFZ) (Treaty of Pelindaba)', http://www.dfa.gov.za/foreign/Multilateral/ africa/treaties/anwfz.htm (3/11/10).

72. Foreign Affairs Parliamentary Media Briefing, 'South Africa's new place in the world', 12 September 1997; Statement by Minister of Foreign Affairs Nzo, to the 52nd Session of the UN General Assembly, 22 September 1997.

73. Interview with Tom Wheeler, Johannesburg, 31 March 2010.

74. *New York Times*, 17 February 2002.

75. Daniel, Naidoo and Naidu, 'SA expansion into Africa', pp. 14–16; Daniel, Naidoo and Naidu, 'The South Africans have arrived', pp. 374–5.

76. Suttner, 'Review'.

77. Vale and Maseko, 'Renaissance', p. 279; Daniel, Naidoo and Naidu, 'The South Africans have arrived', p. 375.

78. Habib, Adam, 'South Africa's foreign policy: hegemonic aspirations, neoliberal orientations and global transformation', *South African Journal of International Affairs* 16 (2009), p. 149.

79. Examples include: Cilliers, Jakkie, 'An emerging South African foreign policy identity', *Institute for Security Studies*, Occasional Paper 39, April 1999; Daniel, Naidoo and Naidu, 'The South Africans have arrived'.

80. Daniel, Naidoo and Naidu, 'The South Africans have arrived', p. 384.

81. Email correspondence with Dr Gary Littlejohn, 24 June 2011.

82. Speech by A. B. Nzo, Minister of Foreign Affairs Budget Vote, Senate, 16 May 1996.

83. Foreign Affairs Budget Vote Remarks by Nzo, House of Assembly, 24 April 1997.

84. Daniel, Naidoo and Naidu, 'The South Africans have arrived', p. 384.

85. Barber, 'The new South Africa's foreign policy', p. 1086.

86. Speech by A. B. Nzo, Minister of Foreign Affairs Budget Vote, Senate, 16 May 1996.

87. SADC, http://www.dfa.gov.za/foreign/Multilateral/africa/sadc.htm (10/9/10).

88. Examples include: Nathan, Laurie, 'The Absence of Common Values and Failure of Common Security in Southern Africa, 1992–2003', Working Paper no. 50, Crisis States Programme (LSE, July 2004), pp. 1–29; Malan, Mark, 'Regional power politics under cover of SADC: running amok with a mythical organ', *Institute for Security Studies* (ISS), Occasional Paper 35 (October 1998); Kent, Vanessa and Mark Malan, 'Decisions, decisions: South Africa's foray into regional peace operations', *Institute of Security Studies* (ISS), Occasional Paper 72 (April 2003).

89. Zaire became the Democratic Republic of Congo (DRC) in 1997 after Laurent Kabila overthrew the rule of kleptocratic President Mobutu. The DRC was invited to join SADC, although it is not located in Southern Africa.

90. 'Communiqué', Summit of heads of state or governments of the Southern African Development Community (SADC), 28 June 1996, Gaborone, http://www.iss.co.za/af/regorg/unity_to_union/pdfs/sadc/communiques/HoS per cent2096x.pdf (5/7/11); Malan, 'Regional power politics under cover of SADC'.

91. During exile the ANC was allied with the Soviet-backed liberation movement, the Zimbabwe African People's Union (ZAPU) led by Joshua Nkomo, who had a bitter rivalry with Robert Mugabe's, Chinese-supported, organization ZANU. In 1987, ZAPU merged into ZANU, forming ZANU PF, and establishing Zimbabwe as a one-party state.

92. Barber, 'The new South Africa's foreign policy', p. 1086.
93. Interview with Andrew Feinstein, London, 1 July 2009; interview with Tom Wheeler, Johannesburg, 31 March 2010.
94. Nathan, 'The Absence of Common Values', July 2004.
95. Ibid.
96. 'Evaluating the Effectiveness of South Africa's Foreign Policy Since 1994', Goedgedacht Forum for Social Reflection, 12 April 2003.
97. Gevisser, *Dream Deferred*, p. 445.
98. Telephone interview with Michael Holman, former African editor for the *Financial Times*, 1 July 2009.
99. Nathan, Laurie, 'Consistency and inconsistencies in South African foreign policy', *International Affairs* 81 (2005), p. 366.
100. *Mail and Guardian*, 21 January 2009.
101. 'Foreign Affairs tries to deny Mugabe's snub', *Southern Africa Report* 16 (August 1998), pp. 4–5.
102. Landsberg, Chris, 'The impossible neutrality? South Africa's policy in the Congo War', in John Clark (ed.), *The African Stakes of the Congo War* (New York, 2004), p. 174.
103. Ibid., p. 170.
104. *The Times*, 20 August 1998.
105. Kent and Malan, 'Decisions, Decisions', ISS (April, 2003).
106. Landsberg, 'Impossible neutrality', p. 170.
107. Southall, Roger, 'SADC's intervention into Lesotho: an illegal defence of democracy?', in Oliver Furley and Roy May (eds), *African Interventionist States* (Aldershot, 2001), p. 157.
108. Ibid., pp. 158–9.
109. Nathan, 'Consistency and inconsistencies', p. 365.
110. Landsberg, 'Impossible neutrality', p. 174.
111. *The Citizen*, 10 December 1998.
112. 'Evaluating the Effectiveness of South Africa's Foreign Policy'.

Chapter 8   A New President, a New Direction? Thabo Mbeki's Renaissance

1. *The Sowetan*, 9 April 1997; Nelson Mandela's closing address at the ANC's 50th National Conference, Mafikeng, 20 December 1997.
2. Alden, Chris and Garth le Pere, 'South Africa's post-apartheid foreign policy: from reconciliation to ambiguity?', *Review of African Political Economy* 31 (2004), p. 287; Gumede, William, *Thabo Mbeki and the Battle for the Soul of the ANC* (Cape Town, 2005), pp. 62–3.
3. Gevisser, Mark, *Thabo Mbeki: the Dream Deferred* (Jeppestown, 2007), p. 658; Johnson, R. W., *South Africa's Brave New World: the Beloved Country Since the End of Apartheid* (London, 2009), p. 55.

4. *The Economist*, 18 December 1997; NEC Election Results, 50th National Conference, Mafikeng, 20 December 1997.
5. *Democratic Governance: a Restructured Presidency at Work*, January 2001, p. 4.
6. Ibid., p. 7.
7. Gumede, *Mbeki*, pp. 124–5.
8. 'Thin-skinned Mbeki will need deft handling', US Embassy Cable (wiki leaks), 23 February 2003, http://wikileaks.org/cable/2001/02/01PRETORIA1173.html (20/3/13).
9. Chothia, Farouk, and Sean Jacobs, 'Remaking the presidency: the tension between co-ordination and centralisation', in Sean Jacobs and Richard Calland (eds), *Thabo Mbeki's World: the Politics and Ideology of the South African President* (Scottsville, 2002), p. 149.
10. *Democratic Governance*, pp. 12, 18.
11. Gumede, *Mbeki*, p. 148.
12. *Business Day*, 27 March 1997.
13. *The Telegraph*, 27 November 2004.
14. *Democratic Governance*, pp. 22–23.
15. Ibid., pp. 21–23.
16. 'Thin-skinned Mbeki'; Interview with Andrew Feinstein, London, 9 July 2009.
17. Mandela, Nelson, 'South Africa's future foreign policy', *Foreign Affairs* 72 (1993), p. 88.
18. For example, see: 'Building a Better World: the Diplomacy of Ubuntu', White Paper on South Africa's foreign policy, 13 May 2011.
19. For example, see Alden and le Pere, 'South Africa's post-apartheid foreign policy', p. 283.
20. 'Developing a Strategic Perspective on South African Foreign Policy', July 1997, http://www.anc.org.za/show.php?id=2348 (8/10/12).
21. Mbeki, Thabo, 'Statement at the African Renaissance Conference', Midrand, 28 September 1998.
22. 'Developing a Strategic Perspective'.
23. 'On efforts to resolve Lockerbie', *Johannesburg SAPA*, 3 February 1995.
24. Mbeki, Thabo, 'Keynote Address of the President of the ANC to the National General Council', 12 July 2000.
25. Alden and le Pere, 'South Africa's post-apartheid foreign policy', p. 145; Feinstein, Andrew, *After the Party: A Personal and Political Journey Inside the ANC* (Johannesburg, 2007), p. 87; Glaser, Daryl, *Mbeki and After: Reflections on the Legacy of Thabo Mbeki* (Johannesburg, 2010), p.10.
26. Murithi, Tim, 'The African Union's evolving role in peace operations: the African Union Mission in Burundi, the African Union Mission in Sudan and the African Union Mission in Somalia', *African Security Review* 7 (2008), pp. 71–82; *Mail and Guardian*, 30 August 2004; *Guardian*, 1 November 2001.
27. Telephone interview with R. W. Johnson, 17 November 2009.

28. Constitutive Act of the African Union, 7 November 2000.

29. Ibid.

30. Ibid.

31. Dates are when these proposals were adopted by the OAU/AU, not necessarily the dates when the measures came into force; there was frequently a large time delay. Protocol Relating to the Establishment of the Peace and Security Council of the African Union, October 2002; Protocol to the Treaty Establishing the African Economic Community Relating to the Pan-African Parliament, March 2001; Protocol of the Court of Justice of the African Union, July 2003.

32. 'Millennium Partnership for the African Recovery Programme', Draft 3a, March 2001, pp. 1–2.

33. *ANC Today* 1/2, 2–8 February 2001.

34. Decisions and Declarations, Assembly of Heads of State and Government, 37th Ordinary Session, 9–11 July, 2001 Lusaka, Zambia; New Partnership for Africa's Development (NEPAD), October 2001, http://www.dfa.gov.za/au.nepad/nepad.pdf (29/6/12).

35. Gumede, *Mbeki*, p. 134.

36. Ibid., pp. 10–11.

37. Ibid., pp. 52–3.

38. 'The New Partnership for Africa's Development (NEPAD): The African Peer Review Mechanism (APRM)', 2003, http://www.dfa.gov.za/au.nepad/nepad49.pdf (29/6/12).

39. Ibid. (29/6/12).

40. *G8 Africa Action Plan*, June 2002, http://www.g8.utoronto.ca/summit/2002kananaskis/africaplan.html (3/7/12).

41. *Mail and Guardian*, 9 July 2003.

42. *Guardian*, 25 June 2010.

43. Johnson, *New World*, p. 326.

44. Mokoena, Refilwe, 'South-South co-operation: the case for IBSA', *South African Journal of International Affairs* 14 (2007), pp. 125–45.

45. Mbeki, Thabo, 'Remarks by the President of South Africa during IBSA Meeting of Heads of State and Government', Brasilia, 13 September 2006.

46. Telephone interview with R. W. Johnson, 13 November 2011.

47. *Mail and Guardian*, 22 June 2006.

48. *Business Day*, 13 April 2011.

49. Interview with Tom Wheeler, Johannesburg, 31 March 2010.

50. Mbeki, Thabo, 'President's State of the Nation Address in Parliament', 8 February 2002.

51. *Business Day*, 6 January 2004.

52. 'Media Programme for the Official Visit to South Africa by Vice President of the Presidium of the Democratic People's Republic of Korea', 15 March 2005, http://www.info.gov.za/speeches/2005/05031516151002.htm. (11/7/12); *Mail and Guardian*, 17 March 2005.

53. 'Deputy Minister Aziz Pahad Concludes his Visit to Iraq in a Positive Mood', 11 February 2003, http://www.info.gov.za/speeches/2003/03021211461002. htm (11/7/12).

54. *Mail and Guardian*, 12 January 2004; *New York Times*, 1 March 2004.

55. *Business Day,* 6 January 2004.

56. *Financial Mail*, 9 January 2004.

57. *Independent*, 1 June 2004.

58. *Business Day*, 18 April 2008.

59. 'South Africa's Main Trading Partners: 1998–2008', South African Revenue Service, http://www.sars.gov.za/home.asp?pid=211 (30/9/12).

60. 'General Assembly elects Belgium, Italy, Indonesia, South Africa', *UN News*, 16 October 2003, http://www.un.org/News/Press/docs/2006/ga10516.doc. htm (18/9/12).

61. *Washington Post*, 16 April 2007; *The Sunday Times* (SA), 8 December 2007.

62. *The Sunday Times* (SA), 8 December 2007.

63. *Mail and Guardian*, 15 January 2007.

64. SAHA, John Barratt Collection, AL3081, A1.7.24.

65. Gruzd, Steven, 'Plurality: Coming or Going?', http://www.saiia.org.za/archi ve-eafrica/plurality-coming-or-going.html (20/9/12).

66. Electoral Institute for the Sustainability of Democracy in Africa, 'Zimbabwe: 2000 General Elections', http://www.eisa.org.za/WEP/zim2000election.htm (20/9/12).

67. *Guardian*, 20 April 2000.

68. 'Report of the UN Fact Finding Mission to Zimbabwe to Assess the Scope and Impact of Operation Murambatsvina' by the UN Special Envoy on Human Settlements Issues in Zimbabwe, July 2005.

69. Norwegian Election Mission Observation Mission, 'Presidential Elections in Zimbabwe 2002, 20 March 2002'; 'Report of the Commonwealth Observer Group, Zimbabwe Presidential election 9 to 11 March 2002'; 'SADC Parliamentary Forum Election Observation Mission, Zimbabwe Presidential Elections 9–10 March 2002'.

70. *The Guardian*, 20 March 2002.

71. 'Interim Statement', the SA Observer Mission on the Zimbabwean Presidential Elections of 9 and 10 March 2002.

72. 'Zimbabwe presidential elections', *ANC Today* 2/11, 15–21 March 2002.

73. Vickers, B, 'Zimbabwe, SADC and CHOGM', *SADC Barometer,* 4 (January, 2004), p. 3.

74. *The Guardian*, 12 December 2003.

75. *The Star*, 9 December 2003.

76. Thabo Mbeki, 'We will resist the upside-down view of Africa', *ANC Today* 3/49, 12–18 December 2003.

77. *The Star*, 9 December 2003.

78. *IOL News*, 14 June 2007.

79. *Mail and Guardian*, 24 March 2003.

80. 'Zimbabwe: SA Economic Aid', Office for the Co-ordination of Humanitarian Affairs, 14 February 2000.
81. *Mail and Guardian*, 31 May 2008.
82. Interview with Andrew Feinstein, London, 9 July 2009.
83. Transcript of an interview with former Australian Prime Minister Malcolm Fraser for ABC Radio, 22 December 2008 http://www.abc.net.au/pm/content/2008/s2453287.htm (8/10/12).
84. *The Namibian*, 29 April 2005.
85. *The Telegraph*, 25 June 2012.
86. *Mail and Guardian*, 12 March 2013.
87. Ellis, *Comrades*, p. 104; Interview with Professor Deon Geldenhuys, Johannesburg, 29 March 2010; Gevisser, *Dream*, p. 437.
88. For greater detail, see: Graham, M, 'The ANC and the 'Myth' of Liberation Solidarity: 'Othering' in Post-apartheid South(ern) Africa', *Africa Insight* (forthcoming, 2014).
89. Melber, H. 2010. The legacy of anti-colonial struggles in Southern Africa: Liberation movements as governments. *Conference on Election Processes, Liberation Movements and Democratic Change in Africa*. 8–11 April. Maputo.
90. *Business Day*, 30 March 2001.
91. *Sunday Times* (SA), 20 January 2002.
92. For HIV/AIDS see: *Guardian*, 1 November 2002; Butler, Anthony, 'South Africa's HIV/AIDS policy, 1994–2004: how can it be explained?', *African Affairs* 104 (2005), pp. 591–614; Special Issue, *Review of African Political Economy* 27 (2000). For corruption see: Feinstein, *After the Party*. For potential opposition to Mbeki see: COSATU 'Secretarial Report to the 1st Central Committee' November 2001, http://www.cosatu.org.za/docs/reports/2001/s ecr-ovr.htm (30/9/12); *Mail and Guardian*, 5 November 2004; *Telegraph*, 9 November 2004.
93. *Mail and Guardian*, 20 September 2008.
94. Chikane, F, *Eight Days in September: The Removal of Thabo Mbeki* (Johannesburg, 2012), pp. 4–5.
95. *Business Day*, 19 December 2007.
96. Chikane, *September*, p. 231.
97. Ibid., p. 232.

Chapter 9   Conclusions

1. During the ANC's exile, the term 'international community' here refers chiefly to the socialist states of the Soviet Bloc; once international communism collapses in 1990, the term is taken to mean the 'West', epitomized by values of liberal democracy and neo-liberalism.
2. The ANC positioned itself to engage both in a socialist struggle, and also one for fundamental human rights and democracy, the latter appealing more to a Western liberal audience. It was successful in doing both.

3. Mandela, Nelson, 'South Africa's future foreign policy', *Foreign Affairs* 72 (1993), pp. 86–97.

4. Lodge, Tom, *Mandela: a Critical Life* (Oxford, 2006), p. 213.

5. Mbeki, Thabo, 'Speech on the Occasion of the Consideration of the Budget Vote of the Presidency', 13 June 2000.

6. Barber, James, *Mandela's World: the International Dimension of South Africa's Political Revolution* (Oxford, 2004), p. 200.

7. Key to this is that the ANC is a nationalist movement, not just a political party, and thus ideological coherence does not necessarily come to it naturally.

8. Such an occurrence during Mandela's presidency arguably represents continuity with the apartheid era, when DFA officials were similarly marginalized by a small group of NP leaders and securocrats who controlled foreign policy. 'Both BOSS [Bureau of State Security] and the Department of Information outmanoeuvred the Department of Foreign Affairs (DFA) as the engine that drove South Africa's foreign policy', Sifiso Ndlovu, 'The ANC's diplomacy and international relations', in SADET, *The Road to Democracy in South Africa*, vol. 2, 1970–80 (Pretoria, 2006), p. 630.

9. Mills, Greg, 'South Africa's foreign policy: from isolation to respectability?', in David Simon (ed.) *South Africa in Southern Africa: Reconfiguring the Region* (Oxford, 1998), p. 74.

10. 'South Africa's Main Trading Partners by Value, 1997–2007', http://www.sars.gov.za/ (3/7/11).

11. *The New Age* (SA), 25 August 2011.

12. *Business Day* (SA), 25 August 2011.

13. *BBC News Online*, http://www.bbc.co.uk/news/world-africa-14610722 (25/8/11).

14. Selebi, Jackie, 'South African foreign policy: setting new goals and strategies', *South African Journal of International Affairs* 6 (1999), p. 210. It must be noted that Jackie Selebi was subsequently sentenced in August 2010 to 15 years in prison, convicted on corruption charges.

BIBLIOGRAPHY

Primary Sources

Archival Sources

ANC Liberation Archive, University of Fort Hare (UFH), Alice

UFH, Dar es Salaam Office, Box 20, File: Declarations 1969, 1989.
——— Lusaka Mission 1923–96, Box 136, Folder 303, Swaziland–SA land deal 1982–3.
——— Lusaka Mission 1923–96, Box 149, Folder 44, Statements Kwanhgwane, Ingwauuma 1982.
——— Zimbabwe Mission, Box 9, Folder 64, SA-Mozambican Relationship 1984.
——— Lusaka Mission 1923–96, Box 148, Folder 27, Discussions between ANC and SA big business 1985.
——— Lusaka and London, ANC Lusaka Additions (Mayibuye II), Box 38, Folder 1, ANC National Consultative Conference 1985, 'NEC (Secretary General's) Report'.
——— Lusaka and London, ANC Lusaka Additions (Mayibuye II), Box 38, Folder 3 (b), ANC National Consultative Conference 1985, 'International Situation'.
——— Zimbabwe Mission, Zimbabwe Additions, Box 4, Folder 34, Correspondence and statements on raid of ANC offices, Harare, 1986.
——— Mozambique Mission, Box 10, File 63: Reports 1986–8.
——— Senegal Mission, Box 1, Folder 2, ANC Campaigns 1986–9.
——— Lusaka Mission 1923–96, Box 9, Folder 33, Negotiations, 1989–91.
——— Liberation Archives, ANC Botswana Mission, Box 1, File 8, ANC Missions 1990.
——— Swedish Mission, Box 88, File: Correspondence: ANC DIA (outgoing faxes, 1990–2).
——— Lusaka Additions (Mayibuye II), Box 36, File 1, Morogoro Conference Resolutions.
——— Lusaka and London, ANC Lusaka Additions (Mayibuye II), Box 32, Folder 1, Contributions ANC units, discussion papers.

————— Lusaka Additions (Mayibuye II), Box 37, File 1, Conference documents and reports.

The Anti-Apartheid Movement (AAM) Archive, Bodleian Library of Commonwealth and African Studies, University of Oxford

MSS Afr. S. 2151 1/2, pp. 151–334, 'Interview with Pallo Jordan, conducted by Howard Barrell, Lusaka, 4 July 1989'.

————— 2/2, pp. 683–921, 'First Interview with Sue Rabkin, Conducted by Howard Barrell, July, 7, 9 and 16 August 1989, Lusaka'.

—————, 'Interview with Ivan Pillay, Conducted by Howard Barrell, 20 and 23 July 1989, Lusaka'.

————— 2/3, pp. 922–1063, 'First interview with Joe Slovo, Conducted by Howard Barrell, August 12–16 1989, Lusaka'.

————— 1/3, pp. 335–535, 'Third Interview with Mac Maharaj, Conducted by Howard Barrell, Johannesburg, 30 November 1990'.

MSS AAM 932, ANC combatants and prisoner of war status, Armed Resistance in South Africa by E. S. Reddy, Director, UN Centre against Apartheid, 6 February 1980.

————— 946, Miscellaneous Papers, 'Memorandum to the Government of Swaziland on the Agreement between Swaziland and the Pretoria regime on Ka-Ngwane and Ngwavuma'.

————— 1027, Memorandum and Leaflets, South Africa's Record of International Terrorism, Tony Gifford, (SWAM/AAM Publication, London, 1981).

————— 948, Miscellaneous ANC, 'African National Congress National Consultative Conference June 1985: Report of the Commission on Foreign Policy'.

————— 1044, Background, 'Roger Martin, Southern Africa: The Price of Apartheid. A Political Risk Analysis, The Economist Intelligence Unit, Special Report No. 1130, July 1988'.

————— 938, Death of Oliver Tambo, ANC Chairperson, Apr 1993, Memoriam O. R. Tambo Programme.

Historical Papers, William Cullen Library, University of Witwatersrand, Johannesburg

ANC AD2186, Box 4, Da9

Institute of Commonwealth Studies Library (ICS), London

PP.SA.ANC.56, 'Hands off Mozambique'.

—————259, 'Statement by comrade Oliver Tambo at a mass rally, Bairro de Liberdade, Maputo, 14 February 1982'.

JQ2026 AFR fol, The Dakar Declaration, 12 July 1987.

Mayibuye Centre Historical Papers (MCH), University of the Western Cape, Cape Town

MCH 70, Survey of the External Mission of the African National Congress of South Africa, February 1965.

————— 236, Draft Foreign Policy by Peter Vale, comments by Rob Davies, and page edits by Renfrew Christie.

The National Archives of the UK, Kew, London

DO 180/6, AR.4/9/50, 'Commonwealth Relations Office Southern Africa Department', African National Congress (ANC) and Pan-African Congress 1961, Document 38, Discussion about Lutuli's prize.

FCO 45/69, Commonwealth Office and Foreign and Commonwealth Office, Liberation Movements 1968 Document 8 – Khartoum Conference, January 1969.

South African Historical Archive (SAHA), University of Witwatersrand, Johannesburg

SAHA, John Barratt Collection, AL3081, A1.2.3
———, A1.3.3
———, A1.3.4
———, A1.3.10
———, A1.3.11
———, A1.3.15
———, A1.5.5
———, A1.6.5
———, A1.6.40
———, A1.6.53
———, A1.6.54
———, A1.7.9
———, A1.7.10
———, A1.7.14
———, A1.7.21
———, A1.7.23
———, A1.7.24
———, A1.7.25
———, A1.7.35
———, A1.7.59
———, A1.7.60
———, A2.4
———, A2.6
———, A2.14

ANC Exile Documents

ANC NEC 1985, 'Take the Struggle to the White Areas Make the Whole of South Africa Ungovernable! Paralyse Apartheid!', *http://www.anc.org.za/show.php?id=*4677 (24/3/11).

Mandela, N., 'Address by Nelson Mandela to the Conference of the Pan-African Freedom Movement of East and Central Africa', Addis Ababa, 12 January 1962, *http://www.anc.org.za/show.php?id=*4297 (7/2/11).

Resha, R., 'Statement by Robert Resha, member of the National Executive Committee of the ANC before the Special Committee against Apartheid', 18 March 1969, *http://www.anc.org.za/show.php?id=*4781 (15/2/11).

Tambo, O. R., 'Statement on behalf of the South Africa United Front', New York, 20 October 1960, *http://www.anc.org.za/show.php?id=*4257 (6/2/11).

ANC Foreign Policy Documents (exile through to political power)

'Decisions and Declarations', Assembly of Heads of State and Government, 37th Ordinary Session, 9–11 July, 2001 Lusaka, Zambia; New Partnership for Africa's Development (NEPAD), October 2001, *http://www.dfa.gov.za/au.nepad/nepad.pdf* (29/6/12).

'Developing a Strategic Perspective on South African Foreign Policy', July 1997, *http://www.anc.org.za/show.php?id=2348* (2/9/10).

'Foreign Policy in a New Democratic South Africa: A Discussion Paper', October 1993, *http://www.africa.upenn.edu/Govern_Political/ANC_Foreign.html* (1/12/09).

'Foreign Policy Perspective in a Democratic South Africa', *http://www.anc.org.za/show.php?id=230* (9/08/10).

'The New Partnership for Africa's Development (NEPAD): The African Peer Review Mechanism (APRM)', 2003, *http://www.dfa.gov.za/au.nepad/nepad49.pdf* (29/6/12).

'Record of Understanding', Meeting between the State President of the Republic of South Africa and the President of the African National Congress Held at the World Trade Centre on the 26 September 1992, *http://www.anc.org.za/show.php?id=4206&t=Transition%20to%20Democracy* (6/7/10).

'Second National Consultative Conference: Report of the Commission on Foreign Policy', 17 June 1985, Kabwe, Zambia, *http://www.anc.org.za/show.php?id=141* (5/7/11).

South African Government and DFA Documents

Act No. 151 of 1993: Transitional Executive Council Act, 27 October 1993, *http://www.info.gov.za/view/DownloadFileAction?id=88467* (17/6/2010).

'African Nuclear Weapons Free Zone Treaty (ANWFZ), 2 June 1995 (Treaty of Pelindaba)', *http://www.dfa.gov.za/foreign/Multilateral/africa/treaties/anwfz.htm* (3/11/10).

'Birth of the African Union', *http://www.dfa.gov.za/docs/2002/au0621.htm* (3/7/11).

'Building a Better World: the Diplomacy of Ubuntu', White Paper on South Africa's foreign policy, 13 May 2011.

'Democratic Governance: a Restructured Presidency at Work', January 2001, *http://www.thepresidency.gov.za/pebble.asp?relid=358* (2/4/15)

First Report of the Technical Committee on the Transitional Executive Council, 13 May 1993, *http://www.nelsonmandela.org/omalley/index.php/site/q/03lv02039/04lv02046/05lv02097/06lv02100.htm* (2/7/2010).

'The Groote Shuur Minute', *http://www.sahistory.org.za/pages/governence-projects/constitution/doc17-groote-schuur.htm* (2/6/11).

The Interim South African Constitution, adopted in 1993, *http://www.info.gov.za/documents/constitution/93cons.htm* (5/5/11).

le Pere, G., 'South Africa's Foreign Policy in a Globalising World An Overview: 1994–2002', The Policy Co-ordination and Advisory Services in the Presidency as part of a 10 year review, *http://www.thepresidency.gov.za/docs/pcsa/irps/pere1.pdf* (2/9/10)

'The Pretoria Minute', *http://www.sahistory.org.za/pages/governence-projects/constitution/doc18-pta-minute.htm* (2/6/11).

SADC, *http://www.dfa.gov.za/foreign/Multilateral/africa/sadc.htm* (10/9/10).

'South African Foreign Policy: Discussion Document', DFA, 1996, *http://www.info.gov.za/greenpapers/1996/foraf1.htm#3.2* (1/7/2010).

'South Africa's Main Trading Partners by Value, 1997–2007', *http://www.sars.gov.za/* (3/7/11).

——— 1998–2008', South African Revenue Service, *http://www.sars.gov.za/home. asp?pid=211* (30/9/12).

'White Paper on South African Participation in International Peace Missions', 21 October 1998, *http://www.info.gov.za/view/DownloadFileAction?id=70438* (2/8/10).

Conference Proceedings and Resolutions

Adopted Resolutions on Foreign Policy, ANC 48th National Conference, Durban, July 1991, *http://www.anc.org.za/show.php?id=113* (23/11/09).

The ANC Freedom Charter, Adopted at the Congress of the People, Kliptown, 26 June 1955, *http://www.anc.org.za/show.php?id=72* (25/11/09).

Communiqué: Summit of Heads of State or Governments of the Southern African Development Community (SADC), 28 June 1996, Gaborone, *http:// www.iss.co.za/af/regorg/unity_to_union/pdfs/sadc/communiques/HoS%2096x.pdf* (5/7/11).

Conference Resolutions from the ANC National Consultative Conference, 14–16 December 1990, *http://www.anc.org.za/show.php?id=120* (22/11/09).

COSATU 'Secretarial Report to the 1st Central Committee', November 2001, *http:// www.cosatu.org.za/docs/reports/2001/secr-ovr.htm* (30/9/12).

'Discussion Document', for Commission on International Relations, ANC 50th National Conference, Mafikeng, December 1997, *http://www.anc.org.za/show. php?doc=ancdocs/history/conf/conference50/discomms3.html#Discuss%20Inter%20 Relations* (2/8/10).

'Extracts from the Political Report of the National Executive Committee of the African National Congress', April 1969, *http://www.anc.org.za/show.php?id=143* (16/2/11).

Fifth Summit Conference of East and Central African States, Lusaka, 14–16 April 1969, *Lusaka Manifesto, http://www.anc.org.za/show.php?id=4836&t=Organisation +of+African+Unity* (16/2/11).

Mandela, N., 'Opening Address to the 48th National Conference of the ANC', *http:// www.anc.org.za/show.php?id=106* (22/11/09).

'Political Report by Oliver Tambo on the National Executive Committee to the National Consultative Conference of the African National Congress', 17 June 1985, Kabwe, Zambia, *http://www.anc.org.za/show.php?id=4464* (3/4/11).

'Resolutions – Role of State and Governance', ANC 50th National Conference, Mafikeng, December 1997, *http://www.anc.org.za/show.php?id=2425* (10/11/10).

Second National Consultative Conference, 'Report of the Commission on National Structures, Constitutional Guidelines and Codes of Conduct', Kabwe Conference, June 1985, *http://www.anc.org.za/show.php?id=136* (4/4/11).

'Statement of the National Executive Committee on the Occasion of the 78th Anniversary of the ANC', *http://www.anc.org.za/show.php?id=71* (28/3/11).

'Strategy and Tactics of the ANC', adopted by the Morogoro Conference of the ANC, Tanzania, 25 April – 1 May 1969, *http://www.ancyl.org.za/docs/political/1969/ Morogoro%20Strategy%20and%20Tacticsg.pdf* (16/2/11).

Tambo, O. R., 'Opening Address to the ANC 48th National Conference, Durban, 2 July 1991, *http://www.anc.org.za/show.php?id=104* (22/11/09).

'Zimbabwe: SA economic aid', Office for the Co-ordination of Humanitarian Affairs, 14 February 2000.

Speeches

'Building Democracy, Securing Economic Development, Advancing Social Justice and Peace', remarks by Mr Alfred Nzo, Minister of Foreign Affairs, at the Council of the Socialist International, Cape Town, 10 July 1995.

'Deputy Minister Aziz Pahad Concludes his Visit to Iraq in a Positive Mood', 11 February 2003.

Foreign Affairs Budget Vote Remarks by Nzo, House of Assembly, 24 April 1997.

Foreign Affairs Parliamentary Media Briefing, 'South Africa's New Place in the World', 12 September 1997 Statement by Minister of Foreign Affairs Nzo, to the 52nd Session of the UN General Assembly, 22 September 1997.

Former Tanzanian President Dr Julius Nyerere speaking to the South African Parliament, Cape Town, 16 October 1997.

'I Am an African', Thabo Mbeki's speech at the adoption of The Republic of South Africa Constitution Bill, 8 May 1996.

Keynote address of Comrade Nelson R. Mandela, Deputy President of the ANC, to the ANC National Consultative Conference, 14–16 December 1990, *http:// www.anc.org.za/show.php?id=123* (22/11/09).

Mr de Klerk's speech at the opening of the South African Parliament, 2 February 1990, *http://www.info.gov.za/speeches/1996/101348690.htm* (18/11/09).

T. Mbeki, 'Speech on the Occasion of the Consideration of the Budget Vote of the Presidency', 13 June 2000.

Parliamentary Briefing Week: The Minister of Foreign Affairs, Mr A. B. Nzo, 13 February 1996.

President G. H. Bush, Address before the Joint Session of Congress on the End of the Gulf War, 6 March 1991.

Speech by O.R. Tambo, Statement of the National Executive Committee on the Occasion of the 60th Anniversary of the ANC, 8 January 1972, *http://www.anc. org.za/show.php?id=2642* (9/8/11).

———— the Minister of Foreign Affairs, Mr Alfred Nzo, Foreign Affairs Budget Vote, Parliament, 8 August 1994.

———— Minister Alfred Nzo to the Council of Ministers on the Occasion of the Accession of South Africa to the SADC Treaty, Gaborone, 26 August 1994.

———— A. B. Nzo, Minister of Foreign Affairs Budget Vote, Senate, 16 May 1996.

———— Nelson Mandela at a breakfast meeting with Business and Media, Harare, 21 May 1997.

Statement by President Nelson Mandela at the OAU Heads of State and Government, Tunis, 13 June 1994.

———— Mr Alfred Nzo, Minister of Foreign Affairs, at the General Debate of the 50th Session of the General Assembly of the UN, 6 October 1995.

O. R. Tambo, Opening address to the ANC National Consultative Conference, 14 December 1990, *http://www.anc.org.za/show.php?id=104* (22/11/09).

———— 'Speech to the ANC Rally at Soccer City, Johannesburg, 16 December 1990, *http://www.anc.org.za/show.php?id=125http://www.anc.org.za/show.php?doc=/ ancdocs/history/or/or90-5.html* (22/11/09).

Thabo Mbeki, 'Statement at the African Renaissance Conference', Midrand, 28 September 1998.

————, 'Keynote Address of the President of the ANC to the National General Council', 12 July 2000.

————, 'President's State of the Nation Address in Parliament', 8 February 2002.
————, 'Remarks by the President of South Africa during IBSA Meeting of Heads of State and government', Brasilia, 13 September 2006.

Newspapers and Journals

African Communist
ANC Today (South Africa)
Business Day (South Africa)
Citizen, The (South Africa)
City Press (South Africa)
Daily Nation (Kenya)
Dawn Economist, The (UK)
Financial Times (UK)
Guardian, The (UK)
Independent, The (UK)
Mail and Guardian (South Africa)
Mayibuye Namibian, The (Namibia)
New Age, The (South Africa)
New Nation (South Africa)
New York Times (USA)
Observer, The (UK)
Sechaba Star, The (South Africa)
Sunday Independent (South Africa)
Sunday Times (South Africa)
Telegraph, The (UK)
Times, The (UK)
Washington Post, The (USA)

Other media sources (accessed via the Foreign Broadcast Information Service unless otherwise stated)

'Abacha: Mandela lacks understanding of diplomacy', *Paris AFP*, 23 November 1995.
'Deputy Minister Pahad on foreign policy priorities', *Johannesburg SABC TV 1 Network*, 29 May 1994.
'DP also criticises Omar', *Johannesburg SAPA*, 25 July 1994.
'Foreign Affairs tries to deny Mugabe's snub', *Southern Africa Report*, 16 August 1994, pp. 4–5.
'Human rights group begins anti-execution campaign', *Paris AFP*, 13 July 1995.
'Lesotho minister discusses recent military uprising', *Gaborone Radio Botswana Network*, 21 April 1994.
'Libya fighting', BBC News Online, *http://www.bbc.co.uk/news/world-africa-14610722* (25/8/11).
'Mandela addresses parliament', *Johannesburg SABC CCV Television Network*, 24 May 1994.
'Mandela comments on cancelling Namibian debt', *Johannesburg SAPA*, 13 December 1994.

'Mandela interviewed on first 100 days', *Johannesburg SABC TV 1 Network*, 18 August 1994.
'Mandela: "no intention" of ending ties with Taiwan', *Johannesburg SAPA*, 6 July 1995.
'Mandela prefers "quiet persuasion" with Nigeria', *Johannesburg Channel Africa Radio*, 1 November 1995.
'Mugabe rules out isolated response to Nigeria', *Johannesburg SAPA*, 18 November 1995.
'Nujoma leaves with debt relief', *Johannesburg SABC TV 1 Network*, 6 December 1994.
'Nzo: commission on Lesotho army working well', *Johannesburg SAPA*, 25 July 1994.
'OAU officially informs government of acceptance', *Johannesburg SAPA*, 23 May 1994.
'On efforts to resolve Lockerbie', *Johannesburg SAPA*, 3 February 1995.
'Pik Botha reacts to UK sanctions decision', *Johannesburg Domestic Service*, 25 September 1985.
'Praises agreement signed in Lesotho', *Johannesburg SAPA*, 14 September 1994.
'Shell to continue Nigerian gas project', *Johannesburg SAPA*, 29 November 1995.
'Simple majority celebrated', *Johannesburg SAPA*, 14 November 1989.
'US, other delegations described', *Johannesburg SAPA*, 9 May 1994.

NGO Reports

Amnesty International, 'South Africa: Torture, ill-treatment and executions in African National Congress camps' (December 1992), *http://www.amnesty.org/en/library/asset/AFR53/027/1992/en/fba1e35c-ed9a-11dd-9ad7-350fb2522bdb/afr530271992en.html* (2/4/11).
Cilliers, J., 'An emerging South African foreign policy identity', *Institute for Security Studies*, Occasional Paper 39, April 1999.
Kent, V., and M. Malan, 'Decisions, decisions: South Africa's foray into regional peace operations', *Institute of Security Studies*, Occasional Paper 72, April 2003.
Malan, M., 'Regional power politics under cover of SADC: running amok with a mythical organ', *Institute for Security Studies*, Occasional Paper 35, October 1998.
'The Report of the Study Commission on US policy toward Southern Africa', *South Africa: Time Running Out*, (Berkeley, 1981).
'Report of the UN Fact-finding Mission to Zimbabwe to Assess the Scope and Impact of Operation Murambatsvina' by the UN Special Envoy on Human Settlements Issues in Zimbabwe, July 2005.
Skosana, X., 'Arms control South Africa style: the dynamics of post-1994 arms export control policy', *Institute for Security Studies*, Occasional Paper 62 (October 2002).
'South Africa: A question of principle. Arms trade and human rights', *Human Rights Watch* 12/5 (A), (October 2000), section vii.
Vines, A., 'Angola: looking beyond elections', *Institute for Security Studies Opinion*, European Union Institute for Security Studies (October 2008).

Primary documents reproduced in secondary sources

Document 13, 'What is Wrong?' Memorandum by Ben Turok before the ANC's Morogoro Conference, April 1969, pp. 383–7.
———— 108, 'Report on meeting of the ANC National Executive Committee, Morogoro, July 15–24, 1977 (abridged)', pp. 696–701.

——— 111, 'Diary of Jack Simons at Novo Catengue camp, Angola, January-March 1979 (abridged)', pp. 707–15.

——— 136, 'A few points on the current state of the struggle in S.A.', ANC intelligence report, mid-1987, p. 608.

Gerhart, G., and C. Glaser, *From Protest to Challenge*, vol. 6, *Challenge and Victory, 1980–1990* (Bloomington, 2010).

Karis, T., and G. Gerhart, *From Protest to Challenge*, vol. 5, *Nadir and Resurgence, 1964–1979* (Bloomington, 1997).

Digital Innovation South Africa (DISA), online archive

'Meetings between Dr Kenneth Kaunda, President of Zambia, and Ministers R. F. Botha, General M. A. de M. Malan and the Administrator General Dr W. A. van Niekerk, April 1984', *http://www.disa.ukzn.ac.za/index.php?option=com_displaydc&recordID=min19840425.035.017.d1.18*.

'Minutes of a meeting between President Kenneth Kaunda and South African Representatives, Lusaka, 25 June 1984', *http://www.disa.ukzn.ac.za/index.php?option=com_displaydc&recordID=min19840625.035.017.d1.18a*.

'Review of the State of Organisation of the Liberation Movement', 1966, Memorandums, *http://www.disa.ukzn.ac.za/index.php?option=com_displaydc&recordID=mem19660000.032.009.013*.

Tom Wheeler's Personal Papers

Internal DFA Document, Multilateral Conference: New York 4–7 February: Proposed agenda items and appointments/briefings, 14 January 1994.

———: Proposed visit of Sub Council on Foreign Relations – New York, 6 January 1994.

'Junketing on a Junk', contribution for the *Meintjieskop Courier* for publication after 27 April 1994.

Interviews (in person, by telephone or via email exchange)

Alan Hirsch, 18 June 2011.

Andrew Feinstein, 1 July 2009 (former ANC MP).

Ann Grant, 7 December 2009 (former Consul and Head of Chancery at the British Embassy in Maputo, Mozambique, 1981–4, and British High Commissioner to South Africa, 2000–5).

Professor Deon Geldenhuys, 29 March 2010.

Enuga S. Reddy, email correspondence 9 November – 1 December 2010 (head of the United Nations Centre against Apartheid).

Gareth von Onselen, 7 September 2009 (The DA's Executive Director of Research and Communications).

Dr Gary Littlejohn, 24 June 2011.

Dr James Brennan, 30 March 2011.

Mark Ashurst, 3 March 2010 (Director of the Africa Research Institute)

Merle Lipton, 11 May 2011.

Michael Holman, 1 June 2009 (former Africa editor of the *Financial Times*, 1984–2002).

Professor Peter Vale, 31 August 2009 and 5 March 2010.
Professor Raymond Suttner, 2 November 2009 (former ANC MP and now academic).
Professor Roger Southall, 14 September 2009.
R. W. Johnson, 13 November 2009.
HRH Prince Dr Seeiso Bereng Seeiso, 30 June 2011 (High Commissioner of the Kingdom of Lesotho for the United Kingdom).
Tom Wheeler, 31 March 2010 (TEC Sub Council on Foreign Affairs Liaison Officer; former ambassador to Turkey and Chief Director: Latin America and the Caribbean Sections).

Secondary Sources

Books

Adam, Heribert, van Zyl Slabbert, Frederik, and Moodley, Kogila, *The Opening of the Apartheid Mind: Options for the New South Africa* (Berkley, 1993).
———, *Comrades in Business, Post-Liberation Politics in South Africa* (Utrecht, 1998).
———, and Moodley, Kogila, *The Negotiated Revolution: Society and Politics in Post-Apartheid South Africa* (Johannesburg, 1993).
Amin, Samir, Chitala, Derrick, and Mandaza, Ibbo (eds), *SADCC: Prospects for Disengagement and Development in Southern Africa* (London, 1987).
Baines, Gary, and Vale, Peter (eds), *Beyond the Border War: New Perspectives on Southern Africa's Late-Cold War Conflicts* (Pretoria, 2008).
Barber, James, *South Africa in the Twentieth Century, a Political History: in Search of a Nation State* (Oxford, 1999).
——— *Mandela's World: the International Dimension of South Africa's Political Revolution 1990–99* (Oxford, 2004).
———, and Barratt, John, *South Africa's Foreign Policy: the Search for Status and Security, 1945–1998* (Cambridge, 1990).
Barrell, Howard, *MK: The ANC's Armed Struggle* (Johannesburg, 1990).
Beinart, William, *Twentieth-century South Africa* (Oxford, 1994).
Benson, Mary, *Nelson Mandela: the Man and the Movement* (Harmondsworth, 1994).
Bond, Patrick, and Khosa, Meshack, *An RDP Policy Audit* (Pretoria, 1999).
———, *Elite Transition: from Apartheid to Neoliberalism in South Africa* (London, 2000).
———, *Talk Left Walk Right: South Africa's Frustrated Global Reforms* (Scottsville, 2004).
Bridgland, Fred, *Jonas Savimbi: a Key to Africa* (Edinburgh, 1986) .
Brittain, Victoria, *The Death of Dignity: Angola's Civil War* (London, 1998).
Cabrita, Joao, *Mozambique: the Tortuous Road to Democracy* (Basingstoke, 2000).
Callinicos, Luli, *Oliver Tambo: Beyond the Engeli Mountains* (Cape Town, 2004).
Crocker, Chester, *High Noon in Southern Africa: Making Peace in a Rough Neighbourhood* (New York, 1992).
Davenport, Richard, and Saunders, Chris, *South Africa: A Modern History* (5th edn, Basingstoke, 2000).
Davis, Stephen, *Apartheid's Rebels: Inside South Africa's Hidden War* (New Haven, 1987).
De Klerk, F. W., *The Last Trek: A New Beginning. The Autobiography* (London, 1999).
Ellis, Stephen and Sechaba, Tsepo, *Comrades against Apartheid: The ANC and the South African Communist Party in Exile* (London, 1992).

Feinstein, Andrew, *After the Party: a Personal and Political Journey Inside the ANC* (Johannesburg, 2007).

Feit, Edward, *Urban Revolt in South Africa, 1960–1964: a Case Study* (Evanston, 1971).

Flower, Ken, *Serving Secretly: Rhodesia's CIO Chief on Record* (London, 1987).

Friedman Steven (ed.), *The Long Journey: South Africa's Quest for a Negotiated Settlement* (Johannesburg, 1993).

———, and Atkinson, Doreen (eds), *South African Review 7: The Small Miracle. South Africa's Negotiated Settlement* (Johannesburg, 1994).

Geldenhuys, Deon, *The Diplomacy of Isolation: South African Foreign Policy Making* (New York, 1984).

Gerhart, Gail, and Glaser, Clive, *From Protest to Challenge*, vol. 6, *Challenge and Victory, 1980–1990* (Bloomington, 2010) .

Gevisser, Mark, *Thabo Mbeki: the Dream Deferred* (Johannesburg, 2007).

Gleijeses, Piero, *Conflicting Missions* (London, 2002).

Glaser, Daryl, *Mbeki and After: Reflections on the Legacy of Thabo Mbeki* (Johannesburg, 2010).

Guimaraes, Fernando, *The Origins of the Angolan Civil War* (Basingstoke, 2001).

Hanlon, Joseph, *Apartheid's Second Front: South Africa's War against its Neighbours* (Harmondsworth, 1986).

———, *Beggar your Neighbours: Apartheid Power in Southern Africa* (London, 1986).

———, *Mozambique: the Revolution under Fire* (London, 1990).

Hughes, Tim, *Composers, Conductors and Players: Harmony and Discord in South African Foreign Policy Making* (Johannesburg, 2004).

Jacobs, Sean, and Calland, Richard (eds), *Thabo Mbeki's World: the Politics and Ideology of the South African President* (Scottsville, 2002).

Jeffery, Anthea, *People's War: New Light on the Struggle for South Africa* (Johannesburg, 2009).

Johnson, R. W., *South Africa: the First Man, the Last Nation* (London, 2004).

——— *South Africa's Brave New World: the Beloved Country since the End of Apartheid* (London, 2009).

Karis, Thomas, and Gerhart, Gail, *From Protest to Challenge*, vol. 5, *Nadir and Resurgence, 1964–1979* (Bloomington, 1997).

Kasrils, Ronnie, *Armed and Dangerous: From Undercover Struggle to Freedom* (London, 1998).

Landsberg, Chris, *The Quiet Diplomacy of Liberation: International Politics and South Africa's Transition* (Johannesburg, 2004).

Larmer, Miles, *Rethinking African Politics: A History of Opposition in Post-colonial Zambia* (Farnham, 2011).

Lelyveld, Joseph, *Move Your Shadow: South Africa Black and White* (London, 1985).

Leon, Tony, *On the Contrary: Leading the Opposition in a Democratic South Africa* (Cape Town, 2008).

Little, Richard, and Wickham-Jones, Mark (eds), *New Labour's Foreign Policy: a New Moral Crusade?* (Manchester, 2000).

Lodge, Tom, *Black Politics in South Africa since 1945* (London, 1987).

——— *Mandela: a Critical Life* (Oxford, 2006).

Mandela, Nelson, *Long Walk to Freedom* (London, 1995).

——— *Conversations with Myself* (Basingstoke, 2010).

Manghezi, Nadja, *The Maputo Connection: ANC Life in the World of FRELIMO* (Auckland Park, 2009).

Marais, Hein, *South Africa: Limits to Change. The Political Economy of Transition* (London, 2001).

Marcum, John, *The Angolan Revolution*, vol. 2, *Exile Politics and Guerrilla Warfare (1962–1976)* (Cambridge, 1978).

Marx, Anthony, *Lessons of the Struggle: South African Internal Opposition 1960–1980* (Cape Town, 1992).

Mckinley, Dale, *The ANC and the Liberation Struggle: a Critical Political Biography* (London, 1997).

Meli, Francis, *A History of the ANC: South Africa Belongs to Us* (Harare, 1988).

Minter, William, *Apartheid's Contras: an Inquiry into the Roots of War in Angola and Mozambique* (London, 1994).

O'Malley, Padraig, *Shades of Difference: Mac Maharaj and the Struggle for South Africa* (New York, 2007).

Pottinger, Brian, *The Mbeki Legacy* (Cape Town, 2008).

Sampson, Anthony, *Black and Gold: Tycoons, Revolutionaries and Apartheid* (London, 1987).
———— *Mandela: the Authorised Biography* (London, 2000).

Saul, John, *The Next Liberation Struggle, Capitalism, Socialism and Democracy in Southern Africa* (Toronto, 2005) .

Seekings, Jeremy, *The UDF: a History of the United Democratic Front in South Africa 1983–1991* (Cape Town, 2000).

Sellestrom, Tor, *Sweden and National Liberation in Southern Africa: Solidarity and Assistance 1970–1994* (Stockholm, 2002).

Shubin, Vladimir, *The ANC: a View From Moscow* (Cape Town, 1999).

Slovo, Joe, *Slovo: the Unfinished Autobiography* (Melbourne, 1997).

Sparks, Anthony, *Tomorrow is Another Country: the Inside Story of South Africa's Negotiated Revolution* (London, 1996).

Spitz, Richard, and Chaskalson, Matthew, *The Politics of Transition: a Hidden History of South Africa's Negotiated Settlement* (Oxford, 2000).

Steenkamp, Willem, *South African Border Wars: 1966–1989* (Gibraltar, 1989).

Stiff, Peter, *Warfare by Other Means: South Africa in the 1980s and 1990s* (Alberton, 2001).

Stockwell, John, *In Search of Enemies* (London, 1979).

Suttner, Raymond, *The ANC Underground in South Africa to 1976* (Auckland Park, 2008).

Taylor, Ian, *Stuck in Middle Gear: South Africa's Post-apartheid Foreign Relations* (Westport, 2001).

Thomas, Scott, *The Diplomacy of Liberation: the Foreign Relations of the ANC since 1960* (London, 1996).

Trewhela, Paul, *Inside Quatro: Uncovering the Exile History of the ANC and SWAPO* (Auckland Park, 2009).

Turok, Ben, *Nothing but the Truth: Behind the ANC's Struggle Politics* (Jeppestown, 2003).

Waldmeir, Patti, *Anatomy of a Miracle: the End of Apartheid and the Birth of the New South Africa* (New Brunswick, 1998).

Articles and Chapters in Books

Alden, Chris and le Pere, Garth, 'South Africa's post-apartheid foreign policy: from reconciliation to ambiguity?', *Review of African Political Economy* 31 (2004), pp. 283–97.

Atkinson, Doreen, 'Brokering a miracle?: the multiparty negotiating forum', in Steven Friedman and Doreen Atkinson (eds), *South African Review 7: the Small Miracle. South Africa's Negotiated Settlement* (Johannesburg, 1994), pp. 13–43.

Barber, James, 'The new South Africa's foreign policy: principles and practice', *International Affairs* 81/5 (2005), pp. 1079–96.

Barratt, John, 'South Africa's outward policy: from isolation to dialogue', in N. Rhoodie (ed.), *South African Dialogue: Contrasts in South African Thinking on Basic Race Issues* (Johannesburg, 1972), pp. 543–61.

Barrell, Howard, 'The turn to the masses: the African National Congress' strategic review of 1978–79', *Journal of Southern African Studies* 18/1 (1992), pp. 64–92.

Butler, Anthony, 'How democratic is the African National Congress', *Journal of Southern African Studies* 31/4 (2005), pp. 719–36.

———— 'South Africa's HIV/AIDS policy, 1994–2004: how can it be explained?', *African Affairs* 104 (2005), pp. 591–614.

Carleton, David, and Stohl, Michael, 'The foreign policy of human rights: rhetoric and reality from Jimmy Carter to Ronald Reagan', *Human Rights Quarterly* 7/2 (1985), pp. 205–29.

Chase, Robert, Hill, Emily, and Kennedy, Paul, 'Pivotal states and US strategy', *Foreign Affairs* 75/1 (1996), pp. 33–51.

Chothia, Farouk and Jacobs, Sean, 'Remaking the presidency: the tension between co-ordination and centralisation', Jacobs, Sean and Calland, Richard (eds), *Thabo Mbeki's World: The Politics and Ideology of the South African President* (Scottsville, 2002).

Coker, Chester, '"Experiencing" Southern Africa in the twenty-first century', *International Affairs* 67/2 (1991), pp. 281–92.

———— 'SA expansion into Africa. Can the leopard change its spots?', *South African Labour Bulletin* 27/5 (2003), pp. 14–16.

Daniel, John, Naidoo, Varusha, and Naidu, Sanusha, 'The South Africans have arrived: post-apartheid corporate expansion into Africa', in John Daniel, Adam Habib and Roger Southall (eds), *State of the Nation: South Africa 2003–2004* (Cape Town, 2004), pp. 368–90.

————, Lutchman, Jessica, and Comninos, Alex, 'South Africa in Africa: trends and forecasts in a changing African political economy', in Sakhela Buhlungu, John Daniel, Roger Southall and Jessica Lutchman (eds), *State of the Nation: South Africa 2007* (Cape Town, 2007), pp. 508–32.

Davies, Robert, and O'Meara, Dan, 'Total strategy in Southern Africa: an analysis of South African regional policy since 1978', *Journal of Southern African Studies* 11/2 (1985), pp. 183–211.

Davis, Nathanial, 'The Angola Decision of 1975: a personal memoir', *Foreign Affairs* 57/1 (1978), pp. 109–24.

Ellis, Stephen, 'The ANC in exile', *African Affairs* 90/360 (1991), pp. 439–47.

Fatton, Robert Jr, 'The African National Congress of South Africa: the limitations of a revolutionary strategy', *Canadian Journal of African Studies* 18/3 (1984), pp. 593–608.

Ginsburg, David, 'The democratisation of South Africa: transition theory tested', *Transformation* 29 (1996), pp. 74–102.

Graham, Matthew, 'Covert Collusion? American and South African relations in the Angolan Civil War, 1974–1976', *African Historical Review* 43/1 (2011), pp. 27–48.

———— 'Coming in from the cold: the Transitional Executive Council and South Africa's reintegration into the international community', *Journal of Commonwealth and Comparative Politics* 49/3 (2011), pp. 359–79.

Habib, Adam, 'South Africa's foreign policy: hegemonic aspirations, neoliberal orientations and global transformation', *South African Journal of International Affairs* 16/2 (2009), pp. 143–59.

————, and Selinyane, Nthakeng, 'South Africa's foreign policy and a realistic vision of an African century', in Elizabeth Sidiropoulos (ed.), *Apartheid Past, Renaissance Future: South Africa's Foreign Policy 1994–2004* (Johannesburg, 2004), pp. 49–60.

Harshe, Rajen, 'Africa: trends in US imperialism', *Social Scientist* 12/11 (1984), pp. 19–33.

Hirschmann, David, 'Southern Africa: détente?', *The Journal of Modern African Studies* 14/1 (1976), pp. 107–26.

Houston, Gregory, 'International solidarity: introduction', in SADET, *The Road to Democracy in South Africa*, vol. 3, *International Solidarity* (Pretoria, 2008), pp. 1–39.

————, and Bernard Magubane, 'The ANC political underground in the 1970s' in SADET, *The Road to Democracy in South Africa*, vol. 2, *1970–1980* (Pretoria, 2006), pp. 371–452.

Huntington, Samuel, 'Democracy's third wave', *Journal of Democracy* 2/2 (1991), pp. 12–34.

Jaster, Robert, 'Evolution of a regional conflict in "war and diplomacy"', in Robert Jaster (ed.), *Changing Fortunes: War, Diplomacy, and Economics in Southern Africa* (New York, 1992), pp. 19–65.

Johns, Sheridan, 'Obstacles to guerrilla warfare – a South African case study', *The Journal of Modern African Studies* 11/2 (1973), pp. 267–303.

Ketelo, Bandile, Maxongo, Amos, Tshona, Zamxolo, Masango, Ronnie, and Mbengo, Luvo, 'A miscarriage of democracy: the ANC Security Department in the 1984 mutiny in Umkhonto weSizwe', in Paul Trewhela (ed.), *Inside Quatro: Uncovering the Exile History of the ANC and SWAPO* (Auckland Park, 2009), pp. 8–45.

Landsberg, Chris, 'Directing from the stalls? The international community and the South African negotiation forum', in Steven Friedman and Doreen Atkinson (eds), *South African Review 7: The Small Miracle. South Africa's Negotiated Settlement* (Johannesburg, 1994), pp. 276–300.

———— 'The impossible neutrality? South Africa's policy in the Congo War', in J. Clark (ed.), *The African Stakes of the Congo War* (New York, 2004), pp. 169–83.

Legassick, Martin, 'Myth and reality in the struggle against apartheid', *Journal of Southern African Studies* 24/2 (1998), pp. 443–58.

Lissoni, Arianna, 'Transformations in the ANC external mission and Umkhonto we Sizwe, c.1960–9', *Journal of Southern African Studies*, Special Issue, *Liberation Struggles, Exile and International Solidarity* 35/2 (2009), pp. 287–301.

Lodge, Tom, 'State of exile: the African National Congress of South Africa, 1976–86', in Philip Frankel, Noam Pines, and Mark Swilling (eds), *State, Resistance and Change in South Africa* (London, 1988), pp. 229–58.

Lyman, P., 'South Africa's promise', *Foreign Policy* 102 (1996), pp. 105–19.

Macmillan, Hugh, 'The African National Congress of South Africa in Zambia: the culture of exile and the changing relationship with home, 1964–1990', *Journal of Southern African Studies*, Special Issue, *Liberation Struggles, Exile and International Solidarity* 35/2 (2009), pp. 303–29.

———— 'The "Hani Memorandum" – introduced and annotated', *Transformation: Critical Perspectives on Southern Africa* 69 (2009), pp. 106–29.

Mandela, Nelson, 'South Africa's future foreign policy', *Foreign Affairs* 72/5 (1993), pp. 86–97.

Mbeki, Thabo, 'South Africa's international relations: today and tomorrow', in Greg Mills (ed.), *From Pariah to Participant: South Africa's Evolving Foreign Relations 1990–1994* (Johannesburg, 1994), pp. 200–6.

Mills, Greg, 'Leaning all over the place? The not-so-new South Africa's foreign policy', in Hussein Solomon (ed.), *Fairy Godmother, Hegemon or Partner? In Search of a South African Foreign Policy* (ISS Monograph Series, 13 May 1997), pp. 19–34.

———— 'South Africa's foreign policy: from isolation to respectability', in David Simon (ed.), *South Africa in Southern Africa* (Oxford, 1998), pp. 72–88.

Mokoena, Refilwe, 'South–South co-operation: the case for IBSA', *South African Journal of International Affairs* 14 (2007), pp. 125–45.

Morrow, Sean, 'Dakawa Development Centre: an African National Congress settlement in Tanzania, 1982–1992', *African Affairs* 97/389 (1998), pp. 497–521.

Murithi, Tim, 'The African Union's evolving role in peace operations: the African Union Mission in Burundi, the African Union Mission in Sudan and the African Union Mission in Somalia', *African Security Review* 7 (2008), pp. 71–82.

Nathan, Laurie, 'Consistency and inconsistencies in South African foreign policy', *International Affairs* 81/2 (2005), pp. 361–72.

Ndlovu, Sifiso, 'The ANC and the world, 1960–1970', in SADET, *The Road to Democracy in South Africa*, vol. 1, *1960–1970* (Cape Town, 2004), pp. 541–71.

———— 'The ANC in exile, 1960–1970', in SADET, *The Road to Democracy in South Africa*, vol. 1, *1960–1970* (Cape Town, 2004), pp. 411–78.

———— 'The ANC's diplomacy and international relations', in SADET, *The Road to Democracy in South Africa*, vol. 2, *1970–1980* (Pretoria, 2006), pp. 615–67.

Nothling, F., 'Co-operation with neighbouring states', in Thomas Wheeler (ed.), *History of the South African Department of Foreign Affairs, 1927–1993* (Johannesburg, 2005), pp. 279–307.

———— 'South Africa, Great Britain and the Commonwealth', in Thomas Wheeler (ed.), *History of the South African Department of Foreign Affairs, 1927–1993* (Johannesburg, 2005), pp. 225–52.

Onslow, Sue, 'The fall of the Berlin Wall and the end of apartheid', *IDEAS Today* 1 (2009).

Ostheimer, Andrea, 'Foreword', in Tim Hughes, *Composers, Conductors and Players: Harmony and Discord in South African Foreign Policy Making* (Johannesburg, 2004), pp. iii–iv.

Pfister, Roger, 'South Africa's recent foreign policy towards Africa: issue and literature', *Centre for International Studies* 29 (2000), pp. 1–32.

———— 'Gateway to international victory: the diplomacy of the African National Congress in Africa, 1960–1994', *Journal of Modern African Studies* 1 (2003), pp. 51–73.

Ralinala, Rendani Moses, Sithole, Jabulani, Houston, Gregory, and Magubane, Bernard, 'The Wankie and Sipolio Campaigns', in SADET, *The Road to Democracy in South Africa*, vol. 1, *1960–1970* (Cape Town, 2004), pp. 479–540.

Rantete, Johannes, and Giliomee, Hermann, 'Transition to democracy through transaction? bilateral negotiations between the ANC and NP in South Africa', *African Affairs* 91 (1992), pp. 515–42.

Sapire, Hillary, 'Liberation movements, exile, and international solidarity: an introduction', *Journal of Southern African Studies* 35 (2009), pp. 271–86.

Sarakinsky, Ivor, 'Rehearsing joint rule: the Transitional Executive Council', in Steven Friedman and Doreen Atkinson (eds), *South Africa Review 7: The Small Miracle. South Africa's Negotiated Settlement* (Johannesburg, 1994), pp. 68–91.

Saul, John, 'Liberal democracy vs. popular Democracy in Southern Africa', *Review of African Political Economy* 24 (1997), pp. 219–36.

Saunders, Chris, 'The Angolan/Namibian crisis of 1988 and its resolution', in Sue Onslow (ed.), *Cold War in Southern Africa: White Power, Black Liberation* (Abingdon, 2009), pp. 225–40.

Schmitz, David, and Walker, Vanessa, 'Jimmy Carter and the foreign policy of human rights: the development of a post-Cold War foreign policy', *Diplomatic History* 28/1 (2004), pp. 113–43.

Schoeman, Maxi, 'South Africa as an emerging middle power: 1994–2003', in John Daniel, Adam Habib and Roger Southall (eds), *State of the Nation: South Africa 2003–2004* (Cape Town, 2004), pp. 349–67.

Selebi, Jackie, 'South African foreign policy: setting new goals and strategies', *South African Journal of International Affairs* 6 (1999), pp. 207–16.

Shubin, Vladimir, 'The Soviet Union/Russian Federation's relations with South Africa, with special reference to the period since 1980', *African Affairs* 95 (1996), pp. 5–30.

Slovo, Joe, 'SACP one of the great pillars of our revolution', *The African Communist* 107 (1986), pp. 15–28.

Southall, Roger, 'The new South Africa in the new world order: beyond the double whammy', *Third World Quarterly* 15 (1994), pp. 121–37.

——— 'Regional security: the 'new' security in Southern Africa', *Southern Africa Report* 10 (1995), pp. 3–6.

——— 'SADC's intervention into Lesotho: an illegal defence of democracy?', in Oliver Furley and Roy May (eds), *African Interventionist States* (Aldershot, 2001), pp. 153–72.

——— 'An unlikely success: South Africa and Lesotho's 2002 election', *The Journal of Modern African Studies* 41 (2003), pp. 1–28.

Spence, Jack, 'South African foreign policy: the "Outward Movement"', in Christian Potholm and Richard Dale (eds), *Southern Africa in Perspective: Essays in Regional Politics* (New York, 1972), pp. 46–58.

——— 'Detente in Southern Africa: an interim judgment', *International Affairs* 53 (1977), pp. 1–16.

——— 'The new South African foreign policy: incentives and constraints' in Francis Toase and Edmund Yorke (eds), *The New South Africa: Prospects for Domestic and International Security* (Basingstoke, 1998), pp. 157–68.

——— 'South Africa: an African exception or just another country?', *Conflict, Security and Development* 7 (2007), pp. 341–7.

Suttner, Raymond, 'Foreign policy of the new South Africa: a brief review', in Samuel Guimaraes (ed.), *South Africa and Brazil: Risks and Opportunities in the Turmoil of Globalization* (Brasilia, 1996), pp. 191–205.

———— 'A brief review of South African foreign policy since April 1994', *Umrabulo* 1 (1996).

———— 'South African foreign policy since April 1994', *African Communist* 145 (1996), pp. 67–76.

Tandon, Yashpal, 'The Organisation of African Unity and the liberation of Southern Africa', in Christian Potholm and Richard Dale (eds), *Southern Africa in Perspective: Essays in Regional Politics* (New York, 1972), pp. 245–61.

Vale, Peter, 'The Search for Southern Africa's security', *International Affairs* 67 (1991), pp. 697–708.

————, and Maseko, Sipho, 'South Africa and the African Renaissance', *International Affairs* 74 (1998), pp. 271–87.

van Aardt, Maxi, 'A foreign policy to die for: South Africa's response to the Nigerian crisis', *Africa Insight* 26 (1996), pp. 107–19.

van der Westhuizen, Janis, 'South Africa's emergence as a middle power', *Third World Quarterly* 19 (1998), pp. 435–55.

Unpublished Theses and Conference Papers

Barrell, Howard, 'Conscripts to their Age: African National Congress Operational Strategy, 1976–1986', D. Phil, University of Oxford (1993).

Evans, Richard, 'South African Foreign Policy and the New World Order', *Institute of Strategic Studies Paper 4* (1993).

Goedgedacht Forum for Social Reflection, 'Evaluating the Effectiveness of South Africa's Foreign Policy since 1994', 12 April 2003, *http://www.goedgedachtforum. co.za/site/index.php?option=com_docman&task=cat_view&gid=38&Itemid=56&li-mitstart=5.*

Nathan, Laurie, 'The Absence of Common Values and Failure of Common Security in Southern Africa, 1992–2003', *Working Paper no. 50, Crisis States Programme* (LSE, July 2004), pp. 1–29.

du Pisani, Andre, 'Post-apartheid South Africa and the Region in the 1990s', paper prepared for BISA Annual Conference, University of Newcastle-upon-Tyne, 17–19 December 1990.

Thomas, Scott, 'The Diplomacy of Liberation: The International Relations of the African National Congress of South Africa, 1920–1985', PhD., LSE (1989).

Vale, Peter, 'Pivot, Puppet or Periphery: the Cold War and South Africa', *The Cold War as Global Conflict International Centre for Advanced Studies*, New York University, Unpublished Working Paper 9 (September 2003).

Internet Sources

Landsberg, Chris, 'Hegemon or Pivot?: Debating South Africa's role in Africa', *http:// www.sarpn.org.za/documents/d0000620/page2.php* (28/10/10).

Neethling, Theo, 'The Emerging South African Profile in Africa: Reflections on the Significance of South Africa's Entrance into Peacekeeping', *African Journal of Conflict Resolution* 2 (2002), *http://www.accord.org.za/publications/ajcr/downloads/ 340-ajcr-volume-02-no-2-2002.html.*

INDEX